DATE DUE

AP 2 4 00			
DE 18 03			

DEMCO 38-296

AN INTRODUCTION TO INTERNATIONAL MONEY AND FINANCE

An Introduction to International Money and Finance

Ramesh F. Ramsaran
Reader in International Economic Relations
Institute of International Relations
University of the West Indies
St Augustine, Trinidad

and London
rld

A catalogue record for this book is available from the British Library.

ISBN 0–333–71786–4

First published in the United States of America 1998 by
ST. MARTIN'S PRESS, INC.,
Scholarly and Reference Division,
175 Fifth Avenue, New York, N.Y. 10010

ISBN 0–312–21261–5

Library of Congress Cataloging-in-Publication Data
Ramsaran, Ramesh.
An introduction to international money and finance / Ramesh F.
Ramsaran.
p. cm.
Includes bibliographical references and index.
ISBN 0–312–21261–5 (cloth)
1. International finance.   I. Title.
HG3881.R283 1998
332'.042—dc21   97–38763
                                                 CIP

This book is printed on paper suitable for recycling and made from fully managed and
sustained forest sources.

10   9   8   7   6   5   4   3
07   06   05   04   03   02   01   00   99

Printed and bound in Great Britain by
Antony Rowe Ltd, Chippenham, Wiltshire

To the memory of my late friend and colleague
Dr Herb C. Addo

Contents

List of Tables   viii

Diagrams   x

Preface   xi

Acknowledgements   xiii

Chapter 1: Emerging Trends in the International Trading
            and Financial System   1

Chapter 2: International Trade and Payments   21

Chapter 3: The International Monetary System   54

Chapter 4: The Foreign Exchange Market, Exchange Rate
            Determination and Exchange Rate Systems   91

Chapter 5: International Banking   127

Chapter 6: The Debt Crisis and the International
            Financial System   155

Chapter 7: International Development Assistance   186

Chapter 8: External Development Finance and the
            Multilateral Financial Institutions   215

Chapter 9: Private Foreign Investment (PFI)   234

Index   255

List of Tables

1.1	Foreign exchange trading over the counter, 1989–95	7
1.2	Markets for selected derivative instruments, 1990–95	9
1.3	The over-the-counter derivatives market at end of March 1995	10
2.1	Composition of world merchandise trade by region, 1983–95	23
2.2	Selected exporters ranked on the basis of the value of merchandise trade, 1973 and 1995	24
2.3	Global net capital flows, 1976–93	27
2.4 (a)	Country A: Balance of payments standard presentation	32
2.4 (b)	Country A: Balance of payments (summary)	33
2.5	Contribution of selected countries to world reserves 1950–96	41
2.6	Composition of the SDR since 1 January 1996 and deriving the US dollar value of an SDR	45
2.7	Growth of international reserves, 1950–95	48
3.1	IMF balance sheet General Department at 30 April 1996	69
3.2	Outstanding Fund credit by facility and policy at end of April 1996	77
3.3	Net annual flow of fund resources to member states 1983–96	77
4.1	Relative shares of currencies traded in selected centres, 1995	92
4.2	The hamburger standard	104
4.3	Exchange rate arrangements adopted by member states of the IMF, 1978, 1984 and 1996	109
4.4	Currency composition and weights of the ECU at 21 September 1989	112
5.1	The world's 25 largest banks in 1995	132
5.2	The magnitude of commercial bank lending to developing countries, 1985–95	146
6.1	External debt of capital-importing developing countries, 1983–94	157
6.2	Outstanding external debt of developing countries by region, 1983 and 1994	158
6.3	Developing countries: selected debt indicators, 1983–95	161

7.1   Distribution of countries by human development group,
       1960 and 1992   189
7.2   Growth of GDP per capita, by economic region and
       income groups of developing countries, 1960–90   191
7.3   The total net flow of financial resources from DAC
       countries to developing Countries and multilateral
       organizations by type of flow, 1980–95   199
7.4   Long-term trends in DAC ODA, 1974/75–1994/95   201
7.5   Total net receipts of ODA by region, 1983/84 and
       1993/94   203
8.1   Selected data on multilateral financial institutions
       (MFIs), 1995   227
9.1   Aggregate net private capital flows to developing
       countries, 1990–96   239
9.2   FDI inflows and outflows, 1983–95   241
9.3   Stock of foreign direct investment, by region and country,
       1980–95   242
9.4   The world's twenty largest corporations ranked by assets
       and revenues, 1995   246

Diagrams

4.1 A supply and demand model of the foreign exchange market   96

Preface

Developments in communication technology, the liberalisation of world trade and the increasing freedom governing capital movements make it difficult for countries to isolate themselves from global trends in financial and goods markets. With the dissolution of the Soviet Union the international economy today is more international than it has ever been in the post-war period. The debt crisis of the 1980s, the failure of development policies predicated on an array of protectionist devices, and the critical dependence by a large number of countries on external sources for development finance, have encouraged more intensive global cooperation. In light of the moves towards greater openness, actors (governments, corporations and individuals) in the national economy are forced to be more alert to the opportunities and challenges created by the new international setting. Reaction has to be informed; and policies have to respond not only to national needs, but must take account of external realities and perceptions. As the sovereignty of nation states has waned and as physical borders lose their significance, international financial organisations, commercial institutions and market forces have become powerful influences in the world economy. Whatever the discipline or the profession, it is difficult to escape the need to understand these influences and the evolving context in which they operate. The world has shrunk in a real sense.

Events, however, do not carry the same significance for people in different corners of the world. Perspectives and interpretation can differ widely. International money and finance is a large and in some ways a complex field. In writing a book in this area one necessarily has to be selective in terms of focus and the material to be covered. Most of the existing texts in the field are heavy on theory, technical jargon, mathematics and the use of diagrams which can be quite intimidating. In most of them very little attention is paid to the perspectives of developing countries, or the impact of international policy decisions on these countries. Developing countries cover a broad range of states and some of them have moved from positions of insignificance to major actors in the world economy, while others have stagnated or slipped backwards.

The book grew out of a course taught at the Institute of International Relations of the University of the West Indies in Trinidad and is designed to provide a non-technical introduction to a range of people interested in understanding the salient issues and arguments in a rapidly changing and challenging field. These include aspiring diplomats, business people, under-graduate students entering the field of economics or international business, government officials and policy-makers. Students with or without an economics or social science background will find the text easily readable. The attention paid to policies and practices as well as the structure and functioning of certain multilateral financial institutions is an attractive feature of this book. A number of issues taken up are discussed from a development perspective, and this helps to highlight the position of developing countries in the international economy and their relationship to the industrial countries. The book covers subjects that should be of interest to readers in both developed and developing countries.

The book is divided into nine chapters. Chapter 1 introduces the reader to the broad trends emerging in the international trading and financial system, and this is followed in Chapter 2 by a discussion on trade and payments which is specifically intended for students without an economics background. Chapter 3 outlines the evolution of the International Monetary System, paying particular attention to the workings of the International Monetary Fund (IMF) and the issues surrounding its operations. The functioning of exchange rate markets and the choice of exchange rate regimes is a confusing field, even for graduate students. Chapter 4 presents a detailed discussion on the concepts and issues in this area. International banking is a fast growing industry, and study of this activity is now an integral part of courses in international monetary economics, international business, transnational cooperation and so on. The reader is introduced to the subject in Chapter 5. The debt crisis of the 1980s threatened to destabilise the international financial system, and ushered in a new era of cooperation between governments, bankers and the IMF. Chapter 6 discusses the debt problem and its impact on the international financial system. International development assistance is not normally covered in texts of this kind, but it touches issues which interest students in several disciplines. Chapter 8 which deals with the structure and performance of multi-lateral development institutions is an extension of Chapter 7. The final chapter discusses the growth of foreign private investment and the changing policy framework which is increasingly being influenced by structural adjustment programs and the emphasis being placed on private initiatives as a major element in the market driven paradigm.

Acknowledgements

In undertaking this work, I have incurred debt, intellectual and otherwise, to a number of people. This book was conceived many years ago, when my students began complaining about the need for a simple, concise and readable text on international money and finance that could meet the needs of readers coming from varied disciplines. The material covered, and the style and approach adopted, were influenced by students who felt intimidated by the jargon. That I was able to finish the manuscript in the last couple years amidst other research assignments is due in no small measure to the encouragement and prodding of my colleagues, both at the University of the West Indies and those from abroad associated with the Caribbean Centre for Monetary Studies. In particular I acknowledge the immense intellectual debt I owe to my late friend and colleague Dr Herb C. Addo who died in 1996. Mr Anselm Francis, the Acting Director of the Institute of International Relations was always responsive to my pleas for help. The librarians at the Institute of International Relations and in particular Randy Balkaransingh provided me with invaluable help in checking the notes and references. Without the dedication of Jackie, Jeanne and Wendy who typed and retyped the manuscript through its several versions, my task would have been immensely more difficult. Finally, my thanks to my wife Nadira for her enduring virtue of forbearance, and for whose neglect I can never fully apologise or compensate.

1 Emerging Trends in the International Trading and Financial System

INTRODUCTION

Because of its duration and the intensity of the conflict, the Second World War was particularly destructive. The pre-war pattern of international trade, payments and specialization which had already collapsed in the 1930s was further fragmented, and the early post-war years witnessed the emergence of a number of groups (for example, the Sterling area in a more formal form, the Franc Zone, the Council for Mutual Economic Assistance and the Dollar area), based on both economic and political concerns. Notwithstanding this division in the world economy and the proliferation of exchange and other forms of trade controls, the need for less commercial restrictions at the global level was recognized even before the war ended.

The persistent efforts to liberalize trade in the post-war period has been accompanied by radical and far-reaching changes in the international monetary and financial system. These changes have not always been predictable. While some were the result of deliberate action designed to accommodate new circumstances, others emerged out of crisis situations. Some also grew out of the reaction to government policies and restrictions, as private operators sought to enlarge the scope of their operations and take advantage of growing opportunities in an increasingly border-less world. In all this, technology has been crucial, as the costs of moving goods, people, money and information are being drastically reduced. By lowering production prices and the costs of communication and transportation, technological progress has not only encouraged trade, but more technology transfers, while the movement of capital has also intensified. These interacting processes have encouraged competition and accelerated the pace of financial and commercial restructurings in an increasingly global capitalist order.

While some government actions and decisions in bilateral and multilateral fora have facilitated the growth of the world economy, its evolution has not followed any neat guidelines, or lent itself to easy predictability.

1

There is no supra-national authority to inform or guide the process. In the globalization process, the nation state has become less significant, and its ability to control actors and undertake economic management even within its own borders has been correspondingly reduced. Investors now move more freely, and developments in transport and communication allow production facilities to be located almost anywhere. The internationalization of markets has challenged traditional notions of sovereignty and reduced national economic autonomy. Despite a growing interdependence in many areas, governments and multilateral institutions often find themselves reacting to events rather than blazing paths of innovation or articulating strategies to manage change. The forces of internationalization have weakened governments' ability to control the money supply or legislate in many areas. They have strengthened the need for intergovernmental co-operation and for stronger and more vibrant international institutions to counter destabilizing forces. Unfortunately, the technologies which have impacted favourably on the growth of legitimate financial activity are also available to illegal operators. The phenomenon of money laundering, for example, is a global concern. The volume of both legal and illegal financial activity is a major feature of the modern financial system.

Trade is widely recognized as perhaps the most critical avenue for encouraging growth, reducing poverty and creating employment. Trade is a resource which could be earned. The relentless efforts to remove commercial barriers are not only reflected in the growth of trade, but in parallel developments in investment and financial markets. In fact, for some time now international financial transactions have been growing at a faster pace than real variables.

SOME RECENT DEVELOPMENTS IN THE INTERNATIONAL ECONOMY

The world economy has been undergoing rapid changes in recent years. Between 1986 and 1996 for example, real GDP in the developed market economies expanded at an annual average rate of around 2.6 per cent per annum as compared to an estimated 4.8 per cent for developing countries as a group. Not surprisingly, countries in some parts of the developing world (for example, those in South and East Asia) have been more dynamic than those in other parts (for example, Africa). China, with a population of 1.2 billion people, is the world's fastest growing economy, averaging 10.5 per cent between 1986 and 1996 ('billion as used in this book means a thousand million). Per capita GDP in real terms increased by over 25 per cent between 1980 and 1995 both in developed and developing countries as groups. In some of the latter, however, per capita income actually fell in the period. In the economies of Eastern Europe and of the former Soviet Union income has also declined as these economies seek to adjust from centrally planned arrangements to market economies. The result of these trends is that while the gap between the industrial countries and some developing countries has narrowed dramatically since the Second World War, with others it has widened.

Increasing per capita income and the reduction of trade barriers have led to an increased opening up of the world economy and larger markets. One of the remarkable features of the post-war period has been the rapid growth of world trade which has been increasing at a faster rate than world output. The developed market economies, however, still account for about 70 per cent of world trade, but a number of developing countries, particularly in South East Asia, have been gaining an increased share of the market place in recent years. The emerging pattern of world trade is a reflection of significant structural shifts in the world economy. The share of manufactures in world merchandise exports rose form 56 per cent in 1980 to about 72 per cent in 1995. There has been a steady shift of world manufacturing output away from Europe and North America to Asia and the evidence now indicates that production levels may now be higher than those in Europe and North America.[1] Japan alone accounted for 11.6 per cent of world export of manufactures in 1995, as compared to 12.4 per cent for the United States. New technologies, less nationalistic stances, cost reducing incentives and increasingly skilled labour forces are encouraging transnational corporations to make greater use of locations in developing countries as competition increases in the world economy. Trade and investment are expanding hand in hand, but some countries have benefitted more than others.

Another significant medium-term trend in international trade has been the growing share of non-merchandise transactions. Service transactions are accounting for an increasing share of world exports of goods and services. The share of 'invisibles' increased from around 25 per cent in 1980 to over a third in recent years. The share of investment income moved from around 10 per cent in the early 1980s to about 16 per cent in the early 1990s. This latter development reflects the increasing globalization of financial services and the more open exchanges and investment policies that have encouraged the growth of trans-border financial transactions. Capital movements now dwarf transactions on current account. Private actors buoyed by the rapid developments in information and communication technology are now operating with greater freedom than at anytime in the post-war period. It was not surprising that the recently concluded Uruguay Round of trade negotiations paid special attention to trade in services. The world export of commercial services alone in 1993 amounted to US$1020 billion as compared to US$3640 billion for merchandise exports.

The emergence of a number of dynamic economies outside North America and Western Europe has not only introduced a greater measure of competition in the world economy and increased market opportunities, but has provided a wider range of models against which economic policies could be discussed and compared. Both in developed and developing countries greater attention is being paid to the supply side of the economy. In the real sector private initiatives are being encouraged, while protectionist tendencies are being abandoned in favour of more open policies. In the financial sector liberalization is now accepted dogma in an increasing number of countries. Major tax reforms have taken place across the globe with a view to increasing efficiency and improving incentives. Measures to increase savings and investment have become an integral part of structural adjustment programmes, designed to reverse economic decline and eradicate poverty.

Policy reforms in both the real and financial sectors now occupy the attention of both national governments and international aid agencies. With the rapid dismantling of trade barriers, competition has increased not only in the goods markets but in the market for investment. The number of stock markets is not only increasing, but are becoming more open. Technology is not only being seen as a way to increase output and efficiency in the real sector, but is revolutionizing operations in the financial industry. The financial landscape is changing daily as new institutions and instruments emerge. International intermediation has taken on enormous proportions and complexity. The developments that have taken place in communications and transport would make it difficult for any country to isolate itself from new ideas and changes taking place elsewhere. While financial markets are being rapidly internationalized with the removal of exchange and capital controls, the goods markets are also being liberalized, regionally and internationally. All indications point to increased globalization of goods and financial markets.

When the International Monetary Fund was set up in 1944, the concern was largely with restrictions on current payments. Article I (iv) of the Fund's Charter states one of its objectives as follows: 'To assist in the establishment of a multilateral system of payments in respect of current transactions between members and in the elimination of foreign exchange restrictions which hamper the growth of world trade.' While Article VII permits capital exchange controls in certain circumstances for limited periods, Article VIII, Section 2(a) clearly states that 'No member shall, without the approval of the Fund, impose restrictions on the making of payments and transfers for current international transactions.' The Fund's Articles have very little to say about capital movements. Article VI, Section 3 reads as follows: 'Members may exercise such controls as are necessary to regulate international capital movements, but no member may exercise these controls in a manner which will restrict payments for current transactions or which will unduly delay transfers of funds in settlement of commitments...'. Section 1 (b) of Article VI permits the use of the general resources of the Fund for capital transactions of reasonable amount required for the expansion of exports or in the ordinary course of trade, banking, or other business. Since capital movements can seriously undermine a fixed exchange rate system, it is clear that the founding fathers of the Bretton Woods monetary system did not foresee the degree and volume of capital movements which emerged subsequently.

Over the years both developed and developed countries have used a variety of measures to protect or improve their balance of payments position. In the 1960s and in the 1970s many newly independent developing countries adopted deliberate policies with respect to private foreign investment with a view to taking control of the 'commanding heights' of the economy, or keeping certain strategic sectors under local control. This policy had more political than economic content and did not work very well. With the decline of traditional foreign exchange earners in the 1970s and 1980s, with increasing cost of imports, and with the decline of private foreign investment, serious balance of payments problems emerged in many cases. Inadequate domestic savings to finance the desired level of investment, mismanagement and poorly conceived macroeconomic policies exacerbated domestic social and economic problems. The 1970s and early 1980s witnessed a significant increase in government domestic and foreign borrowing to finance both consumption and investment. High levels of bank liquidity and aggressive lending by commercial banks contributed to the growth of public debt. With the inability of a number of major debtor countries to service their debt in the 1980s, the period of heady lending and borrowing came to an end with both lenders and borrowers becoming more circumspect in their activities. Resolving the debt problem became a major preoccupation in 1980s and early 1990s, since it threatened the stability of the international financial system with consequences for the international trade and payments system. Recognizing the self interest of the various parties, debtors, creditors and international financial institutions which oversee the international financial system have used a variety of techniques and strategies to diffuse the problem and to encourage capital flows. The stance towards private foreign capital changed radically in the 1980s.

The capital controls instituted in the 1960s did little to stem the international movement of capital, which subsequently contributed to the demise of the fixed exchange rate system. With the growth of resources in private hands, governments' intervention in the market place, be it in respect of the exchange rate system or private investment, came under increasing pressure. The fixed (but adjustable) exchange rate system adopted at Bretton Woods in 1944 collapsed in the early 1970s. Private investors have developed new techniques for dealing with both economic and political risks and for penetrating foreign markets. Banks had to devise new strategies for meeting their clients' needs, or lose business. The growth of the Euro-currency market was a response to this situation, as both savers and lenders felt a need to escape the constraining effects of national controls and regulations. One indicator of the vastly increased scale of capital movements is seen in the fact that gross capital outflows from the main industrial countries (excluding official and short-term banking transactions) came to about US$850 billion in 1993. Such flows averaged around US$500 billion during the 1985–93 period as a whole, compared with only about US$100 billion a year in the first half of the 1980s.[2]

International financial markets have become increasingly sophisticated. Institutional investors are now major players with the opening up of national financial markets. To meet changing portfolio preferences instruments are being issued in several different currencies and the volume of transactions has become increasingly large. It has been estimated that the daily net turnover of foreign exchange transactions in April 1992 was US$820 billion, which was almost three times their value in 1986 and around twelve times the combined GDP of OECD countries on an annualized basis.[3] Total international securities transactions in the Group of Seven countries amounted to US$6 trillion per quarter in the second half of 1993 – about five or six times the value of international trade.[4] A more recent survey reported by the Bank for International Settlements in its *66th Annual Report* shows that in 1995 the daily global foreign exchange market turnover reached an average of US$1,190 billion in April 1995 – an increase of 30 per cent over 1992 when evaluated at constant exchange rates (see Table 1.1). The US dollar was the dominant currency traded, followed by the Deutsche mark and the yen. Among currency pairs, Deutsche mark/dollar trading retained the largest market share, followed by yen/dollar transactions.

Table 1.1   Foreign exchange trading over the counter, 1989–95

Turnover by transactions type[1,2]	1989	1992	1995	% change 1989–92	% change 1992–95
	Daily averages, in billions of US dollars				
Estimated global turnover	590	820	1190	39	45
Spot transactions	350 (59)	400 (49)	520 (44)	14	30
Outright forwards	28 (5)	64 (8)	101 (8)	129	58
Foreign exchange swaps	212 (36)	356 (43)	569 (48)	68	60
Memorandum items:					
Futures	2	5	6	150	20
Options	16[3]	38	42	138	11
	Shares by currency[4]				
US dollar	90	82	84	–8	2
of which: Deutsche mark/dollar		26	23		–3
yen/dollar		19	21		2
Deutsche mark	27	40	37	13	–13
Yen	27	22	24	–5	2
Turnover by location[2,5]					
	Daily averages, in billions of US dollars				
London	184 (26)	290 (27)	464 (30)	58	60
New York	115 (16)	167 (16)	244 (16)	45	46
Tokyo	111 (15)	120 (11)	161 (10)	8	34

[1] Adjusted for local and cross-border double-counting and estimated gaps in reporting.
[2] Percentage shares in brackets.
[3] Estimate.
[4] As a percentage of foreign exchange market turnover adjusted for local double-counting; when shares measure the currency on only one side of a transaction, they sum to 200 per cent. Shares for 1989 are estimated from gross figures. Changes refer to percentage point changes.
[5] Adjusted for local double-counting.

Source: Bank for International Settlements, *66th Annual Report*, 1 April 1995–31 March 1996.

In a liberalized exchange rate setting, daily fluctuations in exchange rates have become the norm, and international portfolio managers are constantly moving from one currency to another as they assess returns and the impact on principal. Lending is increasingly associated with variable interest rates. To deal with currency exposure and interest rate risks a range of instruments has emerged in recent years. Not all the innovations are well known to the public. Interest rates and currency swaps, futures options and caps are now being widely used in the bourgeoning global markets. The new instruments permit the 'unbinding' or separation of risks facing borrowers and investors and in so doing facilitate the hedging of price, interest rate, and exchange rate risk. Competition has been a major driving force in financial innovation.[3] "The essence of a swap contract is the binding of two counter parties to exchange two different payments streams over time, the payment being tied at least in part, to subsequent – and uncertain – market price development'[6] Interest rate swaps are agreements that transform a fixed rate payment obligation in a particular currency into a floating rate obligation in that currency and vice versa. A forward interest rate swap is an agreement under which the cash flow exchange of the underlying interest rate swap would begin to take effect from a specified date. Currency swaps are agreements in which proceeds of a borrowing curency are converted into a different currency and, simultaneously, a forward exchange agreement is executed providing for a schedule of future exchanges of the two currencies in order to recover the currency converted. The combination of a borrowing and a currency swap produces the financial equivalent of substituting a borrowing in the currency obtained in the initial conversion for the original borrowing. Options are contracts that allow the holder of the option to purchase or sell a financial instrument at a specified price within a specified period of time from or to the seller of the option. The purchaser of an option pays a premium at the outset to the seller of the option, who then bears the risk of an unfavourable change in the price of the financial instrument underlying the option. Futures and forward contracts are contracts for delayed delivery at a specified future date of a specified instrument at a specified price or yield.[7]

'Derivatives' is a term which is usually applied to futures, options, and interest rate and currency swaps. Essentially, as the name suggests, derivatives are instruments that are linked to or derived from an underlying security or commodity market. For example, financial futures contracts were derived from the foreign exchange market while interest rate swaps were derived from the Euro-bond market.

The growth of derivative markets are playing an increasingly greater role in transforming the management and allocation of risk. Bank participation in derivative markets in recent years has been increasing, giving rise to concerns about riskiness of individual banks and of banking systems as a whole. In the US, for example, the total amount of interest rate, currency, commodity and equity contracts at commercial and savings

Table 1.2   Markets for selected derivative instruments, 1990–95

Instruments	Notional amounts outstanding in billions of US dollars					
	1990	*1991*	*1992*	*1993*	*1994*	*1995*
Exchange-traded instruments	2 290.4	3 519.3	4 634.4	7 771.1	8 862.5	9 185.3
Interest rate futures	1 454.5	2 156.7	2 913.0	4 958.7	5 777.6	5 863.4
Interest rate options[1]	599.5	1 072.6	1 385.4	2 362.4	2 623.6	2 741.7
Currency futures	17.0	18.3	26.5	34.7	40.1	37.9
Currency options[1]	56.5	62.9	71.1	75.6	55.6	43.2
Stock market index futures	69.1	76.0	79.8	110.0	127.3	172.2
Stock market index options[1]	93.7	132.8	158.6	229.7	238.3	326.9
Over-the-counter instruments[2]	3 450.3	4 449.4	5 345.7	8 474.6	11 303.2	17 990.0
Interest rate swaps	2 311.5	3 065.1	3 850.8	6 177.3	8 815.6	–
Currency swaps[3]	577.5	807.2	860.4	899.6	914.8	–
Other swap-related derivatives[4]	561.3	577.2	634.5	1 397.6	1 572.8	–

[1] Calls and puts.
[2] Data collected by the International Swaps and Derivatives Association (ISDA) only; the two sides of contracts between ISDA members are reported once only.
[3] Adjusted for reporting of both currencies; including cross-currency interest rate swaps.
[4] Caps, collars, floors and swaptions.
– not available.

Source: Bank for International Settlements, *66th Annual Report*, 1 April 1995–31 March 1966.

banks soared from US$6.8 trillion in 1990 to US$11.9 trillion in 1993, an increase of 75 per cent [8] Table 1.2 gives some indication of the annual turnover of the markets for selected derivative instruments in recent years, while Table 1.3 shows the state of the over-the-counter (instruments traded outside organized exchanges) derivatives market at the end of March 1995. Between 1990 and 1995 the notional amounts of over-the-counter (OTC) instruments outstanding increased by more than five times as compared to four times for exchanges-traded instruments. The value of outstanding OTC contracts stood at US$40.6 trillion at the end of March 1995.

It is widely accepted that saving and investment are crucial to the growth process. At both the domestic and international levels, the role of financial intermediation is not only to encourage saving but to make this saving available to investors. Savers and investors have different needs and as they seek new opportunities, competition compels financial intermediaries to engage in a constant process of self-examination and innovation. Deregulation, more open investment policies, the removal of capital

Table 1.3   The over-the-counter derivatives market at end of march 1995[1]

Market risk category and instrument type	Notional amounts outstanding		Gross market values		Gross market values as a % of notional amounts outstanding
	billions of US dollars	% share[2]	billions of US dollars	% share[2]	
Foreign exchange	13 095	100	1 048	100	8
Forwards and foreign exchange swaps[3]	8 699	72	622	71	7
Currency swaps[4]	1 957	11	346	22	18
Options[5]	2 379	17	71	7	3
Other products	61	0	10	0	16
Interest rates	26 645	100	647	100	2
Forward rate agreements	4 597	17	18	3	0
Swaps	18 283	69	562	87	3
Options	3 548	13	60	9	2
Other products	216	1	7	1	3
Equity and stock indices	579	100	50	100	9
Forwards and swaps	52	9	7	14	13
Options	527	91	43	86	8
Commodities	318	100	28	100	9
Forwards and swaps	208	66	21	78	10
Options	109	34	6	22	6
Total	40 637		1 773		4

[1] Adjusted for local and cross-border double counting.
[2] To put the shares accounted for by different foreign exchange instruments on a comparable basis, percentages have been calculated on data that exclude figures for currency swaps and options reported by dealers in the United Kingdom.
[3] Data are incomplete because they do not include outstanding forward and foreign exchange swap positions of market participants in the United Kingdom.
[4] Notional amounts excluding data from reporting dealers in the United Kingdom amounted to $1307 billion.
[5] Notional amounts excluding data from reporting dealers in the United Kingdom amounted to $1995 billion.

Source: Bank for International Settlements, *66th Annual Report*, 1 April 1995–31 March 1996.

controls, the adoption of sound macroeconomic policies (often under pressure from the international aid agencies) have led to increased capital mobility. While governments continue to borrow for various purposes, private investors, multilateral institutions, financial and non-financial companies are also players in the market. Funds are raised through a variety of investments differentiated by risks, returns, currency, maturity, and so forth. The terms on which lending institutions borrow also determine the terms on which they lend. For instance, since 1982 the International Bank for Reconstruction and Development (IBRD) has moved away from fixed rate lending to variable rate loans to help mitigate its interest rate risk. The IBRD derives most of its resources from borrowing in international capital markets.

With the opening of their markets, with strong economic growth in some cases, with the dismantling of interest rate controls and with the adoption of more rigorous macroeconomic policies, private capital flows to developing countries have been increasing. Net private capital flows to developing countries increased from annual average of US$10.2 billion in 1973–77 to US$114.3 billion in 1989–95.[9] A substantial part of these flows, however, have been concentrated in a few countries in Asia and the western hemisphere. Funds raised in international credit markets by both developed and developing countries (including the Transition Economies) increased from US$279.1 billion in 1985 to US$832.2 billion in 1995.[10] Of this latter figure, 55 per cent took the form of bonds and 44 per cent the form of bank loans. The bond market has become increasingly diverse and versatile. Global bonds which are launched in both domestic and international markets now encompass a wide range of currencies, maturities (up to forty years), issue sizes and categories of borrowers. Increasingly, the products offered are tailor made or of a 'niche' variety. One example is the development of the 'dragon' bond market for issues in Asia aimed at tapping the financial resources of the rapidly growing Asian economies.[11]

Financial institutions have become less specialized both in terms of the areas in which they operate and in the products they offer. The availability of financial instruments for hedging exchange risks has been critical in the integration of domestic and foreign financial markets. Foreign investors have shown an increased willingness to buy government bonds. The holdings of bonds issued by the governments of eleven major countries almost tripled between 1983 and 1988 growing from US$213 billion to US$583 billion.[12] More than half of all cross-border holdings of bonds consists of government bonds, close to 90 per cent of which have been issued in domestic markets, and the rest in Euro-markets, where they are commonly known as sovereigns. The rest is corporate bonds (including state enterprises) which except for US domestic bonds are largely Eurobonds.[13] One of the main reasons for the growth in the market for government bonds has been the persistence of large government fiscal and balance of payments deficits and the fact that financial institutions have devised new ways to market government securities, such as the use of zero-coupon instruments and futures and options contracts common in the government debt market.[14]

While net international bank credit fell in the early 1990s, banks are still important players in international credit markets. Not all banks have been affected in the same way by the relative decline in bank lending. While the international assets position of these institutions in certain countries has increased, in others it has declined. The fall-off in the creditworthiness of a number of countries and their inability to borrow have forced them to seek other forms of financing. Increasing financing needs make governments important players both in domestic and foreign markets. Measures are rapidly being introduced with a view to making government securities increasingly marketable.

With the emergence of the debt problem in the 1980s, greater emphasis was placed on private investment to restart or accelerate the growth process, and the freeing-up of both the real and financial sectors was seen as a necessary prerequisite. With the liberalization of domestic financial markets have come the progressive removal of barriers and regulations governing capital movements. The lines between domestic and international capital markets have become more difficult to discern. The Bank for International Settlements in its *64th Annual Report* has noted that the interdependence of markets worldwide has continued to increase and this has led to further blurring of 'the distinctions between bank credit and securities issues, domestic and international paper, cash instruments and derivatives, and between different categories of derivative products.'[15]

DEVELOPMENTS IN THE INTERNATIONAL MONETARY SYSTEM

Since the end of the Second World War, the international monetary and financial system has undergone radical changes. The Bretton Woods monetary system founded in 1945 was intended to avoid both the rigidity of the gold standard and the self-defeating policies of the inter-war years. The key role assigned the US dollar in the new international monetary system stemmed from the fact that at the end of the War the dollar was the major currency being used in international transactions or as a reserve asset and store of value. The dollar was the only convertible currency at the time, and with the US holding about three quarters of the world's monetary gold stock, the US did not find it difficult to buy and sell gold for dollars (or convertible currency) at US$35 an ounce. At the end of the war the destruction of productive capacity in other industrial countries left the US as the world's major supplier. The demand for US goods for reconstruction purposes and the seriously impaired export capacity of the European countries resulted in a dollar shortage.

The position of the United States as the dominant economic power at the end of the war came increasingly under challenge in the 1950s and 1960s. By 1973 West Germany was second only to the United States as an exporter, with Japan, France and the United Kingdom in third, fourth and fifth places respectively. With the growth of dollar liabilities and the loss of gold reserves in the 1950s, confidence in the US dollar started to wane. Throughout the 1960s there were suggestions that gold should be revalued, which was another way of saying the dollar should be devalued. It was felt, particularly by France, that the devaluation of the dollar against gold would have increased the supply of world reserves and reduced dependence on the dollar as a reserve currency.[16] The arguments against gold revaluation were considered weak. The principal ones were: (1) a devaluation of the dollar against gold would not have solved the adjustment problem if other countries devalued against the dollar; (2) an increase in the gold price would have benefited South Africa and the Soviet Union; and (3) the gold standard was too rigid. It was felt by some that a devaluation of the US dollar would have dealt both with the 'liquidity' problem and the 'confidence' problem.[17]

The major reluctance to devalue the dollar stemmed from the conviction that such action would destabilize the system. The US had agreed to provide the world with liquidity, but while doing so had failed to appreciate the consequences for its economy of the increasingly competitive situation to which the European countries in particular were moving. In the face of persistent US deficits, the Europeans refused to undertake upward revaluation to any significant extent. In fact, what happened was a number of *ad hoc* arrangements were put in place to help prop up the US dollar. These included the formation of the gold pool in 1961 by the Group of Ten countries with the aim of maintaining the price of gold in the free gold market at around US$35 an ounce by selling gold from the pool when there were upward pressures on the price in the market and by buying gold if the price tended to fall. This worked for a while, but with the decline in confidence in key currencies in the late 1960s following the devaluation of the sterling in 1967 and the withdrawal of France in 1968, the arrangements collapsed. Thereafter a two-tier market developed with the official price remaining at US$35 per ounce and a free market with price responding to demand and supply.

Whatever the difficulties affecting the Bretton Woods system in the 1960s, it was widely felt there could be no return to the gold standard, however great the value that was placed on stable exchange rates. A strong US dollar was a major premise of the Bretton Woods system, but with the serious loss of gold reserves resulting from net capital outflows, the link between the US dollar and gold could not be maintained, and in August 1971 the relationship was severed, creating a climate of uncertainty in the international monetary system. The US had always argued that the dollar's role in the Bretton Wood's system had made it difficult to use the exchange rate as an instrument of adjustment without throwing the whole system into chaos.

When the link with gold was cut in 1971, the US dollar was devalued by 15 per cent. Since then it has undergone further depreciations against the major currencies. Yet it is a currency in high demand. In some countries (for example, the Bahamas and Panama) the US dollar circulates side by side with the local currency. There is evidence that the US dollar serves as an important substitute for the domestic currency of many Latin American nations.[18] In a large number of developing countries, particularly in those where inflation rates are high or where exchange controls are stringent, it is the most sought after asset. It is seen as a medium for retaining the value of savings or as insurance for access to foreign goods and services. Unofficial markets for US dollars exist in most developing countries still operating foreign exchange controls. In fact, these markets often give a better indication of the equilibrium or market rate than that in the controlled formal sector where regulations can seriously distort the effects of structural changes in the economy on the exchange rate. While the unofficial or black market may be used by residents to satisfy what some may regard as legitimate needs, there tends to be other players as well, who buy and sell foreign exchange to support activities such as narcotics trading, smuggling, and so on. The importance of the dollar can also be seen in the fact that it carries the largest weight in the Special Drawing Right (SDR) and accounts for the largest component of the Euro-currency market.

The severed link between gold and the US dollar came just before the major currencies went on float, in fact (if not in law) putting an end to the fixed exchange rate system which the major industrial countries had struggled to keep during the 1960s. The developing countries, however, still preferred a fixed but adjustable exchange rate system and their initial reaction was to continue to peg to a major currency. Later a few floated, while others chose to peg to the SDR or their own basket. Members of the European Monetary System peg their currencies to the European Currency

Unit and to each other, while floating against other currencies. A large number of countries have miscellaneous arrangements. Of course, pegging to a currency that is floating is not the same as pegging to one that has a fixed relationship with other currencies within an internationally agreed set of rules. While the international financial system is now less crisis prone, the exchange rate question remains far from settled. International adjustment is still a thorny issue. The United States has been able to run a persistent balance of payments deficit and not make more fundamental adjustments largely because it is a reserve currency country. The US can finance imports by merely printing dollars, once other countries are willing to accept this currency. Other countries, of course, can do the same once the latter conditions obtains.

A major issue that still haunts the international monetary system is the question of adjustment. Specifically, the question is how to operationalize a set of rules to which both surplus and deficit countries can comply. The present relationship between the United States and Japan epitomizes the problem, but the implications are much larger. A number of developing countries with external payments problems have been forced to undertake structural adjustment programmes, in many cases with heavy social costs. The burden of adjustment has been inequitably shared. Too often is the assumption made that the factors behind the economic difficulties are all at the domestic level. The multilateral financial institutions who are at the forefront of the campaign to reform economic policies clearly do not exert the same influence on the industrial countries that they do on the developing nations whose influence on the operations of these bodies is relatively insignificant. Following the outbreak of the debt crisis even the commercial banks now operate very closely with the IMF and the World Bank who have come to regard the banks as partners in the adjustment process.

The Fund itself has become more powerful in recent years as its resources have grown to accommodate a wider range of facilities. During the oil boom years of the 1970s and early 1980s, countries seeking finance turned to the commercial banks partly to escape the conditionalities of the Fund and perhaps more importantly because the Fund did not have the volume of resources available to the commercial banks. With many countries unable to raise new loans or service old ones they turned increasingly to the Fund for assistance. Many of the commercial banks insist on a Fund programme before they agree to reschedule loans. The Fund's function is no longer confined to providing balance of payments support, but is now a major protagonist for structural adjustment, an objective on which both the World Bank and the Fund collaborate. The distinction between the two institutions has grown increasingly blurred in some respects.

In recent years both the Fund and the Bank have been at the forefront of the move for a more open world trading system and more liberalized national economies. There has not only been growing pressure to remove trade barriers, but also to reduce exchange controls and to free up the financial markets. The large number of countries experiencing fiscal and balance of payments problems and needing Fund assistance have given the Fund greater control over their policies which, not surprisingly, have become increasingly more market influenced. With the entry of the states of the former Soviet Union and Eastern Europe into the IMF and World Bank, these two Washington-based institutions now preside over a global effort to establish market-based economies to which there appears to be no ideological challenge.

The international monetary and financial system in the 1990s differs in fundamental ways from what prevailed in the early post-war years. Gold is no longer a formal part of the system and the fixed exchange rate system has given way to more flexible exchange rate arrangements which were near inconceivable two decades or so ago. At the end of June 1996 out of 181 members of the Fund only 43 chose to peg their respective currencies to a single major currency, 100 had arrangements that were described as 'managed' or 'independently' floating and 20 were pegged to a currency composite other than the SDR. With the relative decline of the US economy and currency in recent decades, the international use of the US dollar has also declined. For some time the international monetary system has been evolving in a multi-currency direction, and with the changes taking place in the global economy this process is likely to continue.

It needs to be noted, however, that notwithstanding the relative decline of the US economy as reflected in world manufacturing output and world exports, the US dollar remains the world's most widely used currency. As indicated earlier, the US dollar still accounts for over 50 per cent of identified official holdings of foreign exchange reserves, as compared to around 70 per cent in the early 1980s. At the end of June 1986 20 countries were still pegging their currencies to the US dollar. In many developing countries with high inflation rates and in some of the 'transition' states of the former USSR, residents have abandoned the domestic currency as a store of value and have sought foreign currency, particularly the widely available US dollar as a refuge for financial savings. In many relatively low inflation countries, the US dollar was and still is a highly preferable currency for various reasons. With financial liberalization, residents in many developing countries have been allowed to hold foreign currency deposits as a part of a strategy to attract capital and increase foreign reserves. The dollarization ratio (the ratio of foreign currency deposits to broad money, inclusive of foreign currency deposits) currently stands at nearly 85 per cent in Bolivia, 70 per cent in Uruguay and 65 per cent in Peru.[19]

The growth of foreign reserves and the renewed confidence shown in foreign exchange as a means of international payments has now raised doubts about the earlier undertaking that the SDR should become the principal reserve asset in the international monetary system (Article XXII of the IMF Agreement). The establishment of monetary union in Europe and the decision to move towards a single currency (the Euro) which is intended to eventually replace national currencies also raises questions for the future role of the SDR and also for the role of non-European currencies in the international payments system. What the recent experience has taught us, however, is that regardless of what governments do, the private markets are adept at finding ways and means at meeting new challenges and opportunities.

CONCLUDING OBSERVATIONS

The increasing shift to market-oriented policies, particularly in developing economies and in the transition economies of the former Soviet Union and Eastern Europe, has strengthened the forces of globalization in both the goods, investment and capital markets. The globalization process, however, has had a differential impact on various countries. Opening up has been more favourable to some than others. Liberalization and deregulation which come as part of the adjustment package have not reversed the downward spiral in a number of states unable to attract capital on the desired scale.

Experience has shown that where adjustment is being undertaken without the promise of growth, poverty reduction and employment creation, it does not attract support. These objectives, however, require investment which can be financed from both domestic and foreign savings. The widespread removal of currency controls and the greater emphasis being placed on private investment as an engine of growth has created a very competitive international situation. Developing countries are not only competing among themselves, but with the 'transition' states of the former USSR and Eastern Europe as well as with the developed countries themselves. Equity markets in a number of developing countries have experienced robust growth in recent years. Not only have the types and volume of securities increased but the quality of information has improved. The need to provide jobs and encourage both local and foreign investment are forcing governments to pursue more responsible macroeconomic policies in a world where market forces are becoming increasingly predominant. The Mexican currency crisis at the end of 1994 shows how easily favourable trends can be reversed. The assistance provided by the United States and the IMF to Mexico also shows how other countries and international institutions cannot afford to be indifferent to problems of their neighbours, trading partners or individual members in a world that has become increasingly interdependent.

If the cliché 'no nation is an island' ever needed proving, developments in the world economy in the 1970s and 1980s did this without a doubt. The early 1990s have accelerated many of the trends that emerged in the previous two decades. Information technology and developments in telecommunications have indeed shrunk the world to village size, forcing changes in policies and facilitating the greater movement of goods, services and capital. The world economy has now moved to a new level of interdependence. No country in the world, be it exporter or importer, could now be indifferent to the price of oil. The debt crisis became an issue not because of altruistic or moral reasons, but because it posed a real threat to the stability of the international financial system. The creditworthiness of debtor countries was not the only thing at stake. The creditor financial institutions in the metropolitan centres faced real threat of collapse, and even though that threat has retreated somewhat, it is widely recognized that the debt crisis has deeper roots and is not simply a problem for the debtor countries. There is now a link between debt and the environment. There is also a recognition that mitigation of the debt burden must be an integral part of any effort to restore growth in indebted countries.

The exchange rate is a major factor affecting competitiveness and no central bank could afford to ignore relationships between the domestic currency and other currencies; nor could it fail to take account of trends in interest rates in the world's money centres, given the absence or ineffectiveness of controls and the need to borrow from time to time. LIBOR (the London inter-bank offered rate) is now a household word in debtor countries. So, too, is the Paris Club and the International Monetary Fund (IMF). Not everyone understand 'derivatives', but the word appears with increasing frequency not only in financial journals, but in daily newspapers. The collapse of a bank in one centre can produce financial tremors in other centres. The flight of capital from one country can trigger flights elsewhere. It is now recognized that inflation in the industrial countries can easily be transmitted to other nations.

Though trade barriers persist, and nationalism is far from dead, the increasing trends towards liberalization and globalization make for the easy flow of goods, services and capital. It is difficult to insulate national policies from external developments in a situation where information travels quickly and the foreign investor is a highly sought after 'animal'. One study in the United States concluded that 'foreign economic variables exert a statistically significant influence on US short-term interest rates and their collective influence has been expanding somewhat relative to economic variables.[20]

Notes

1. See Bank for International Settlements (BIS) *64th Annual Report* (April 1993–March 1994), p. 73.
2. *Ibid.*, p. 148.
3. *Ibid.*, p. 174.
4. *Ibid.*
5. See Morgan Guaranty Trust Co., *World Financial Markets*, December 1986.
6. Morgan Guaranty Trust Co., *World Financial Markets*, 2 April 1995.
7. See the World Bank, *Annual Report*, 1995, p. 160.
8. See K. Simons, 'Interest Rate Derivatives and Asset-Liability Management by Commercial Banks', *New England Economic Review* (January/February 1995), pp. 33–41.
9. See International Monetary Fund, *World Economic Outlook*, May 1996 (Washington, DC: IMF, 1996), p. 35.
10. See the United Nations, *World Economic and Social Survey, 1996* (New York: UN, 1996), p. 339.
11. BIS, *64th Annual Report, op. cit.*, p. 105.
12. Morgan Guaranty Trust Co., *World Financial Markets*, 22 November 1989.
13. *Ibid.*
14. Morgan Guaranty Trust Co., *World Financial Markets*, December 1986.
15. BIS, *64th Annual Report, op. cit.*, p. 95.
16. A. H. Meltzer, 'US Policy in the Bretton Woods Era,' Federal Reserve Bank of St Louis, *Review*, Vol. 73 (May/June 1991), pp. 58–83.
17. *Ibid.*
18. See M. Melvin and J. Ladman, 'Coca Dollars and the Dollarization of South America', *Journal of Money, Credit and Banking*, Vol. 23 (No. 4, November 1991), pp. 752–63.
19. See R. Sahay and C. A. Végh, 'Dollarization in Transition Economies', *Finance and Development*, Vol. 32 (March 1995), pp. 36–9. See also G. Calvo and C. Végh, 'Currency Substitution in High Inflation Countries', *Finance and Development*, Vol. 30 (March 1993), pp. 34–7.
20. L. J. Radeki and V. Reinhar, 'The Globalization of Financial Markets and the Effectiveness of Monetary Policy', Federal Reserve Bank of New York, *Quarterly Review*, Vol. 13, (Autumn 1988), pp. 18–27.

Further Reading

Buckley, A., *The Essence of International Money*, Prentice Hall, New York, 1990.

Daniels, R. Z. and L. H. Radebaugh, *International Business, Environments and Operations*, 6th edn, Addision-Wesley Publishing Company, New York, 1992.

Das, D. K. (ed.), *International Finance, Contemporary Issues*, Routledge, New York, 1993.

Dunning, J. H., *The Globalization of Business*, Routledge, London, 1993.

Federal Reserve Bank of Atlanta, *Financial Derivatives, New Instruments and their Uses*, Federal Reserve Bank of Atlanta, Georgia, 1993.

Grabbe, J. O., *International Financial Markets*, Elsevier, New York, 1986.

Hodgson, J. J. and M. G. Herander *International Economic Relations*, Prentice Hall International Inc., Englewood Cliffs, 1983.

International Monetary Fund (Staff Team), *Development in International Exchange and Payments Systems*, IMF, Washington, DC, 1992.

Kenen, P. B., *The International Economy*, 3rd ed Cambridge University Press, Cambridge, 1994.

Kenwood, A. G. and A. L. Lougheed *The Growth of the International Economy, 1820–1980*, George Allen & Unwin, London, 1983.

Kim, T., *International Money and Banking*, Routledge, London, 1993.

Kreinin, M. E., *International Economics*, 6th ed, The Dryden Press, New York, 1991.

Michie, J. and J. G. Smith (eds.), *Managing the Global Economy*, Oxford University Press, London, 1995.

Odell, J. S., *US International Monetary Policy: Markets, Power and Ideas as Sources of Change*, Princeton University Press, Princeton, 1982.

Pilbeam, K., *International Finance*, Macmillan, London, 1992.

Sakamoto, Y. (ed.), *Global Transformation: Challenges to the State System*, The United Nations University Press, New York, 1994.

United Nations, *Global Outlook 2000*, United Nations, New York, 1990.

Wallace, I., *The Global Economic System*, Routledge, London, 1992.

2 International Trade and Payments

THE CHANGING MATRIX OF INTERNATIONAL TRADE

As indicted in the previous chapter, one of the salient features of the post-war period has been the rapid expansion of international trade. Between 1985 and 1995, for example, the value of world merchandise exports grew from US$1860 billion to around US$5000 billion or by more than 150 per cent.

In virtually every year of the post war period, the growth of world merchandise trade has exceeded the growth of world merchandise output. Overall, the volume of world merchandise trade is estimated to have increased at an average annual rate of slightly more than 6 percent during the period 1950–94, compared with close to 4 percent for world output. This means that each 10 percent increase in world output has on average been associated with a 16 percent increase in world trade. During those 45 years, world merchandise output has multiplied $5^{1}/_{2}$ times and world trade has multiplied 14 times both in real terms.[1]

This trend is continuing. In 1993, for example, the volume of world exports increased by 8 per cent as compared to 2 per cent for world real GDP. The growth of trade and investment, of course, tends to lead to a greater range and volume of financial transactions.

The ongoing integration of the world economy, the relative openness of markets, increasing currency convertibility and the numerous opportunities which expanding markets are presenting to newcomers will continue to fuel this expansion. Recognizing the need for larger markets and the link to growth, there has been a number of recent initiatives aimed at reducing or eliminating barriers to trade in both goods and services. An increasing number of countries are joining the General Agreement on Tariffs and Trade (GATT) which has served as the major international forum for discussions aimed at removing trade barriers since the Second World War.[2] There have been several 'rounds' of such discussions. The most recent, which was started in Uruguay in 1986 concluded in December 1993. This round was regarded as not only the most ambitious to date but the most complex, focusing as it did on some sensitive areas such as agriculture, trade related investment measures, anti-dumping and services. The results, which include the formation of the World Trade Organisation to oversee the operation of the international trading system, and lower industrial tariffs point to a more open world economy.

In addition to the efforts being made at the international level to liberalize trade, there have been several initiatives at the bilateral and regional levels in recent years to create larger markets. The on-going discussions between Japan and the United States (the Structural Impediments Initiative) is one such move. The Australia/New Zealand closer Economic Trade Agreement is another, as is the Free Trade Agreement between Canada and the United States. By the beginning of 1994 this latter was expanded to include Mexico and became the North American Free Trade Area (NAFTA) which in time is expected to be open to other countries of the hemisphere. In Europe, the formation of the Single European Market and its potential enlargement would further enhance this region as a major force in the international economy. Many developing countries themselves are adopting new approaches to economic cooperation following early failures. Some developed countries have also offered trade concessions to developing countries, but these are confined to particular groupings and to particular products. Almost all WTO members are involved in at least one regional arrangement designed to further liberalize trade. Under IMF/World Bank monitored structural adjustment programmes trade liberalization at the individual country level is proceeding in a number of countries which traditionally have used trade barriers of various kinds as a development strategy. The import substitution model which involves a highly protectionist policy has lost a great deal of its attractiveness.

While regionalism can complement multilateral efforts in freeing up international trade there are fears that some of these groupings can become inward looking and perhaps become involved in trade wars. Not surprisingly, NAFTA is being seen as the Americans' response to what is taking place in Europe and the Pacific rim where Japan is a major player. Regional arrangements, however, rather than become closed clubs, are likely to attract other neighbouring countries fearful of being adversely affected. This phenomenon is taking place in Europe, and will no doubt also take place in NAFTA.

The global pattern of world trade has undergone fundamental changes since the early post-war years. In 1950, for example, the United States is estimated to have accounted for 17 per cent of world exports. By 1995 this had fallen to 11.6 per cent, though the US was still the world's leading exporter, closely followed by Germany (10.1 per cent) and Japan (8.8 per cent).[3] Together these two latter countries, still suffering the effects of the Second World War, accounted for about 5 per cent to 6 per cent of world exports in the early 1950s. Not surprisingly, among the world's leading exporters are the other industrialized nations such as France, the United Kingdom, Italy, Canada, Netherlands, Belgium and Luxembourg, all of whom exported more than US$150 billion worth of goods respectively in 1995. Among the first 20 leading exporters are to be found the newly industrializing countries such as Hong Kong, Taiwan, the Republic of Korea, Singapore, Mexico, Malaysia and China. China has been moving up the ladder at a phenomenal pace. It is worth noting that the United States' trade with China increased more than it did with Canada. Not surprisingly, the major exporters are also among the major importers. In 1995 the United States accounted for US$771 billion or 14.9 per cent of world imports followed by Germany (8.6 per cent) and Japan (6.5 per cent). While the trade of many developing countries has been increasing, the share of world trade by North America, Western Europe and Asia (see Table 2.1) would suggest that the trade of the developed market economies and of the newly industrializing countries of Asia has grown at a faster rate. Of the US$5 trillion world merchandise exported in 1995, the developed countries accounted for two thirds, selling more than 70 per cent to other developed countries. The developing countries provided about 29 per cent, with almost half coming from South East Asia (excluding China). The economies in transition provided the rest, about 4 per cent.[4]

Table 2.1 Composition of world merchandise trade by region, 1983–95 (percentage shares)

Region	Exports			Imports		
	1983	1993	1995	1983	1993	1995
North America	15.4	16.8	15.9	17.8	19.4	18.7
Latin America	5.8	4.4	4.6	4.4	4.8	4.9
Western Europe	39.0	44.0	44.8	39.8	41.9	43.5
Central/Eastern Europe and the former USSR	9.6	2.8	3.1	8.3	2.6	3.9
Africa	4.4	2.4	2.1	4.6	2.4	2.4
Middle East	6.7	3.4	2.9	6.2	3.2	2.6
Asia	19.1	26.2	26.6	18.9	25.7	24.2
	100.0	100.0	100.0	100.0	100.0	100.0

Source: WTO, *International Trade, Trends and Statistics*, 1994 and 1995.

While trade has been growing internationally, intraregional trade has also been growing in some cases. In the case of North America, the share of intraregional merchandise exports in total exports increased from 33.2 per cent in 1983 to 36.0 per cent in 1995. In the case of Western Europe the comparable increase was from 65.8 to 68.9 per cent; in the case of Asia the proportion moved from 22.5 per cent to 50.9 per cent; and in the case of Latin America the figured increased from 18.4 per cent to 20.8 per cent. While intraregional trade has been growing, interregional trade is by no means insignificant. Over 25 per cent of North America's exports go to Asia and around 20 per cent to Western Europe. More than half the exports of Central/Eastern Europe and the former USSR are sold in Western Europe. Asia provides a market for more than 40 per cent of the exports of the Middle East. The developed countries continue to be major trading partners for developing countries. Almost half the exports of Latin America are sold in North America, while a similar situation obtains for Africa in Western Europe. Asia provides a market for more than 40 per cent of the exports of the Middle East.

Of particular significance in recent years is the pace at which a number of developing countries are moving up the rank of leading exporters. Honk Kong moved from 25th place to 9th between 1973 and 1995, Taiwan from 28th to 14th, the Republic of Korea from 39th to 12th, Singapore from 33rd to 13th and Thailand from 51st to 22nd. Brazil, however, dropped on the scale from 19th to 26th in the period (see Table 2.2).

Table 2.2   Selected exporters ranked on the basis of the value of merchandise trade, 1973 and 1995

Countries	Rank	
	1973	1995
Hong Kong	25	9
Taiwan	28	14
Republic of Korea	39	12
China	22	11
Singapore	33	13
Mexico	45	18
Brazil	19	26
Malaysia	41	19
Indonesia	44	27
Thailand	51	22
India	42	31

Source: GATT, *International Trade,* various issues.

Goods (or merchandise) are not the only items traded internationally. Of growing importance in recent years is the export of commercial services which in 1995 amounted to over US$1000 billion or 20 per cent of world merchandise exports. This trade is dominated by the developed countries, with the United States being the leading exporter and importer accounting for 17 per cent of exports and 12.0 per cent of imports in 1995. In terms of the composition of the exports of services from both developed and developing countries, the share of business services has increased significantly from both groups since 1970.[5]

While the growth of both exports and imports does not follow any smooth or easily predictable pattern, the value of exports tends to fluctuate more because of the number of factors affecting volume and price changes. Primary commodities still account for almost one quarter of world trade and for just under half of the exports of the developing countries.[6] When the value of world imports exceeds the value of exports the deficit in the external accounts can be financed either from reserves or from capital inflows (investment, aid or loans), or from both. An examination of the current account position of some of the major countries in the world economy in recent years can be quite revealing. For instance, the data for the United States in the period 1983–95 show this country as having a trade deficit in every year of the period. The positive services inflows were not sufficiently large to offset the trade deficits in any year. Net capital inflows (dominated by direct investment, portfolio and other short-term capital) far exceeded the current account deficits. Germany, on the other hand showed a persistent positive trade balance in the period and a persistent net capital outflow. Japan's external accounts displayed a similar pattern. For the developing countries as a group the trade balances were generally positive, but these were offset by investment income (interest, profits, dividends) paid abroad. This was typical of Latin America, Africa and West Asia. For capital importing developing countries, direct investment flows dropped significantly in the 1980s, but started to increase again in the early 1990s. Service payments, relating to private debt were generally greater than new credit flows. With respect to official flows, interest payments on the public debt continue to offset most of the new credits. For the poorer developing countries grants provide a relatively significant flow.

Countries are able to operate persistent current account deficits, once net capital flows are positive. Capital inflows, however, are not easily predictable since capital moves in response to a complex set of factors. A government's policy may be influenced by the desired level of investment and the actual level of domestic savings. The extent of its own intervention will be influenced by the kind of role it envisages for itself. A government may borrow to finance both consumption and investment; how much it is able to borrow, however, will be influenced by its ability to repay and how creditors view future prospects and repayment record. Governments which are members of the International Monetary Fund (IMF) can use the facilities of this organization to finance balance of payments deficits, but access is governed by rules and conditionalities. Private capital moves in response to rates of return and risk. Rates of return are determined not only by the level of interest rates or profit rates, but by the tax regime. Besides economic risks, other risks may arise from political factors, convertibility, the exchange rate and government regulations. Interest rates and expected profits alone cannot explain the movement of private capital.

Between 1988 and 1995, total net external financing requirements of developing countries amounted to around US$1040 billion. Non-debt creating flows (such as direct and portfolio investment) contributed 40 per cent, net external borrowing 59 per cent and IMF credit and loans less than one per cent.[7]

The removal of capital controls and the emergence of a wide range of new financial instruments in various currencies have allowed financial capital to become more mobile than real capital (direct investment) or goods. The move to a policy of greater convertibility and the ease with which such assets can be traded in domestic and international markets have contributed to this mobility and the integration of financial markets. Interest rates, bond and stock prices and even capital gains in one country increasingly mirror movements in other countries. According to recent trends noted earlier, gross capital outflows from the main industrial countries may now be in excess of US$1000 billion. The persistence of such sizable capital flows for almost a decade has resulted in a sharp increase in the proportion of financial assets held by non-residents. According to one calculation, non-resident holdings now amount to around 20–25 per cent of total outstanding government bonds in the Group of Ten countries other than Japan.[8]

Net capital flows have also become large (see Table 2.3). In the 1980s the movement of funds was largely among the industrial countries but the flow of funds to developing countries from both loans and investment dropped significantly. In recent years, however, this trend has been reversed, but for some countries, particularly those in Africa, the situation is still bleak. In 1995, the developing countries were able to borrow US$81.1 billion in international capital markets – more than US$51 billion above the level of 1985. An increasing share of these arrangements were bonds, a form of lending that was once open only to a few countries and in limited amounts.[9]

Despite the tendency to treat trade in goods and services as a topic that could be studied quite separately from money and finance, it is difficult to separate the movement of goods and services from the international flow

Table 2.3   Global net capital flows, 1976–93, in US$ billions, annual averages

Countries	1976–80	1981–85	1986–90	1991	1992	1993[1]
United States	–9.3	53.9	99.7	–13.5	24.4	42.3
Japan	–0.3	–23.0	–63.9	–90.0	–118.8	–108.0
Western Europe	27.1	2.6	15.3	75.0	55.7	–20.6
Developing countries of which:	15.8	40.9	37.4	126.4	143.0	159.5
Asian NIEs[2]	4.1	3.5	–6.0	3.5	5.0	7.2
Other Asia	6.4	15.2	22.3	36.0	48.1	50.0
Latin America	22.6	12.5	8.8	34.2	57.5	67.4

Note: Changes in net official monetary position are excluded. A minus sign
         indicates a capital outflow.
        [1] Partly estimated;
        [2] Excluding Hong Kong.

Source: Bank for International Settlements, *64th Annual Report*, 1 April 1993–31
March 1994.

of monetary assets. True, some trade takes the form of barter, that is the
exchange of goods for goods. Countries who suffer from a shortage of
foreign currency (that is currencies or monetary assets such as gold) that
are acceptable to other nations as payments for goods and services, often
have little choice but to engage in barter.

Trade in goods and services constitutes only one of the many economic
transactions that take place between states. Public and private gifts (unilateral
or unrequited transfers) also cross national borders. Private investment is an
integral part of the world economy. In fact it is often difficult to separate trade
from investment since the latter tends to create trade. Governments, public
enterprises and private companies also borrow money from abroad and these
debts have to be serviced. The external economic transactions of a country
are generally summed up in an account known as the 'balance of payments'
which can tell how well or how badly a country has performed externally
over a period of time. In the following section we undertake an analysis of
this account. This is followed by a discussion on international liquidity.

UNDERSTANDING INTERNATIONAL FINANCIAL RELATIONS
THROUGH THE BALANCE OF PAYMENTS

Terms such as 'trade balance', 'services balances', 'current account
balance', 'capital account balance' or balance of payments 'deficit and

surplus' (or balance of payments equilibrium or disequilibrium) are bound to crop up in any discussions relating to economic relations between two countries. These terms can be confusing to the average person, but they help to define the 'balance of payments' which is essentially a summary record of all economic transactions between the residents (firms, individuals and government) of a country and foreign residents (the rest of the world) over a given period of time, usually one year. In compiling their balance of payments accounts countries have come to follow certain common practices, even though there can be small variations in presentation. Such a situation facilitates comparison. The IMF has helped greatly in clarifying certain critical concepts. For balance of payments purposes 'a country means those individuals and business enterprises, including financial institutions, that have a permanent association with a country's territory together with that country's governmental authorities at all levels.'[10] Residents include all those economic units whose economic activity is subject to direction and control by the national authorities. All enterprises that are engaged in production in the domestic territory are regarded as residents, even if they are owned by foreigners.

The balance of payments is not a mere statement of money receipts and payments. It includes all transactions which at some stage (whether sooner or later) give rise to monetary settlement in cash or against credit of varying duration. It also includes some economic transactions even if they will never give rise to monetary settlements (for example goods granted under a foreign aid program). The balance of payments is intended to record systematically all the flows of real resources between a country (that is residents) and the rest of the world, and all the changes in its foreign assets and liabilities.[11] As such the balance of payments tells at a glance how well or how badly a country is doing on the economic front. It not only shows the trading positions, but the extent of borrowing from or lending to the rest of the world and movements in assets and liabilities. It shows how deficits are financed or surpluses disposed of. In sum, it reflects the depth of interaction with the international economy.

There are several points that we need to note about the balance of payments. The term 'balance of payments' or 'balance of international payments' itself can be misleading. Some observers feel the term 'balance of international transactions' would be more appropriate.

Transactions are not classified according to actual receipts or payments of money that may or may not occur. Instead, they are classified according to the direction of payment that they would typically entail sooner or later, whether or not money is paid in each transaction. Commodity imports, for example, appears as the debit or 'payments-to-foreigners' side of a country's balance of international payments and not because the act of bringing goods into a country in itself is an outpayment – of course it is not – because commodity imports typically have to be paid for. A particular import is still classified this way even if it is not paid for (it may come as a gift or as part of a barter deal, or the importer may default on his obligation to make payments.[12]

It should be noted that even though the balance of payments presentation may sometimes seem illogical and confusing, under IMF guidelines member countries have come to adopt a number of common conventions, concepts and definitions which tend to facilitate international comparison.[13] There are, of course, some variations in presentation and detail to suit individual country's needs.

A second point that we need to note is that it is a record – a record in the sense that it reflects inward and outward movements of goods, services and assets, which continually cross a country's borders and which by international agreements are included in the balance of payments. There are some transactions, of course, which escape the authorities and therefore do not show up in the balance of payments. Secondly, it adopts the approach of a double entry bookkeeping system, that is, every payment (debit) has a receipt counterpart (credit) and vice versa. Most transactions appear for the first time in the currency or capital account and then for the second time in the cash compartment (the financing section) of the capital account.[14] By tradition credit entries are made in the left-hand column and debit entries in the right-hand column. In summary statements a net outflow (for example imports greater than exports) is usually associated with a minus sign, while a net inflow (for example exports greater than imports) would carry a plus or no sign.

This convention does not apply to the capital (monetary or settlements) account of the balance of payments. If, for example, total credits in the current and capital (non-monetary) accounts were greater than total debits, for the two sides to balance in the overall position, the adjusting items in the settlements or financing account would have to appear on the debit side which would reflect the disposition of the surplus. One way to interpret this is to say that the settlements (financing account) pays to the reserves (stock) account so much and so much. Of course, if total debits in the current and capital (non-monetary) accounts were greater than total credits, the adjusting items would appear on the credit side of the settlements account, if the two sides were to balance. One way to read this is to say the settlements account receives from reserves so much and so much.

In summary form the overall surplus (current and capital accounts) would be offset by a figure with a negative sign in the settlements account (reserves of foreign exchange have increased) and an overall deficit by figures with a positive sign (reserves of foreign exchange have decreased). In the summary statement – as that shown in Table 2.4(b) – an overall deficit (a figure with a negative sign) will be counterbalanced by a figure with a positive sign (indicating a reduction in reserves or assets). An overall surplus (a figure with a positive sign), on the other hand, will be accompanied by a figure with a negative sign in the reserves account (indicating an increase in assets or reserves). Because of the double entry system of bookkeeping, the balance of payments always balances in an accounting sense.

Two further points are worth noting. In the case of barter both entries are in the goods and services account. Secondly, official agencies are not always able to pick up all transactions between residents and non-residents and, therefore, an 'errors and omissions' item which is a statistical residual is associated with all balance of payments accounts.

Though exports represent an outflow of goods (or services) the payment received (or to be received) is an inflow and is recorded as a credit item in the current account. To the extent that export receipts lead to an increase in foreign reserves, this change would be indicated by a minus sign. Imports are inflows of goods and services, but payments to suppliers are an outflow and treated as a debit item. When payments are made out of reserves, the decrease is associated with a plus sign. A decrease is often indicated in summary statements by a plus sign, but the sign is generally left out. It is common to speak of goods (merchandise) exports as *visible* exports, and goods imports as *visible* imports. The difference between these two items is referred to as the balance of *visible* trade. An explanation is required with respect to the treatment of services which are commonly referred to as 'invisibles'. Services cover a wide range of transactions relating to transport, tourism, finance and investment. Payments in the form of interest, dividends, profits, reinsurance, royalties, consultant fees, and so on are included in the services account.

The 'exports' and 'imports' items in the balance of payments are normally associated with terms such as f.o.b., c.&f., and c.i.f. which are placed next to them. They refer to the terms of purchase (or sale) and give an indication of what the figures contain, or do not contain. Exports are generally associated with f.o.b. terms, that is, all the exporter is required to do is deliver the goods over the ship's rail, where delivery and change of title take place. Exports f.o.b. means that the figures reflect the basic cost of the goods and perhaps the cost for packing and transport to the docks. The importer then takes responsibility for transporting the goods to wherever he wants them. 'Imports' with 'c.&f.' next to it means that figures include both basic cost and the cost of freight. If the goods were insured, the term would become c.i.f., that is, cost, insurance and freight. Trade transactions are associated with a number of other terms such as f.a.s. (free alongside ship), f.o.r. (free on rail), ex works (basic price) and FRANCO (free to the importer's premises). The inclusion of freight and insurance costs explains why the value of a product at the importer's port would differ from the value given to it at the exporter's port. On top of the c.i.f. value an importer may have to pay other charges and taxes to which a profit margin is then added. These costs are generally passed on to the consumer.

It should be pointed out that the balance of payments is structured in terms of transactions, rather than in terms of how payments are made, or how foreign currency is earned or spent. Foreign exchange earned by an aircraft (owned by residents) or the transport of people or goods is no different from foreign exchange earned from the export of merchandise. When visitors go to a particular country, the foreign currency spent in the form of hotel charges, goods, drinks, transport or handicrafts purchases are treated as foreign exchange earned, and show up in the balance of payments of the host country as credit items. What is a credit (receipt) for one country is, of course, a payment (debit) for another.

Because of the double entry accounting approach total credits (which by convention are put in the left hand column) are always equal to total debits and in this sense (accounting) the balance of payments always balances. In a non-accounting sense, however, very rarely would total payments to the rest of the world be exactly equal to total receipts, either in the sub-accounts or overall. There can be a surplus (when total receipts are greater than total payments) or deficit (total payments are greater than total receipts) in any one of the sub-accounts as well as in the overall position, that is in the current and capital (non-monetary) accounts taken together. A surplus in one sub-account can be offset by a deficit in another sub-account, (and vice versa) so that the overall position may not be the same. When one speaks of a surplus or deficit, it is always useful to specify the account being referred to.

Earlier, mention was made of the 'reserves' account and a little more needs to be said on this. 'International reserves' refer to assets which governments use to settle debts with each other. 'International liquidity' is commonly used to describe the 'stock' or availability of such assets. The foreign reserves or international liquidity account can be regarded as a kind of savings account closely associated with foreign earnings and spending. Unlike the balance of payments which is a 'flow' account the reserves account is a 'stock' account. It is closely related to the balance of payments account, but is not part of it. The state of the foreign reserves gives a good indication of how well the country is doing on the trade front. It is also an index of import capacity and helps to define the country's credit worthiness when it tries to borrow on international capital markets.

Balance of payments concepts can best be illustrated with the use of an example. Table 2.4(a) and 2.4(b) shows fictitious 1990 and 1995 accounts for Country A in standard and summary form respectively. Basically, as can be seen the balance of payments is divided into two parts: the current account and the capital account. The current account has three sections: (a) the goods or trade (merchandise) acccount; (b) the services account; and (c) the unilateral transfers account. The capital account is divided into two main parts: one shows the movement of capital associated with private

Table 2.4 (a)   Country A: balance of payments standard presentation in US$ million

		1990		1995	
		Credit	*Debit*	*Credit*	*Debit*
A.	*Goods or merchandise*	*1 000*	*900*	*500*	*800*
	Exports (f.o.b.)	1 000	nil	500	nil
	Imports (c.i.f.)	nil	900	nil	800
B.	*Services*	*210*	*290*	*352*	*320*
	Freight	80	85	21	58
	Non-merchandise insurance	20	55	8	46
	Travel	95	50	300	105
	Investment income	13	85	4	98
	Other services	2	15	19	13
C.	*Un-requited (uni-lateral) transfers*	*60*	*27*	*70*	*85*
	Private	35	16	60	66
	Government	25	11	10	19
D.	*Current account*	*1 270*	*1 217*	*922*	*1 205*
E.	*Capital*	*68*	*192*	*523*	*148*
	Direct investment	44	126	480	102
	Other private long term	17	53	22	17
	Other private short term	2	nil	3	23
	Central government	5	13	18	6
F.	Allocation of SDR's	*10*	nil	nil	nil
G.	Net Errors and Omissions	*6*	nil	nil	15
H.	Total (A to G)	*1 354*	*1 409*	*1 445*	*1 368*

Table 2.4 (b) Country a: balance of payments (summary) in US$ million

		1990	1995
A.	*Merchandise* (net)	*100*	*-300*
	Exports	1 000	500
	Imports	900	800
B.	*Service* (net)	*-80*	*+32*
	Freight	-5	-37
	Non-merchandise insurance	-35	-38
	Travel	45	195
	Investment income	-72	-94
	Other services	-13	6
C.	*Un-requited transfers*	*33*	*-15*
	Private	19	-6
	Government	14	-9
D.	*Current account*	*53*	*-283*
E.	*Net capital movements*	*-124*	*+375*
	Direct investment	-82	378
	Other private long term	-36	5
	Other private short term	2	-20
	Central government	-8	-12
	Allocation of SDRS	10	nil
F.	*Allocation of SDRs*	*10*	nil
G.	*Net errors and omissions*	*6*	*-15*
H.	*Overall surplus or deficit*	*-55*	77
I.	*Change in reserves*	*55*	*-77*
	(minus means increase)		
	Commercial banks	3	nil
	Central Government	nil	nil
	Central bank:		
	Reserves assets	35	-60
	Reserve position in the IMF	12	-17
	Special Drawing Rights	5	nil

sector and government activities, while the other is termed the financing or settlements account. As can be seen Table 2.4(a) the results in 1990 show that the trade (or merchandise) account was positive (surplus or favourable) while the services account was negative (deficit or unfavourable). In 1995 the reverse position obtained, that is, the trade account was negative and the services account was positive. Both individuals and governments make and receive gifts in the form of goods, services, securities and money to foreign governments and residents. Gifts are one way (unilateral or unrequited) transfers. In other words, there is no corresponding movement in kind or cash in the opposite direction, as happens in the case of imports and exports. A good example of a unilateral transfer is the money sent back home by immigrants living abroad. Some governments make available financial resources (grants) to other governments who are not required to repay as happens in the case of imports and exports, or when a loan is made. In other words, there is no *quid pro quo*. In the case of a loan, there is a change in both the assets and liabilities position of the receiving country and this would be put in the capital account. The country from which the gift is made would show the transfer as a debit item, while the receiving country would show it as a credit item. The balance of payments account divides the unilateral or unrequited transfers into two parts: public (government) and private. Capital is often classified in terms of long term and short term and also in terms of public (government) and private. Long-term capital tends to be used in reference to real investment and financial claims with a maturity of one year or more. Real investment includes not only producing facilities, but buildings and land. Short-term capital tends to be associated with a maturity period of less than one year. Investments give rise to profits, interest and dividends which may be re-invested or remitted back to the investor's home country. Countries whose residents invest heavily abroad have a greater inflow of investment income than countries whose residents undertake very little foreign investment. This explains why the GNP of the industrial countries tend to be greater than their GDP.

The country from which the investment originates will show the transaction as a debit item, while the receiving country will show it as a credit item. The earnings, however, would be recorded in the services account (of the current account) with inflows being placed in the credit column and outflows in the debit column. The sum of the goods account, the services account and the unilateral transfers account gives us what is commonly called the *current account balance*.

The capital account is normally divided into two parts. The first shows the movement in investment funds (both long term and short term) and loan capital. Direct investment occurs when foreign investors acquire or establish an enterprise in which control is retained. Portfolio investment refers largely to securities (debentures, stocks, bonds, and so on) purchase in which the motivation is a guaranteed return rather than control. It should be noted that the repayment of a loan (the principal) is recorded in the capital account while the interest payments are placed in the current account.

The second part of the capital account focuses on changes in the country's foreign reserves, and is commonly referred to as the *financing or settlements account*. The items in this account are seen as 'below the line' or 'accommodating' items. These transactions are not undertaken for their own sake but can be regarded as residual changes in the country's assets/liability (liquidity) position as a result of transactions that have taken place 'above the line'. The latter are termed 'autonomous' in that they are undertaken for their own sake in response to changes in prices, interest rates, income, and so on. The distinction between 'autonomous' and accommodating' is based on motivation, and therefore is not always easy to make. A grant for example, may be made with the aim of helping a poor country, but may be specifically aimed at assisting that country to finance a balance of payments deficit.

An examination of Table 2.4(b) will show that Country A had an overall deficit of $55 million in 1990, that is, the total debits under Sections A to G were greater than the total credits. The deficit was largely financed by drawing on reserves assets and to a lesser extent by using the tranche credit and SDR facilities at the Fund. The movement of commercial bank funds also helped. It should be pointed out that some countries put capital movements associated with commercial banks 'above the line' in cases where governments exercise little control over the foreign operations of these institutions. In cases, however, where the banks are allowed to hold only small working foreign exchange balances and their operations are strictly monitored by the central bank, their position could easily be above or below the line. Note that for the credit and debit columns for 1990 to be equal in Table 2.4(a), the $55 million (the financing item) would have to be on credit side, even thought the situation is one of deficit. One way to read this is to say that the current account receives (credit) from the reserves account (debit) the sum of $55 million. In 1995 Country A had an overall surplus of $77 million, even though it had a current account deficit of $283 million. The latter was more than offset by direct investment inflows. A surplus could be used in one of three main ways or in a combination of them. It could be used to augment the country's foreign reserves which could be used to finance deficits in subsequent years. Alternatively, it could wholly or partly take the form of loans to other countries, or it could be used to settle debt incurred in the past. The debt could have been to private financial institutions, other governments or international or regional agencies like the IMF, the World Bank, the Inter-American Development Bank and the Caribbean Development Bank. In Table 2.4(b)

Country A used $60 million of the $77 million in 1995 to increase its reserves and $17 million to repay money borrowed from the IMF. Note that in Table 2.4(a) the balancing item of $77 million would have to be on the debit side if the two columns are to balance. This could be read as saying that the balance of payments account paid (deficit) to the reserves account (credit) the sum of $77 million.

All countries' balance of payments show an item called 'errors and omissions' which could relate either to the debit or credit side. The reason for the presence of this residual item is very simple. Some of the figures that appear in the accounts are derived from several sources which may not always provide complete information. Documents can also go astray and the statisticians frequently have to make estimates on the basis of what is available. The item also reflects unreported flows of private capital. It also should be noted that for countries participating in the Special Drawing Right (SDR) arrangement of the IMF, the balance of payments also shows movements in SDR holdings, since SDRs can be used in external settlements with other countries.

The balance of payments accounts are important to governments in helping to formulate monetary, fiscal and trade policies. In open economies, domestic demand tends to have a close relationship with the country's reserves position. The trends in the balance of payments also help governments in fashioning their trade policies. Some governments may wish to focus on particular items which they consider critical to policy making. One such concept is the *basic balance* which includes the current account and long-term capital transactions only.

The balance of payments accounts can tell a great deal about a country's economic structure and the features of its economy. Some countries, for instance, produce so few goods that they depend on foreign sources for a wide range of products. In a number of cases earnings from exports of goods alone are not able to pay for needed imports. Some countries run perpetual trade deficits, but this is possible because of the foreign exchange they earn from the export of services (for example tourism) or from transfers. For some economies, remittances are more significant than for others. Movements in the capital account can give an indication of investors' confidence in the economy. In situations where there are buoyant capital inflows over a prolonged period of time, these can conceal serious problems in the current account.

An overall deficit in any one year does not mean that the country has a balance of payments problem. A deficit could occur for a variety of reasons. A drop in the price of commodities which the country exports, a rise in import prices or import volume, reduced investment flows, capital flight or a drop in foreign demand for the country's exports can individually or collectively lead to a deficit. Depending on the underlying cause, a deficit may be reversed quickly. However, persistent deficits can result in the erosion of the country's reserves, leading to a contraction of import capacity, that is, its ability to buy needed imports. Borrowing (be it from private financial institutions, other governments, multilateral institutions such as the IMF) may provide temporary relief. Persistent borrowing itself soon leads to heavy service payments, which can take a significant proportion of foreign exchange earnings. Inability to service debt makes it difficult to raise new loans, in the absence of which the country's investment programme may be curtailed significantly. For countries which have experienced persistent balance of payments problems and have exhausted the borrowing option, they may have no recourse but to turn to the IMF for assistance. Assistance from this institution is for the most part conditional upon accepting its advice.

BALANCE OF PAYMENTS ADJUSTMENT IN THE INTERNATIONAL SYSTEM

As we shall see later the International Monetary Fund (IMF) was set up to provide short-term balance of payments assistance to member states experiencing balance of payments difficulties. Such assistance was intended to discourage countries from instituting measures to restrict trade – measures which could invite retaliation and inhibit the growth and development of world trade. The exchange arrangements were also designed to avoid competitive devaluations and the 'beggar thy neighbour' type of policies that emerged in the 1930s. Not surprisingly a major purpose of the Fund was to facilitate 'expansion and balanced growth of international trade'.

Despite this objective, the Fund Articles of Agreement are not very clear on the sharing of the burden of adjustment between surplus and deficit countries. Under the fixed exchange rate system a member state was required to sell foreign currency when the demand was greater than the supply, and to buy foreign exchange when the reverse situation prevailed. This was necessary to maintain the rate within agreed margins. Of course, when monetary authorities were hard pressed for reserves in an environment where great store was placed on stable exchange rates, crises easily developed. Eventually, the whole fixed exchange rate system was abolished, though there are many countries which still peg their currencies to a major currency. To the extent that there are exchange or other forms of controls the rate adopted may not be the market rate, that is the rate that brings supply and demand into equilibrium.

The Fund's rules (Article 8) prohibit member states from imposing restrictions on the making of payments and transfers on current international transactions without the approval of the Fund. The same Article also prohibits discriminatory currency arrangements or multiple currency practices without the Fund's authorization. While there was a commitment that all restrictions on current payments would eventually be removed and member states would move towards full convertibility, in practice only a small number of countries (mainly the industrial ones have been able to abolish all exchange controls). In practice, most developing countries because of external payments difficulties have retained a variety of controls on trade and payments, though under structural adjustment programmes these are being gradually removed. The GATT Articles also make provision for retention of controls on trade in certain circumstances. One of the difficulties in freeing up international trade is that even when tariffs are reduced or eliminated, countries have come up with a range of non-tariff barriers which are just as potent as tariffs in restricting trade. For political, security and other reasons some sectors are very sensitive and governments tend to use a variety of devices to shield them from foreign competition.

A balance of payments problem (in the sense of a persistent external deficit reflecting itself in the run-down of a country's reserves) can emerge in response to a variety of developments. A decline in the prices or volume of goods or services exported is a frequent factor. If imports do not drop correspondingly, the tendency is to use reserves (or borrowing) to pay suppliers. Of course, an increase in the volume or prices of imports without increased foreign exchange earnings will also impact on the country's reserves or debt position. It is worth pointing out that the level of reserves is affected not only by current transactions, but what takes place in the capital account as well. Reduced flows of foreign investment or a flight of capital will also be reflected in the foreign position. Inflows from foreign loans and debt repayments can also increase or decrease the level of reserves.

Faced with a balance of payments problem, there are several types of measures or policies which a government can adopt. Some of these would be subject to constraints arising from membership of regional and international organizations which carry with it, as indicated before, certain obligations. It can increase tariffs or institute quantitative restrictions with a view to discouraging imports. At a time when governments are under pressure to adopt a more open stance towards international trade, this is becoming increasingly more difficult to do, notwithstanding the exception clauses in the Charter of international organizations. The other approach which can be taken where a fixed exchange rate policy is in place is to devalue the currency. A devaluation is normally intended to increase the price of imports in local currency and reduce the price of exports to foreigners. Such a move is expected to improve the trade balance, but this does not always turn out to be so; whether or not there is improvement depends on the existence of certain conditions and the structure of the economy. The responsiveness of exports and imports to changes in the exchange rate, for example, may be crucial to the net outcome. As the exchange rate changes one cannot assume that all other things will remain equal. Higher prices (in domestic currency) for imported inputs and increased wages and salaries instigated by higher prices for imported goods and services could offset the devaluation advantage. The effects of a devaluation on the income of the devaluing country also has to be taken into account. The possible outcomes tend to be examined through the 'elasticity' and 'absorption' models or approaches to devaluation. Another form of analysis, of which there are several variants, and widely referred to as the 'monetary approach' to the balance of payments, links balance of payments problems to disturbances in the stock, demand and supply of money.[15]

Of course, if the local currency is floating, the greater demand for foreign currency would lead to a depreciation of the local currency to a point where supply and demand for foreign currency would be once more equal. In other words, the deficit would be eliminated through the exchange rate mechanism. In practice, a combination of policies is used to deal with payments deficits, including monetary and fiscal policy which can be used to reduce domestic demand. A government can reduce its own expenditure, and also the spending power of the private sector through an increase in taxation. The Central Bank can also use its power to influence the commercial banks to reduce lending, or not to lend for specified kinds of transactions. The Central Bank can do this through 'moral suasion' or through changes in reserve requirements or in the discount rate, that is, the rate at which the Central Bank as lender of last resort lends to the commercial banks in times of difficulty.

For a while, a country may postpone the adopting of corrective measures by borrowing in private external markets to finance an external deficit. The extent to which a government can borrow would depend on its creditors' assessment of its ability to service its debt. Fear of the conditions for which the IMF is reputed often leads developing countries in particular to turn to this institution as a last resort. Invariably, IMF assistance comes with conditions the impact of which has been the subject of a great deal of controversy.

Even the development lending institutions are now loath to provide financial assistance without a structural adjustment programme of some kind in place.

INTERNATIONAL LIQUIDITY

At the domestic level, an individual's assets may take several forms. He may have cash at home, savings in financial institutions, stocks and bonds, land, house, a car, and so on. Cash in hand may be regarded as the most 'liquid' of these assets since it can be used for immediate payments. In place of currency, credit is being increasingly used to make cash settlements, so that access to credit has to be treated as part of an individual's money balance. The concept of liquidity as commonly used at the domestic level has as its main measuring yardstick nearness to cash. Financial savings, therefore, would tend to be regarded as more liquid than a car or house which could take some time to be disposed of before they can be converted into a means of payment. An individual's assets is often structured to meet not only his immediate needs, but may need to conform to some notion of future requirements. Payments or settlement needs have to be balanced against the desire for income from assets and contingency concerns.

In the same way that an individual needs money balances to meet his daily transaction needs, a country also has to keep in stock assets that could be used to make payments to other countries. What is acceptable to other trading countries as a means of settlements help to determine what it is prepared to accept for export of its own goods and services. International liquidity, therefore, refers to the stock of assets that can be used to settle financial claims among countries. In the same way that there is no precise definition of money, not everyone agrees on what should be included in international reserves. In practice, foreign or international reserves is comprised of gold, foreign exchange, Special Drawing Rights (SDRs) and Reserve Position in the Fund. The stock of official gold reserves was declining even before the decision was taken in 1976 to abolish the official price of gold and to eliminate the obligation to use it in transactions with the Fund. Official gold reserves fell from 1193.58 millions of ounces at the end of 1965 to 1018.2 million of ounces at the end of 1975. By the end of August 1996, the figure had further declined to 904.88 millions of ounces. If the latter figure were valued at the London market price of US$386.45 per ounce it would have amounted to 293.5 billions of SDRs (US$427.8 billion), as compared to 1044.0 billion SDRs for foreign exchange. Fund-related assets (namely) reserve positions in the Fund and SDRs amounted to 56.7 billion SDRs. Table 2.5 shows reserves held by selected countries at the end of June 1996. Japan had the largest stock 145.6 billion SDRs (13.6 per cent of the total) followed by Taiwan with 59.5 billion SDRs (5.6 per cent), and Germany

Table 2.5 Contribution of selected countries to world reserves[1], 1950–96, in millions of SDRs

Countries	1950 (end of)	1970 (end of)	1980 (end of)	1996 (end of June)
Industrial countries of which	*37 662*	*70 783*	*211 893*	*562 921*
France	791	4 960	24 301	21 377
Germany	190	13 609	41 430	62 238
Italy	741	5 352	20 466	36 293
Japan	605	4 840	20 164	145 635
Netherlands	543	3 241	10 669	22 445
Spain	121	1,818	9 813	34 992
Switzerland	1 579	5 132	15 190	27 023
United Kingdom	3 443	2 827	16 851	27 758
United States	24 266	14 487	21 479	59 325
Developing countries of which	*10 355*	*22 397*	*142 888*	*507 925*
Brazil	...	...	...	40 274
China (People's Republic)	...	...	2 444	61 834
Guyana	...	20	10	198
India	2 057	1 007	5 745	12 891
Jamaica	29	139	82	565
Kenya	...	220	388	487
Maurllius	...	46	72	604
Mexico	297	744	2 393	11 430
Nigeria	110	222	8 049	1 572
Republic of Korea	27	610	2 304	25 319
Saudi Arabia	...	662	18 536	6 920
Singapore	88	1 012	5 149	50 014
Taiwan	47	622	1 839	59 490
Thailand	291	905	1 310	26 959
Trinidad and Tobago	...	43	2,182	392
Venezuela	378	1 021	5 579	5 437
World Total	*48 448*	*93 180*	*354 781*	*1 070 846*

Note: The figures include gold valued at 35 SDR per ounce.
[1] Mainly members of the IMF.
... not available

Source: IMF *International Financial Statistics,* various issues.

with 62.2 billion SDRs (5.8 per cent). The share held by Singapore was higher than that of several developed countries. The figures reflect the strides made by countries such as Korea, Taiwan, Singapore and Thailand as exporters since 1950.

At the end of the Second World War, the United States emerged as the strongest economy in the world, and it was not surprising that the US dollar came to perform the role of an international currency in the absence of one. While the US dollar became the lynchpin of the Bretton Woods system, gold was not completely abandoned. The system set up was in fact a gold-exchange system. Member states of the Fund could declare a par value either in terms of gold or the US dollar and since the US government had undertaken to buy and sell gold at US$35 per ounce, a par value with respect to either one could easily be converted to one involving the other asset.

An asset that is widely acceptable and can be used as an accounting unit and as a store of value facilities trade. The US dollar fulfilled these functions in the early post-war years. The absence of other assets which could pose serious competition made countries willing to hold US dollars, and this was the fundamental reason why the United States, despite a persistent deficit in its balance of payments, was able to finance a great deal of its activities abroad by printing money. What was initially a dollar shortage became a dollar glut. This ability to make claim over other countries' goods and services or other assets by printing money is often seen as one of the main advantages of being a reserve currency country. But there are disadvantages as well, as we shall see later.

One of the major issues featuring in the discussions on the international monetary system in the 1960s centred on the question of international liquidity. The concern was not only about adequacy, but distribution among countries and the supply of each type of liquidity. Perhaps of even greater concern was the lack of control over the growth of reserves. Following the end of the Second World War both US dollars and gold were being used by countries to settle their international payments. Because of the position of the United States as the principal supplier of goods in the early post-war years the largest use of reserves was to make payments to the United States. In 1947 the US had a trade surplus of US$10 billion. At the end of 1938 the United States' holding of gold totalled US$14.6 billion, but by 30 June 1947 this had risen to US$21.4 billion and to almost US$25 billion by 1944. The much talked about 'dollar shortage' prevailed until about the mid-1950s. Military spending abroad in the 1950s increased the dollar holdings of foreign central banks. Loans to foreign governments and investment abroad by private firms and individuals contributed to the deficit in the capital account. The relatively large deficits which began in the late 1950s reflected mainly a rising net outflow of capital, and since the mid-1960s a dwindling trade surplus that soon turned into a rapidly increasing deficit. The US had committed itself to buy and sell gold at US$35 per ounce, and in keeping with this, foreign central banks did not hesitate to exchange dollars for gold which was seen as a more stable asset. The US gold reserves dropped from US$24.6 billion in 1949 to US$12 billion in 1967. Over this period the ratio of official liabilities to gold reserves increased from 0.28 to 2.96. By 1971 when the link with gold was cut it had further declined to 6.12 and by 1975 to 11.19.

Although the founders of the Bretton Woods system chose to base it on a gold-exchange standard, there were already questions surrounding the future role of gold in the international payments system. When the Bretton Woods system was set up it was believed that the link with gold would add an element of stability to the system. A major question, however, that became increasingly prominent was the divergence between gold production and the needs of international trade. World gold production in 1958 was valued at US$1.051 billion and during the 1960s annual production showed little tendency to increase. Production in 1968 was valued at US$1.4120 billion, of which South Africa accounted for more than three quarters. Official holdings remained almost stagnant during the 1960s.

In the 1960s a number of techniques were discussed for creating additional reserves. One of these was an extension of the ability of a member to make automatic and unconditional purchases from the Fund. Another was investment by the Fund in member countries. Instead of using these methods, a decision was taken by the late 1960s to create a new reserve asset called the Special Drawing Right (SDR) to supplement existing reserve assets. The IMF Articles of Agreement was amended for the first time on 28 July 1969 and on 6 August the Special Drawing Account came into being. The SDR is not a currency, but an asset created on the books of the Fund to be used both as a reserve asset and as a means of payment.[16] It was called a 'drawing right' instead of a 'reserve asset' in deference to the French. When a country experiencing balance of payments problems wishes to convert its SDRs, the Fund designates a participant in a strong balance of payments and reserve position to provide currency in exchange for SDRs. Let us assume Brazil is the country experiencing difficulties and wishes to use part of its SDR holdings. Let us also assume that the UK is the country designated by the Fund to provide Brazil with foreign currency. Brazil's holdings of SDRs in the IMF's special drawing account ledger will go down, while the UKs will increase. Brazil gets foreign exchange which it can use to make payments or purchase other currencies. Subsequently Brazil may be asked to accept SDRs from some other country (including the UK) and to furnish foreign exchange, Brazil's holdings of SDRs would increase, while that of the country desiring foreign currency would decrease. A participant is not obligated to provide currency for SDRs beyond the point at which its holdings of SDRs in excess of its net cumulative allocation are equal to twice its net cumulative allocation. It is easy to see why SDRs are regarded as part of the international reserves. There are certain rules governing the use of SDRs and these are discussed in the following sections.

The SDR is an international reserve asset which the Fund can create as and when it determines that there exists a long-term global need to supplement existing reserves.[17] The Board of Governors periodically decides (an 85 per cent majority vote is needed) how much would be allocated, but decision among the countries participating in the account depends on quotas. SDRs were first allocated in 1970–72, and the last was made in 1979–81. The need for new allocations has been a controversial matter. Total net cumulative allocation to date amounts to 21.4 billion. Of this, holdings of participants accounted for 19.6 billion at the end of April 1996, holdings by prescribed holders for 1.0 billion and General Resources Account for 0.8 billion. Although SDRs are not allocated to the Fund, the Fund may acquire, hold, and dispose of SDRs through the General Resources Account. The Fund receives SDRs from members in the settlement of their financial obligations to the Fund and uses SDRs in transactions and operations between the Fund and its members. The Fund earns interest on its SDR holdings at the same rate as all other holders of SDRs. It should be noted that the use of SDRs is not confined to members of the IMF. There are a number of prescribed holders who do not receive SDR allocations but who can acquire and use SDRs in transactions and operations with participants in the SDR Department and other prescribed holders under the same terms and conditions as participants. As of 31 April 1994, there were 15 prescribed holders.[18]

At the time the SDR was created, a number of questions remained unsettled. One was whether the new asset was optimally defined. Another was how 'long-term global need' was to be measured and met. This latter question has become particularly interesting in the context of the 1978 Amendment to the Fund's Charter which pledges to make the SDR the principal reserve asset in the international monetary system (Article VIII Section 7). Another question, of course, related to the distribution of SDRs, which some countries felt should be based on need rather than on quotas. At the moment, industrial countries account for over 75 per cent of SDRs held by participants. There are some countries which have never received an allocation.

In order to make the SDR an attractive asset, it was to be made as closely comparable to gold as possible. As such, it was defined in terms of gold as being worth one thirty-fifth of an ounce at the then official price, that is equal to one United States dollar at the then prevailing dollar price of gold. With the floating of major currencies in 1973, par values were no longer observed, and in order to guard against fluctuations in individual exchange rates a decision was taken in 1974 to determine the daily value of the SDR by reference to a basket of 16 currencies most widely used in international trade. This particular basket was used between 1 July 1974 and 30 June 1978. Between 1 July 1978 and 1 December 1980, a new set of weights and amounts were introduced with basically the same currencies. The Danish krone and the South African rand were removed, and the Saudi Arabian riyal and the Iranian rial were brought in. In order to make the SDR more usable as a private unit of account the composition of the basket was simplified and the 16 currencies were replaced by those of the five major trading nations from 1 January 1981. Under the basket technique, the SDR is valued as the sum of fixed amounts of several currencies. The currencies included were those most widely used in international trade and payments. The weight assigned is intended to reflect the currency's importance in trade as well as its importance in financial markets. Columns (1) and (2) of Table 2.6 shows the weights and corresponding amount of each of the five currencies in the basket, which was last revised on 1 January 1996. The basket is reviewed every five years with a view to including the currencies of the five member countries of the Fund with the largest exports of goods and services during the five-year period ending

Table 2.6 Composition of the SDR since 1 January 1996 and deriving the US dollar value of an SDR

Currencies	(1) Percentage weight	(2) Amount of currency units	(3) Exchange rate per US dollar[1]	(4) US dollar equivalent Col. (2) ÷ Col. (3)
US dollar	39	0.582	1.0	= 0.5820
Deutsche mark	21	0.446	1.5219	= 0.2930
Pound sterling	11	0.105	1.5485[a]	= 0.1626[b]
French franc	11	0.813	5.1525	= 0.1578
Japanese yen	18	27.2	109.42	= 0.2486
	100			US$1.4404

[1] End of June 1996.
[a] US dollars per pound.
[b] (col. 2) × (col. 3).

12 months before the effective date of the revision, and to determine initial weights for those currencies reflecting their relative importance in international trade and finance during the same period.

The value of the SDRs (in terms of US dollars) at any point in time would depend on the exchange rates of the component currencies prevailing at that time. For example, using the exchange rate at the end of September 1996, the value of the SDR at that time (assuming the present composition of the SDR was the same then) would be derived as in Table 2.6. At the end of June 1996, the value of one SDR would have been equal to US$1.4440. To convert figures expressed in US dollars to SDRs, all that is required is to divide the figures by the US dollar value of the SDR at the particular point in time. In the same way, figures expressed in SDRs can be converted to US dollars by multiplying by the US dollar value of one SDR.

In order to increase the attractiveness of the SDRs, it was decided that interest should be paid on the new asset. In the beginning, the United States felt that the interest rate should be low in order to minimize the competition with the US dollar as a reserve asset. Increasingly, however, the rate assumed market rate proportions, rising from an initial 1.5 per cent to 5 per cent per annum in 1974. Since the beginning of 1981 the rate of interest on the SDR has been calculated using interest rates on selected short-term instruments in the domestic money markets of the five countries whose currencies are included in the SDR basket. With effect from 1 January 1991, these interest rates are the market yield on three-month US Treasury bills, the three-month inter-bank deposit rate in Germany, the three-month rate for treasury bills in France, the three-month rate on certificates of deposit in Japan, and the market yield on three-month UK Treasury bills. The weekly (Monday–Sunday) interest rate on the SDR is computed as the sum, rounded to the nearest decimal places, of the products of the respective interest rates, the currency amount and the exchange rates in effect on the preceding Friday.[19]

The Fund not only pays interest on holdings of SDRs, but levies charges at the same rate on allocations. Participants whose holdings exceed their allocation earn net interest, while those whose holdings are below allocations pay net charges at a going rate.

At the time of its creation there were numerous restrictions associated with the use of the SDRs. For instance, the reconstitution initially required each participant to maintain a minimum average holding of SDRs of 30 per cent of its net cumulative allocation over successive five year periods. Other reserve assets had a similar feature, and this weakened the SDR. The required holding requirement has now been eliminated. Restrictions on the sale of SDRs for currency by agreement with another participant have also been liberalized. Under the Second Amendment to the Fund's Articles of Agreement a participant may enter into transactions by agreement with all other participants, without any requirement of Fund approval of the particular transaction or the type of transaction and without any balance of payments need.

In the second amendment when the official price of gold was abolished, members pledged to make the SDR the principal reserve asset, and the Fund's own unit of account became the SDR. The SDR is also used as a unit of account, or the basis for a unit of account, by a number of other international and regional organizations and conventions. It is also being used to denominate financial instruments and transactions outside the Fund by the private sector and some governments (private SDRs).

A few countries also peg their currencies to the SDR and also use it as a unit of account. Despite these developments, the amount of SDRs in existence continue to form only a small proportion of international reserves (less than 2 per cent in 1995). Foreign exchange which contributed only 28 per cent to international reserves in 1950 has increased its share in recent years to between 80 and 90 per cent (see Table 2.7).

What the experience with the SDR has proved, notwithstanding its description as paper gold, is that fiat cannot be used to determine how countries hold their reserves. The attractiveness of a particular asset depends on four main criteria:[20]

1. an absence of exchange controls so people can spend, transfer, or exchange their reserves denominated in that currency when and where they want them,
2. an absence of applicable credit controls and taxes that would prevent assets denominated in the currency from bearing a competitive rate of return relative to other available assets;
3. political stability, in the sense that there is a lack of substantial risk that points (1) and (2) will change within or between government regimes;
4. the currency is in sufficient use internationally for the costs of making transactions in the currency not to be prohibitive.

Notwithstanding the adversities suffered by the US dollar in recent years, this currency still accounted for over 56.4 per cent of official holdings of foreign exchange at the end of 1995. The next most important currency was the Deutsche mark with 13.7 per cent followed by the Japanese yen with 7.1 per cent. The yen's share increased from 5.8 per cent in 1984 as both developed and developing countries have found it increasingly attractive as a reserve asset. Although official holdings of gold have been

Table 2.7 Growth of international reserves, 1950–95 (end of period) in million SDRs

Composition of	1950 Value	%	1960 Value	%	1970 Value	%	1980 Value	%	1995 Value	%
Foreign exchange	13 332	27.6	18 494	30.8	45 333	48.7	292 781	82.5	892 550	91.0
Reserve position in the Fund	1 671	3.4	3,570	6.0	7 697	8.3	16 836	4.7	36 673	3.7
SDRs	–	–	–	–	3 124	3.3	11 808	3.3	19 773	2.0
Gold (at 35 SDR per oz.)	33 445	69.0	37 917	63.2	37 026	39.7	33 356	9.4	31 816	3.2
Total	48 448	100.0	59 981	100.0	93 180	100.0	354 780	100.0	980 812	100.0
Gold holdings (mn. ozs)	955.56		1 083.34		1 057.89		953.05		908.90	

Source: IMF *Financial Statistics,* various issues.

falling, gold still performs a limited monetary function. Some countries have used it as collateral to obtain international credit, while some others have used it to pay off debt. For private investors gold can be an attractive investment, particularly when interest rates are falling (reduced opportunity cost of holding the metal) or there are disturbances in currency markets. One of the factors militating against a greater monetary function for gold is, of course, the huge fluctuation in prices which can lead to capital losses. The London price of gold increased from US$37.37 per ounce in 1970 to US$140.25 per ounce in 1975 and to US$589.50 per ounce in 1980. In recent years the price has averaged between US$300 and US$400 per ounce.

Many of the issues that came to the fore when the SDR was created are still around in various forms. Two developments which have radically changed the scenario since that time are the severing of the link between the US dollar and gold, and the abandonment of the fixed exchange rate system, both of which arrangements were the source of endless controversies and periodic crises. As indicated before, the SDR, despite its increasing role as an accounting device, is still far from becoming the world's major reserve asset. The US dollar performs that role and the US is still the major supplier of international reserves. There has been a great deal of controversy about the extent to which the US has benefitted from this role. A country whose currency is used as a reserve asset can finance its balance of payments deficits by printing money, once other countries have confidence in that currency and are willing to accept it as payments for goods and services. In other words a reserve currency country can access the real resources of other countries for the cost (paper, ink, labour, and so on) of creating international money. Because the latter is so small compared to the social value of the goods acquired, it is often said that the reserve country derives 'seigniorage'[21] from such arrangements and this may be one reason why the United States and other industrial countries have not pushed very hard to have the SDR emerge as a major international asset. Of course, if this were to happen more countries would share in the seigniorage. Conceding to a multilateral organization the right to issue an international asset that could displace national currencies would deprive the industrial countries (particularly the United States and to a lesser extent Germany and Japan) of a major advantage in the world economy.

The United States has often argued that there is a cost attached to being a reserve currency country, and this was particularly so when it was obliged to sell gold to official holders of US dollars. A stable price for gold was essential to the arrangement so that even when it was losing its competitiveness it could not easily devalue its currency (increase the price of gold) which would have led to a run on its gold stock. Foreign holders of dollars fearful of real losses would have hurried to exchange their dollars for gold.

With the gold factor now largely removed from the international monetary system and with the US now able to pursue more flexible exchange rate arrangements, the US balance of payment deficits have continued, and this may point to problems other than the exchange rate. The US continues to play the role of the world's most important provider of international money, albeit in a rapidly changing international financial environment characterized by increasing convertibility and greater freedom in the movement of capital.

CONCLUDING OBSERVATIONS

The link between international reserves and the growth of international trade is well recognized. Without the means to pay for imports, the demand by countries for each other's goods and services will be affected, and this, of course, would have a deflationary effect on the world economy. Questions relating to adequacy of world reserves, the creation and distribution of reserves and what should comprise such reserves are fundamental to an international monetary system seeking to promote international trade. Yet the Bretton Woods agreement failed to provide a systematic means for increasing the reserves of IMF member countries in a world of growing trade and output.[22]

In the post-war period the United States' balance of payments deficit have provided a significant part of world reserves. The link with gold made the US dollar an attractive asset, but this arrangement itself had a built-in problem reflected in what came to be known as the (Robert) Triffin dilemma. It was argued that if the United States' deficits were eliminated the world would lose a source of new reserves, and if the deficits continued the increased US liabilities to the rest of the world relative to the US gold stock would lead to a loss of confidence in the US dollar and the willingness to hold this currency.[23] It was in response to this concern and in the context of a perceived shortage of international reserves that the SDR was created. It was to be under the control of the IMF and would supplement existing reserve assets. It would meet reserves need 'as and when it arises' taking into account 'long-term global need'.

Although there was a commitment in the Second Amendment to this Fund's Charter to make the SDR the principal review asset, allocation, to date accounts for only a small proportion of total world reserves. The changed circumstances in recent years has also raised questions about its future which was discussed at a recent Seminar. The following major conclusions and recommendations emerged:[24]

● The SDR does not appear likely to become the principal research asset of the international monetary system. Nor does the SDR appear destined to evolve from an unconditional line of credit into a fully-fledged world currency.

● The SDR should not be abolished, however, because it possesses the ability to serve as a valuable 'safety net' should the international monetary system run into serious difficulty.

● Attention should be paid to the 'equity issue' arising from the distribution of SDRs and the fact that many IMF members have never received an SDR allocation.

● One argument against further allocation is that countries can meet their reserves needs by borrowing in private capital markets. Not all countries, however, enjoy such access. The reserve currency countries can obtain borrowed reserves at significantly lower costs than other countries.

● The coming into being of the 'Euro' in Europe may also raise questions about the future role of the SDR.

The SDR represents unconditional finance. While private capital markets have grown, not all countries enjoy access to it. Even those that do, acquire reserves at great cost. In this context, questions were also raised in terms of whether the benefits of the SDR would not be enhanced if allocations were targeted to specific countries. The Seminar was inconclusive on a number of issues. The international monetary system, of course, evolves on the basis of crises.

Notes

1. See World Trade Organization, *International Trade: Trends and Statistics, 1995*, Vol. 1 (Geneva: WTO, 1995), p. 15.
2. At the end of August 1996, there were 126 members of the World Trade Organization (WTO) which succeeded the GATT in January 1995.
3. See WTO, *International Trade, op. cit.*, p. 13.
4. See United Nations, *World Economic and Social Survey 1996* (New York: UN 1996), p. 55.
5. *Ibid.*, p. 279.
6. See United Nations, *World Economic and Social Survey* (New York: UN, 1994), p. 71.

7. International Monetary Fund, *World Economic Outlook*, March 1996 (Washington, DC: IMF, May 1996), p. 162.
8. Bank for International Settlements (BIS), *64th Annual Report*, (April 1993 to March 1994) Basle, 1994, p. 148.
9. United Nations, *World Economic and Social Survey, 1994* (New York: UN, 1994), p. 103.
10. Paul Host-Madsen, *Balance of Payments, Its Meaning and Uses* (Washington, DC. IMF, 1967), p. 1.
11. *Ibid.*, p. 3–4.
12. L. B. Yeager, *International Monetary Relations* (New York: Harper and Row, 1966), p. 36.
13. See IMF, *Balance of Payments, Concepts and Definition* (Washington, DC: IMF, 1969).
14. See P. B. Kenen, *The International Economy, 3rd ed.* (Cambridge: Cambridge University Press), p. 307.
15. For an excellent discussion of these approaches see M. E. Kreinin, *International Economics, 6th ed.* (New York: The Dryden Press, 1991).
16. See IMF, *Annual Report*, 1994, p. 144.
17. *Ibid.*, p. 100.
18. The prescribed holders of SDRs are the African Development Bank, African Development Fund, Andean Reserve Fund, Asian Development Bank, Bank of Central African States, Bank for International Settlements, Central Bank of West African States, East African Development Bank, Eastern Caribbean Central Banks, International Bank for Reconstruction and Development, International Development Association, International Fund for Agricultural Development, Islamic Development Bank, and Nordic Investment Bank. See IMF, 1994 *Annual Report*, p. 144.
19. IMF, *Annual Report*, 1994, pp. 144–5.
20. See J. V. Grabble, *International Financial Markets* (New York: Elsevier, 1986), p. 22.
21. The term 'seignior' or 'seigneur' was used to address a feudal lord or the lord of a manor. The term 'seigniorage' goes back to a time when the seignior or master of a feudal manor was able to extract seigniorage gains from his vassals by forcing them to use in all transactions pieces of paper (money) with his signature. To obtain this 'money' the vassals had to sell real goods and services to the seignior. The gains (seigniorage) accruing to the latter was the difference between the costs incurred to create goods and services acquired. This practice, of course, has its modern counterpart in government's ability to create money. At the national level one may argue that the seigniorage is shared. The Concise Oxford Dictionary defines seigniorage as 'a profit made by issuing currency, especially by issuing coins rated above their intrinsic value.'

    At the international level it can be similarly argued that when a government can use its printing press (create money) to acquire 'real' goods from other countries, it enjoys seigniorage to the extent that the value of these goods exceed the cost of creating that money (its intrinsic value).

22. See R. Solomon, 'The History of the SDR' in M. Mussa, J. M. Boughton and P. Isard eds, *The Future of the SDR in Light of Changes in the International Financial System* (Washington, DC: IMF, 1996), p. 25.
23. *Ibid.*
24. IMF, *Survey*, September 1996, p. 21.

Further Reading

Andersen, K. and R. Blackhurst (eds) *Regional Integration and the Global Trading System.* Harvester/Wheatsheaf, London, 1993.

Baldwin, R. E. and J. D. Richardson, *International Trade and Finance*, Little Brown and Company, Boston, 1986.

Classens, S. and S. Gooptu, 'Can Developing Countries Keep Foreign Capital Flowing In', *Finance and Development*, Vol. 31 (March 1994), pp. 62–65.

Euromoney, *The 1995 Guide to Emerging Currencies*, Euromoney Publications, London, 1995.

Flickenschild, H. M., *et al. Developments in International Exchange and Payments Systems*, IMF, Washington, DC, 1992.

Folkerts-Landau, D. and Takatoshi Ito, *International Capital Markets: Developments, Prospects and Policy Issues*, Washington, DC, August 1995.

Gold, J., *Special Drawing Rights, Character and Use*, IMF, Washington, DC, 1970.

Goldstein, M. and D. Folkerts-Landau, *International Capital Markets Systemic Issues in International Finance, Part II.* IMF, Washington, DC, August 1993.

Host-Marsden, P., *Balance of Payments, Its Meaning and Use*, IMF, Washington, DC, 1967.

International Monetary Fund, *International Capital Movements Under the Law of the International Money Fund*, Washington, DC, 1977.

International Monetary Fund, *Balance of Payments Manual*, IMF, Washington, DC, 1993.

Kuhn, M. G., *Official Financing for Developing Countries*, IMF, Washington, DC, 1994.

Mussa, M. *et al.* (eds) *The Future of the SDR in Light of Changes in the International Financial Systems*, IMF, Washington, DC, 1996.

Page, S., *How Developing Countries Trade*, Routledge, London, 1994.

Parboni, R., *The Dollar and its Rivals*, NLB and Verso Editions, London, 1981.

Richardson, J. O., *Understanding International Economics*, Little, Brown and Company, Boston, 1980.

Shiells, C., 'Regional Trade Blocs: Trade Creating or Diverting', *Finance and Development*, Vol. 32 (March 1995), pp. 30–32.

Trebilcock, M. J., *The Regulation of International Trade*, Routledge, London, 1995.

Whiting, D. P., *International Trade and Payments*, Macdonald and Evans Ltd., Estover, Plymouth, 1978.

3 The International Monetary System

At the domestic level a national currency performs three major functions – a medium of exchange, a unit of account and a store of value. The pricing of goods and services in terms of the local money and the latter's status as legal tender facilitates domestic trade. A currency also allows the storing of purchasing power for future use. With respect to trade between countries, there is no international currency issued by a supranational central bank. The functions of money have largely been performed by metal, mainly gold and silver, or by the currencies of the major powers. In the post-war period, the US dollar has been the main money performing the role of an international currency. The pricing of goods and services, the settling of debt and the keeping of reserves in US dollars have reduced information and transaction costs. To enhance the role of the dollar as an international currency, the US government assumed specific responsibilities within the institutional arrangements that came into force at the end of the Second World War. Those arrangements while reflecting the economic imperatives and intellectual fervour of the time, were filled with compromises that left many critical questions hanging in the air. Many of the problems which the founding fathers of the Bretton Woods system grappled with are still with us today.

The post-war international monetary system has been undergoing rapid and fundamental changes as events in the international economy are forcing reforms in some of the early arrangements and practices. The system set up at Bretton Woods drew on the experience of the 1930s and the inter-war period, but the framers obviously could not foresee all of the developments which later came to destabilize the system. For the first two decades or so after the end of the Second World War that system served the international economy well, and this is reflected in the rapid growth of trade in the post-war period. Before we discuss the present day monetary system, it would be useful to reflect back on the gold standard and the inter-war experience since current arrangements are better understood against the background of history.

THE GOLD STANDARD

At various times a variety of commodities (for example, shells, cattle, rum, tobacco, cigarettes) have been used as money. 'Gold and silver had been used for monetary purposes long before the nineteenth century. In Europe as trade expanded from the thirteenth century onward, these two precious metals gradually displaced all other monetary commodities. For hundreds of years they were used simultaneously without any provision for regulating their value.'[1] Of all the commodities, however, gold has had the greatest fascination not only for its beauty and ornamental worth but for a range of other qualities such as utility and value, portability, indestructibility, homogeneity, divisibility, stability of value and cognizability.[2] Unlike silver it does not tarnish and it is not corroded by acid.[3]

The 18th century was largely a bimetallic standard. Effectively, Britain was on a gold standard from 1717, though she did not formally go into one until 1816. The international gold standard, however, did not come into being until the 1870s when other European countries followed. The United States remained on a bimetallic standard (gold and silver) until 1900. Russia and Japan joined the group in 1897, but China never made the switch from silver to gold. Though the gold standard period is often stated as 1870–1914, the period of full operation was from 1897 to 1914. In this period the demand for gold increased significantly as countries began to accumulate gold for monetary reserves as well as for coining.

What were the essential features of the gold standard? The ground rules were 'a fixed price for gold with gold coin forming either the whole circulation of currency within a country or circulating with notes representing and redeemable in gold. On the international plane it means completely free import and export of gold, with all balance of payments deficits settled in gold. Thus in theory gold disciplines the economy of a country.'[4]

Adjustment under the gold standard was explained by the price-specie-flow mechanism which operated on two main assumptions: (1) each country's money supply consists of gold or paper currency backed by gold and it stands ready to buy and sell gold at a fixed price; and (2) the quantity theory of money holds so that a decrease in the country's money supply leads to a decrease in its general price level, while an increase in the money supply leads to an increase in prices. This can be expressed in the equation of exchange: $MV = PT$ where M is the country's money supply; V is velocity of circulation; P is price level; and T is physical output.

V depends on institutional factors and T represents full employment output. It was argued that these tend to remain stable in the short term so that an increase in *M* leads to a proportionate increase in *P* and vice versa External adjustment takes place through movements in prices, Higher domestic prices impact adversely on exports and also, together with the increased purchasing power, encourage residents to buy more from abroad. The opposite happens if there is a deficit, that is, the money supply and the price level fall leading to an increase in exports and a decrease in imports. In this analysis there is an assumption of perfect flexibility in interest rates, prices and wages. In practice, of course, there were no perfect markets or flexibility in wages and prices. Adjustment was not automatic. In times of difficulty suspension of convertibility seemed to have been a common resort. Interventions by central banks to influence the domestic money supply in the desired direction was also a practice. Also contributing to the working of the system were migration, the movement of capital and the use of protectionist measures.

The First World War had a profound effect on the international monetary system. The financing of the war and the post-war reconstruction led to significant increases in national monetary liabilities – and inflation. Gold production did not increase at the same rate so that the ratio of gold reserves to money supply fell. When the war ended in 1918 only a few countries remained nominally on the gold standard. These included the United States and some of the European neutrals (for example, the Netherlands, Sweden and Switzerland).[5] Despite widespread agreement that the gold standard should be restored, the return for many countries was a slow and almost painful process. Between 1922 and 1929 most countries returned to gold. With Britain's entry in 1925, the standard was widely considered as restored even though countries such as Spain and Portugal were still outside the restored area. But the arrangements adopted were not the same as those obtaining before the war.

> What had happened is most accurately described as a return to the gold basis for national currencies in the belief that, as before 1914, this would ensure exchange stability. What was restored was the legal form of the gold standard. Those who could see beyond the symbols knew that the restored gold standard was a facade. They knew that the popular faith in gold as an assurance of both price and exchange stability rested upon an illusion reflecting prewar conditions that no longer existed.[6]

In fact what Britain went back to in 1925 was not the gold standard, but the gold bullion standard under which gold coins did not circulate freely internally and could not be exchanged for other coin. Notes in large amounts could, however, be redeemed for bullion bars of specified weight.

Despite this situation, gold continued to hold the fascination of men and monetary authorities because of its natural qualities, one of these being its high value/weight ratio or density. It is still the most internationally acceptable medium of exchange. Its scarcity which has often been a cause of concern in the context of the adequacy of international liquidity ironically has contributed to its 'valuableness'. Between 1492 (when Columbus discovered America) and the end of 1967 it is estimated that only 70 000 tons were mined.[7] Monetary gold today forms only a small part of the world's total gold stock. At the end of June 1996 this was estimated to be about 905 million fine troy ounces held by IMF member states. Valued at the London market price this was worth 240 billions of SDRs. As we shall see later, when the Bretton Woods system was adopted in 1944, gold still held sway over the minds of its authors.

THE INTER-WAR YEARS

The 1914–18 war significantly disturbed the international pattern of production and trade that had taken root during the 19th and early part of the 20th century. With the outbreak of the war, resources shifted to war-related activities in the countries involved, and this led to a decline in a wide range of exports from Europe. Such shortages stimulated production in consuming nations (including the less developed countries) who continued to protect the newly created industries even after the war ended. Protectionism not only took the form of tariffs, but also import and export licensing, quotas, prohibitions and exchange controls. The European countries themselves during the 1920s intensified their restrictive policies adopted during the war years as they sought to protect not only industry, but agriculture as well. After the war, restrictions began to be used for a wider range of objectives such as protecting infant industries and defending the balance of payments. The efforts to restore international trade in the 1920s were overwhelmed by the growing economic nationalism of the period, which grew out of a preoccupation with problems at the individual country level. In this situation, international policy-making was increasingly pushed into the background as the 'beggar thy neighbour' syndrome took hold, with each country trying to benefit at each others expense.

Behind the protective measures national production grew, both in Europe and elsewhere. With many countries producing or growing the same things, finding export markets become a major challenge. Even the United States which emerged from the war as the greatest industrial power in the world and soon became the world's major creditor nation also fell victim to the protectionist ethic that grew increasingly strong in the 1920s. In the absence of competition, the pattern of world production did not reflect comparative advantage as resource allocation was determined by national needs and policies rather than by international demand.

During the 1920s agricultural prices were kept up by a variety of government devices such as commodity pools and guarantee prices. Following the collapse of the New York stock market in October 1929, raw material prices declined steeply, affecting both efficient and inefficient producers. This development, combined with the inability to raise loans in the American market, severely affected the ability of debtor countries to service their debt. Raw material producers tried to deal with the situation by exporting more, and this in turn led to steeper increases in tariffs and the adoption of licensing and quota systems in consuming countries. But default was inevitable. Capital flight and the inability to raise loans worsened the external position of debtor countries. The movement of capital from one centre to another severely undermined exchange stability, eventually leading to the abandonment of the gold standard.

Britain abandoned the gold standard in September 1931, in a situation where London was still the world's major clearing centre and sterling the main currency for settling international obligations. With the subsequent depreciation of sterling, payments settlements became confused and chaotic amidst growing controls in the form of bilateral arrangements and exchange and quantitative trade controls. To complicate the situation a banking panic set in 1931 and to help ease the difficulties a moratorium on war debts and reparation payments was put into effect. International trade contracted and world growth was affected. The United States eventually left the gold standard in April 1933 following a period of capital flight and loss of gold reserves.

The inter-war gold standard was structurally flawed. International efforts in the rest of the 1930s to achieve currency stabilization failed, even though it was widely felt that if the pre-war international monetary mechanism could be restored, there could be a return to multilateral trade. The 1930s in fact turned out to be a period of economic warfare, with countries trying to gain at each other's expense. The depressed state of economic activity provided the rationale for increasing state intervention which spread to all areas of economic management. Two observers put it this way:

> The economic nationalism even spread to the field of monetary policy, where despite the professed reverence for the gold standard mechanism, the independent national control of the domestic supply of money came

to supplant the pre-war principle of the international gold standard, according to which any nation's stock of money was dependent upon the ebb and flow of gold. By giving to the central bank the power to influence strongly the supply of money inside the country, the government tended to insulate the national monetary system from international forces and in doing so, it impaired the very mechanism upon which so much faith in future economic progress rested.[8]

In the climate of economic nationalism rampant in the 1930s, countries of the world community failed to appreciate the benefits of interdependence and multilateralism. The world also failed to adjust to the changed conditions prevailing after the end of the war. Britain was in no position to continue to play a lead role and the United States was not prepared to fill the void. Eventually the need was seen for a set of rules which could govern the economic behaviour of states and for arrangements which could provide assistance in times of payments difficulties. Even before the Second World War ended discussions had already started for the setting up of an international monetary system designed to provide a set of rules which could encourage world trade. The view that national welfare could not be separated from international cooperation had taken a stronger hold.

THE INTERNATIONAL MONETARY SYSTEM OF TODAY

The present day international monetary system has its beginnings in the International Monetary System and Financial Conference of the United and Associated Nations held in July of 1944 at Bretton Woods, New Hampshire in the United States. This is regarded as the most significant world economic conference ever held. Both developed and developing countries were represented at this conference and although 44 nations signed the Bretton Woods agreement, it represented largely the outcome of discussions between the United States and Great Britain. The British views were presented by John Maynard Keynes while for the United States Harry Dexter White was the main advocate. The main elements of what came to be known as the Keynes Plan (proposals for an International Currency or Clearing Union) were as follows:

1. He called for the setting up of a new international organization that would act like an international central bank for central banks. The International Clearing Union, as he chose to call this new organization, would issue a new international currency or reserve asset called 'bancor'.

2. The quotas for each country in the Union were to be fixed as half of the average of imports and exports over the past five years. These quotas determined the limits up to which debtors could borrow. Interest rates were to rise as the debt to the Union increased. Creditors would be required to pay charges to the Union if their balances rose above a quarter of their quota. In other words the responsibility for adjustment was placed on both deficit and surplus countries.

3. He suggested the creation of US$26 billion in bancor deposits to help finance the expansion in world trade and aid post-war recovery.

4. 'Bancor' was to be defined in terms of gold, but it was not to be convertible into gold. Members of the Union would not be able to demand gold. Bancor would be available only for transfer to another clearing account. The value of bancor would be expressed in terms of gold, but this value could change from time to time by the Union. Member countries could obtain bancor in exchange for gold but could not obtain gold in exchange for bancor.

5. It was proposed that the debit balances, when they arose, should take the form of overdrafts and not of specific loans. A rate of interest would be charged on both debit and credit balances. This was intended to share the burden of adjustment among both debtor and creditor countries.

The Keynes Plan provided for a special position for the United States and the United Kingdom as founder members. It suggested that these two should be able to out vote the remainder of the members and that the head office of the Union should be in London, with the governing board meeting alternately in London and Washington.

The White Plan

1. The US was opposed to the amount of liquidity creation proposed by Keynes on the grounds of its potential inflationary effects. Unlike the Clearing Union the White Plan suggested resources should come from subscriptions totalling at least US$5 billion.

2. The Plan proposed the setting up of a 'Stabilization Fund' which would exercise greater control over exchange rates. The latter would be fixed by the Fund and changed only with the consent of 80 per cent of the voting power.

3. The White Plan made no provisions for the payment of interest by surplus countries.

4. The Fund could determine the rates at which it would exchange one member's currency for another's. A guiding principle was stability in

exchange relationships. Changes in the rates were to be made only when essential to correction of a 'fundamental disequilibrium' and only with the consent of 80 per cent of members' votes.

5. The Fund was to be managed by a Board of Directors. Each member would appoint one Director and the Board would elect a Chairman and a small operating committee, whose members would devote their full time to the Fund's work.

6. Each member of the Board would have 100 votes, plus one vote for the equivalent of every million dollars subscribed in gold or currency to the Fund by his government.

The Bretton Woods agreement signed in 1945 reflected the American position in major areas and can be summarized as follows:

1. A new institution called the International Monetary Fund (IMF) was created and was to oversee the operation of international monetary arrangements. The Fund would also lend foreign exchange to any member who was short of foreign exchange. Such lending, however, was not to be automatic but would be conditional on the borrowing member's willingness to accept policies laid down by the Fund in letters of agreement.

2. The US dollar and the British pound would be the reserve currencies, and member states were to maintain their foreign exchange reserves principally in these currencies.

3. Fund members would be required to declare a par value for their respective currencies and would have to maintain the exchange rate for their currencies within 1 per cent of the declared par value. The fact the US dollar would be the principal reserve currency meant pegging to the US dollar and buying and selling US dollars to keep market exchange rates within the agreed margins. Under a separate arrangement the US agreed to buy gold from or sell gold to foreign official monetary authorities at $35 per ounce in settlement of international financial transactions. In effect the US dollar was pegged to gold, so that any other currency pegged to the US dollar was also pegged to gold.

4. Par value could change only with Fund approval. Such approval would be given in cases of 'fundamental disequilibrium'. While this term was not defined, in theory it was seen as 'a condition of persistent disequilibrium not amenable to monetary fiscal and other economic measures, except at the cost of significant unemployment or retarded growth.'[9]

5. After a transition period, it was agreed that currencies would become convertible, that is, they should be traded without restrictions.

To carry out its functions, the Fund needed gold and currencies, and these were to come from subscriptions. Each member was assigned a quota and this determined its financial and organizational relations with the Fund. Quotas determine members' subscriptions to the Fund, their relative voting power, their maximum access to financing from the Fund and their shares in SDR allocations. Those with larger quotas also enjoy greater access to Fund resources and greater influence over decision making.

Unlike some other organizations where every member has one vote that may have the same weight as the others, in the IMF and World Bank voting is weighted. Each member is assigned a quota which approximately determines its voting power and the amount of foreign exchange it may draw from the Fund.

Each member has 250 votes plus one additional vote for each part of its quota equivalent to 100 000 special drawing rights. Decisions are normally made by a majority of the votes cast, but there are areas where a special majority is needed. For instance, a change in the exchange rate arrangements requires an 84 per cent majority of the total voting power. At the end of April 1996, the United States had the most votes (17.78 per cent) followed by Germany (5.54 per cent), Japan (5.54 per cent), France (4.98 per cent), and the United Kingdom (4.98 per cent). This means that the United States has a veto power in any decision requiring over 82.22 per cent of the votes.

Initially, quota payments took the form of 25 per cent in gold and 75 per cent in the member's own currency. The amount of a member's quota is expressed in terms of SDRs and is equal to the subscription the member must pay in full to the Fund. Up to 25 per cent of the subscription has to be paid in reserve assets specified by the Fund (SDRs or usable currencies) and the remainder in the member's own currency. Each member has 250 basic votes plus one additional vote for each SDR 100 000 of quota. A member's voting power is important for two reasons:

1. Many of the principal policy and operational decisions of the Fund require a certain majority of votes, for example, an adjustment of quota needs an 85 per cent majority of the Board of Governors, as does the allocation of SDRs and sales of the Fund's gold; a 70 per cent majority is required for the determination of charges.
2. The voting power of a member has a bearing on the member's representation on the Board. The five members with the largest quotas each

appoint their Executive Director, as can the two members with the largest net creditor positions in the Fund over the past two years. The remaining Directors are elected by groups or constituencies of members, and since a member's voting power depends on the size of its quota, quotas have a bearing on the formation of these groups as well.

Under the Fund Articles, the Board of Governors is required to conduct a general review of quotas at intervals not longer than five years and to propose any adjustments that it deems appropriate. The Articles of Agreement, however, do not indicate how a member's quota should be determined. In practice, quotas tend to be related to economic factors (for example, national incomes, the value of official reserves, the variability of current receipts, external trade and payments) though they are not strictly determined by them.

Membership of the Fund was made open to all members of the United and Associated Nations, provided they agreed to:

(a) abandon within a year all restrictions and control over foreign exchange transactions with member countries except with the approval of the Fund;

(b) to alter their exchange rates only with the consent of the Fund, except for a narrow range to be fixed by the Fund and permitted to all member currencies.

Until recently the IMF, like the World Bank and the GATT, was largely a western institution. One of the notable developments of recent years is the number of states of the former USSR and East European countries which have joined the Fund or have applied for membership.[10] The USSR had participated in the Bretton Woods Conference but eventually decided against joining. With the new members the Fund is increasingly becoming a more universal organization. As of 30 April 1996, the IMF had a membership of 181 with several more applications pending.

RELATIONSHIP WITH THE WORLD BANK

Article V Section 8 of the World Bank's (IBRD) Articles of Agreement requires this institution to 'cooperate with any general international organization and with public international organizations having specialized responsibilities in related fields.' In making decisions on applications for loans or guarantees relating to matters directly within the competence of any international organization of the types just described and participated in primarily by members of the Bank, the latter is required 'to give consideration to the views and recommendations of such organization.' There is no such requirement in the IMF's Charter.

Though the Fund and the World Bank have different Charters and different mandates they are expected to collaborate in the interest of promoting 'sustained economic growth, stability and development in member states.'[11] Not only do conflicts arise from time to time in terms of who has primary responsibility for certain issues, but the questions of duplication of work and the efficient use of staff resources have also been a source of concern. In 1986 a set of guidelines for collaboration were drawn up and these are reviewed on a regular basis. According to these guidelines, the Fund's primary responsibility is in the area of macroeconomic policy and the related policy instruments and institutions, while the Bank's primary responsibility is in the area of structural reform and resource allocation to the public and private sectors.[12]

The distinct roles of the IMF and World Bank[13]

The IMF	The World Bank
• Oversees the international monetary system and promotes international monetary cooperation	• Seeks to promote economic development and structural reform in developing countries
• Promotes exchange stability and orderly exchange relations among its members	• Assists developing countries through long-term financing of development projects and programs
• Assists members in temporary balance of payments difficulties by providing short-to-medium term financing, thus providing them with the opportunity to correct maladjustments in their balance of payments	• Provides special financial assistance to the poorest developing countries through the International Development Association (IDA)
• Supplements the reserves of its members by allocating SDRs if there is a long-term global need	• Stimulates private enterprises in developing countries through its affiliate, the International Finance Corporation (IFC)

- Draws its financial resources principally from the quota subscription of its members

- Acquires most of its financial resources by borrowing on the international bond market

THE INTERNATIONAL MONETARY FUND IN OPERATION[14]

When the Articles of the Fund were drafted it was assumed that two other organizations would be established, not only to help bring order in the post-war world economy, but to help in the reconstruction effort. One of these was the International Bank for Reconstruction and Development (IBRD) which would provide capital or development resources. The other was to be a trade organization whose main aim would be the removal of the barriers to international trade. Membership in the Fund is a prerequisite for membership in the Bank.

The Fund Agreement has been in force since 27 December 1945, when it was signed by 29 governments, representing 80 per cent of the original quotas in the Fund. Three consequences followed at once or in due course;[15] (1) an international institution came into existence; (2) the member countries of the Fund became subject to new rules of public international law, the observance of which the Fund supervises; and (3) the Fund acquired assets consisting of gold and the currencies of members, which are administered by the Fund in accordance with the Articles to help members observe these rules. Membership in the Fund is confined to sovereign states. Before admitting a country to membership, the Fund satisfies itself that the country is a state that conducts its own international affairs and that the obligations of the Articles can be performed. A country need not belong to the United Nations to become a member of the Fund.

It was agreed that the Fund should have a Board of Governors, an Executive Board, a managing director, and a team of staff. Traditionally, the managing director has been a European and the President of the World Bank an American. The present President of the World Bank, Mr J. D. Wolfensohn, though born an Australia, is a naturalized US citizen. The highest authority of the Fund is exercised by the Board of Governors, on which each member country is represented by a Governor and an Alternate Governor. Normally, the Board of Governors meets once a year. The Governors may take votes by mail or other means between annual meetings. The Board of Governors has delegated many of its powers to the Executive Directors in Washington. However, the conditions governing the admission of new members, adjustments of quotas, election of Directors and certain other important powers remain the sole responsibility of the Board of Governors.

The Executive Board (the Board) is the Fund's permanent decision-making body. As of 30 April 1996, the Board comprised 23 Executive Directors appointed by member countries or elected by individual countries or group of countries. Chaired by the managing director, the Board usually meets several days a week to conduct Fund business. The Interim Committee of the Board of Governors on the International Monetary Fund is an advisory body made up of 23 Fund Governors, ministers, or others of comparable rank, representing the same constituencies as in the Fund's Executive Board. The Interim Committee normally meets twice a year, in April or May, and at the time of the annual meetings in September or October. It advises and reports to the Board of Governors on the latter's supervision of the management and adaptation of the international monetary system, considering proposals by the Fund's Executive Board to increase quotas or amend the Articles of Agreement, and dealing with sudden disturbances that might threaten the international monetary system.

When a state becomes a member of the Fund it agrees to abide by the rules to which all members are subject, and therefore assumes specific obligations. Under Article IV, for instance, 'each member undertakes to collaborate with the Fund and other members to assure orderly exchange arrangements and to promote a stable system of exchange rates. In particular, each member shall:

   (i) endeavour to direct its economic and financial policies toward the objective of fostering orderly economic growth with reasonable price stability, with due regard to its circumstances;

  (ii) seek to promote stability by fostering orderly underlying economic and financial conditions and a monetary system that does not tend to produce erratic disruption;

 (iii) avoid manipulating exchange rates or the international monetary system in order to prevent effective balance of payments adjustment or to gain an unfair competitive advantage over other members; and

 (iv) follow exchange policies compatible with the undertakings under this Section.

In order to carry out its mandate to 'exercise firm surveillance over the exchange rate policies of its members' with a view to promoting the balanced growth of world trade and an orderly and stable system of exchange rates, the Fund undertakes on-going analyses of economic and financial conditions in member states. Members may also be required to furnish the

Fund with information on such things like holdings of gold and foreign currencies, international trade, investments and payments, exchange controls, government accounts, money and credit, capital flows, wages, prices, national income, interest rates etc. The Fund carries out its surveillance in several ways. Under Article IV the Fund holds annual consultations with each member country 'to ensure that members' domestic macro-economic and structural policies – which have an important bearing on exchange rates – are conducive to sustained economic growth and price stability. A Fund staff team visits each member country regularly (usually, once a year) to collect economic and financial information and to discuss with authorities their general economic strategy and policies, as well as prospects for the domestic economy and the member's balance of payment position.'[16] The data collected allows the Fund to appraise the member's economic performance and policies, discuss policy options and to make recommendations. Another form of surveillance is more multilateral in nature and is conducted through Executive Board discussion of the world economic outlook twice a year. 'These world economic outlook discussions serve as a framework for assessing the interaction of the economic policies of the Fund's members – particularly the large industrial countries – and to discuss prospects for the international economy under various policy assumptions. They also allow for a cooperative and systematic monitoring of global economic conditions.'[17] Besides these two mechanisms for surveillance, the Board periodically discusses exchange rate developments and financial market conditions in the major industrial countries, and assesses their impact on the world economy.

Consultation under Article IV begins with Fund staff reviewing policies, institutional developments and statistical data on all aspects of a member's balance of payments, capital flows, national accounts, government accounts, money and credit wages prices and interest rates. This review is followed by discussions with the local authorities to evaluate the effectiveness of economic policies since the last consultation and to advise on modifications if necessary in order to obtain the desirable objectives.[18]

In effect, a state on joining the Fund surrenders part of its sovereignty in the interest of promoting order in global economic and financial conditions. How the Fund has interpreted its mandate has been the subject of a great deal of controversy, particularly in developing countries where it is often accused of interfering in the domestic affairs of these countries and lacking a social conscience. The Fund for its part argues that its 'surveillance responsibilities are sufficiently general to allow it to express its views on a wide range of policies affecting a member's economy and global economic environment'.[19] The principles which inform the Fund's appraisal of members' policies are therefore not irrelevant; but judging from the criticisms levelled against the Fund, particularly by developing countries, it would appear that these countries do not exert a great deal of influence on the formulation of these principles or on the *modus operandi* of the Fund generally. There is, in fact, a certain kind of theory and ideology underlying the Fund's perspectives and recommendations, which have become more explicit in recent years with the Fund's broader interest not only in stabilization, but in structural adjustment and in the proferring of advice and technical assistance in a wide variety of fields. The Fund places a high store on a market-based economy. Restrictions, controls and government interference on ownership of the means of production are seen as leading to distortions and as preventing the economy from performing at its peak level. Misallocation of resources results in inefficiency and discourages exports and this helps perpetuate balance of payments problems which in turn creates pressures leading to the institution of trade and exchange controls. These 'views' may not be particularly important to a member which does not feel the need for the Fund's assistance. Over the years the Fund has grown increasingly powerful as its membership has increased, as its resources have grown, as its range of assistance has widened and as other organizations and private financial institutions have sought to work more closely with it. Not surprisingly, the scope of the Fund's surveillance or supervision does not remain static and increasingly touch issues that pertain to almost every aspect of the economy.

SOURCES AND USE OF FUND RESOURCES

As can be seen in Table 3.1 the bulk of the Fund's resources come from members' quotas. At the end of April 1996 the Fund's total assets/-liabilities amounted to 151.3 billion SDRs, and of this quotas amounted to 95 per cent. Under Article 111, Section 2(a) of the Fund's Articles of Agreement, the Board of Governors is required to conduct a review of quotas at intervals of not more than five years. The Eleventh Review which is to be completed within a five-year period beginning on 3 January 1995, is underway.

Each member of the Fund has a quota, expressed in SDRs, that is equal to its subscription in the Fund.

The formula used for determining members' initial quota and increases in quota has undergone some change since the early years of the Bretton Woods Agreement. Initially the major variables in the formula included average import and export flows, gold holdings, and dollar balances and

Table 3.1 IMF balance sheet General Department at 30 April 1996
(in millions of SDRs)

Assets	1996
General Resources Account	
Currencies and securities...............................	144 181.4
SDR holdings..	824.7
Gold holdings.......................................	3 624.8
Charges receivable....................................	1 199.8
Interest and other receivables	64.1
Other assets	141.7
Total General Resources Account.......................	150 036.5
Special Disbursement Account	
Investments	–
Structural adjustment facility loans	1 544.8
Interest receivable	6.0
Total Special Disbursement Account	1 550.8
Total Assets	151 587.3
Quotas, Reserves, Liabilities, and Resources General Resources Account	
Quotas	145 318.8
Reserves..	1 875.9
Special contingent accounts	1 633.5
Liabilities	
Borrowing	
Remuneration payable..............................	232.7
Interest payable	–
Other Liabilities ,,,,,,,,,,,,,,,,,,,,,,,,,,,,,,,,,	*141.0*
	373.7
Deferred income from charges	*834.7*
Total General Resources Account.......................	*150 036.5*
Special Disbursement Account	
Accumulated resources	1 547.2
Deferred income	3.6
Total Special Disbursement Account	*1 550.8*
Total Quotas, Reserves, Liabilities and Resources	*151 587.3*

Source: IMF, *Annual Report*, 1996.

national income. In 1963 new quota formulas were introduced. The present method dates back to the Eighth General Review of Quotas in 1982/83. GDP is now used in place of national income in the formulas, and holdings of reserves were redefined to include in addition to gold and foreign exchange holdings of SDRs, ECUs (European Currency Units), and reserve positions in the Fund. The number of quota formulas was reduced from ten to five. These employ the more broadly based data for current receipts and payments (debits and credits on goods, services and private transfers) in place of the corresponding data for visible trade. Under the Fund's Agreement the Board of Governors is required to conduct a general review of quotas at intervals not exceeding five years and to make adjustments that reflect growth of the world economy and charges in the economic positions of members.

A member must pay up to 25 per cent of its quota in SDRs or in currencies of other members selected by the Fund, with their concurrence; it pays the remainder in its own currency. Subsequent increases are also to be paid partly in the member's own currency and the remainder in the form of reserve assets. (The 1978 revision was an exceptional one in which members were permitted to pay the entire increase in their own currencies). Incidentally, a member's quota is not increased until the member consents to the increase and pays the subscription.

As indicated earlier, a member's quota determines its voting power in the Fund, which is based on one vote for each SDR 100 000 of its quota plus 250 basic votes to which each member is entitled. A member's quota also determines its access to the financial resources of the Fund and its share in allocation of SDRs.

When the Fund agrees to assist a member state in balance of payments difficulties it in effect agrees to sell SDRs or currencies of other members in return for that member's own currency. Repayment by a member largely takes the form of repurchasing its own currency by paying to the Fund SDRs or currencies of other members specified by the Fund. Fund resources are intended to provide temporary relief and therefore great attention is paid to repayment. The Third Amendment to the Fund's Articles of Agreement provides that a member's voting and certain related rights may be suspended by a 70 per cent majority of the total voting power, if the member persists in its failure to fulfill its obligations under the Articles. Member countries, therefore, do not easily fall into an arrears position. At the end of April 1996, obligations overdue by six months or more amounted to 2.2 billion SDRs. Liberia, Somalia, Sudan and Zaire accounted for the bulk of overdue obligations.

Financial resources are made available to member states through a variety of facilities and policies. These differ in terms of the type of balance of payments need they seek to address, in the length of repurchase period, and in the degree of conditionality attached to them. Basically these facilities and policies can be divided into the regular (general) facilities, temporary facilities and special facilities. For ordinary operations the Fund derives its finances from:

1. resources in the General Resources Account, which are used to provide balance of payments financing to all members, and are derived from members' subscriptions and the Fund's borrowing. Incidentally, most of the transactions between member countries and the Fund take place through the General Resources Account. This account reflects the receipt of quota subscriptions, purchases and repurchases, collection of charges or member's use of Fund credit and payment of remuneration on creditor positions in the Fund, and repayment of principal and interest to the Fund's lenders. Assets held in the General Resources Account include (a) currencies (including securities) of the Fund's member countries, (b) SDR holdings, and (c) gold.

    The Fund makes its resources available to its members under policies on the use of its resources by selling to members, in exchange for their own currencies, SDRs or currencies of other members. When members make purchases, they incur an obligation to repurchase the Fund's holdings of their currencies, within the period specified by the Fund, by the payment to the Fund of SDRs or currencies of other members specified by the Fund. The Fund's policies on the use of its general resources are intended to ensure that their use is temporary and will be reversed within the relevant purchase period.

2. resources in the Special Disbursement Account, which are used for concessional balance of payments assistance to low income developing members through the structural adjustment facility (SAF), and are derived from the reflow of Trust Fund resource;

3. resources in the Enhanced Structural Adjustment Facility (ESAF) Trust, which are used for concessional balance of payments assistance to low income developing members through the ESAF, and are derived from members' loans and donations.

The rules governing access to the Fund's general resources apply uniformally to all members. General resources are used to finance certain special facilities that are open to all members.

Disbursement of the agreed amount normally takes the form of tranches (segments) over a stipulated period of time. The Fund employs certain standards in relation to each tranche and these are reflected in the conditions associated with the agreement for use of the Fund's resources. With each draw down the Fund's holdings of the member's currency increases.

RESERVE TRANCHE

Each member has a *reserve tranche* position in the Fund which is equal to its quota minus the Fund's holding of the country's currency in the General Resources Account, excluding holdings arising out of purchases under all policies on the use of the Fund's general resources. A member may purchase up to the full amount of its reserve tranche, without conditions at any time. By definition, a reserve tranche purchase does not constitute a use of Fund credit and is not subject to charges or to an expectation or obligation to repurchase.

As indicated earlier, the Fund makes its assistance available through a variety of policies and facilities. These can be divided into regular, special, and facilities for low-income countries. The Fund's tranche policies and Extended Fund Facility fall into the regular category. The special facilities include the Compensatory and Contingency Financing Facility (CCFF), the Buffer Stock Financing Facility and the Systemic Transformation Facility. Special Facilities are often ad hoc and can be short lived as was the case with the two oil facilities created in the 1970s to assist member countries in dealing with the effects of the oil price increases. At present there are two facilities designed to help low-income countries – the Structural Adjustment Facility (SAF) and the Enhanced Structural Adjustment Facility (ESAF).

Regular facilities

Credit tranche policies

The credit tranche policy is the Fund's regular or basic lending policy. Credit is made available in four tranches or segments, each equivalent to 25 per cent of a country's quota, and even larger access can be authorized.

A *first credit tranche* purchase is defined as one that raises the Fund's holdings of the purchasing member's currency in the credit tranches to no more than 25 per cent of quota. The first tranche is used in cases of small balance of payments difficulties and is easily accessible once a member demonstrates that it is making reasonable efforts to overcome its difficulties. Performance criteria and purchase installments are not used. Repurchases are made in $3^{1}/_{4}$–5 years.

Access to *upper credit tranches* depends on a member's willingness to undertake a substantial and viable programme to overcome its balance of payments difficulties. Resources are normally provided in the form of stand-by arrangements that include performance criteria and purchases in installments. Re-purchases are made in $3^1/_2$–5 years.

Until 1975 Fund resources were provided exclusively through what was known as stand-by arrangements (see Appendix 3.1). These arrangements typically cover periods of one to three years, and focus on appropriate exchange rate and interest rate policies aimed at overcoming short-term balance of payments difficulties. Members make purchases (or drawings in tranches or segments) of 25 per cent of quota each. For drawings within the first credit tranche, the member is required to show reasonable efforts to overcome its balance of payments difficulties. Performance criteria such as budgetary and credit ceilings, appropriate exchange and interest rate policies, and avoidance of restrictions on current payments and transfers are not applied. Purchases in the upper credit tranches require substantial justifications; the member must have a strong and viable programme. Performance criteria are applied and purchases are made in installments. Repurchases (or repayments) on all drawings are made in $3^1/_2$–5 years.

Extended Fund Facility

This facility was adopted in 1974 in response to criticisms that not only were the resources from the Fund inadequate to undertake the kinds of reforms necessary for correcting the balance of payments difficulties attributed to structural as well as macroeconomic problems, but the period was too short. Under extended arrangements the Fund supports medium-term programs that generally run for three years, although it may be lengthened to four years where this would facilitate sustained policy implementation and achievement of balance of payments viability over the medium term. Typically, a program states the general objectives for the three-year period and the policies for the first year; policies for subsequent years are spelled out in annual reviews. Performance criteria are applied and repurchases are made in $4^1/_2$–10 years except in the case of purchases made with resources borrowed under the enlarged access policy.

Special facilities

Compensatory Financing Facility (now the Compensatory and Contingency Financing Facility)

The Compensatory Financing Facility was introduced in 1963 and liberalized in 1975. In August 1988, it was replaced by the Compensatory and Contingency Financing Facility. One purpose of this facility is to provide financial assistance to members, particularly primary commodity exporting countries, that are experiencing balance of payments difficulties resulting from shortfalls in export earnings or to meet increases in cereal import costs. Such shortfalls must be temporary and largely attributable to circumstances beyond the member's control. For members whose balance of payments problems go beyond the effects of an export shortfall, the use of the compensatory financing element requires that the member cooperate with the Fund in finding appropriate solutions to its balance of payments difficulties. In 1979 compensatory financing was broadened to include tourist receipts and worker remittances in calculating the export shortfall, and in 1981 a further extension allowed compensation for countries faced with an excessive rise in the cost of specific cereal imports. An export shortfall is defined as the amount by which export earnings or cereal import costs deviate from their medium-term trends.

With the addition of the new element in 1988 the facility now provides contingency financing to protect members' economic adjustment programmes from adverse movements in key external economic variables affecting current account transactions. It provides advance assurances of financial protection in the event of a disruptive external shock. Contingency financing covers deviations in certain key economic variables from 'baseline' forecasts. These variables could include export earnings, import prices, international interest rates, worker remittances tourism receipts, and other variables affected by external conditions beyond members' control. The contingency element is symmetrical; if the member experiences an external shock that has a positive net balance of payments impact, it is expected to add to its international reserves, where these are low; if reserves are adequate the member is expected to forego further borrowings from the Fund under the associated arrangement, or make early repayments on previous contingency financing loans.

A member using the CCFF may draw under the compensatory mechanism up to 40 per cent of its quota for export shortfalls and 17 per cent for the excess costs of cereal imports. Under the contingency mechanism, a member may also draw up to 40 per cent of quota to cover applicable external contingencies. (Contingency financing associated with any particular arrangement is generally limited to 70 per cent of the amount of the arrangement). In addition, the Fund allows an optional drawing of up to 25 per cent of quota to supplement either the compensatory or contingency element, at the member's choice. Cumulative purchases under the compensatory, contingency and cereal elements at any one time are limited to 122 per cent of quota.

Following a review in April 1990, a decision was taken to increase the flexibility of the CCFF in order to adapt the facility to the particular needs of members. For example, in determining the coverage of contingency financing, it was agreed to focus on those key external components of the member's current account that are highly volatile, are easily identified and whose movements are clearly beyond the authorities' control. It was agreed that due consideration should be given to the effects on the current account of changes in excluded external variables that are widely recognized to have been influenced substantially by developments in world markets. The need for greater flexibility in determining the threshold was acknowledged. Re-purchases are made in $3^{1}/_{2}$–5 years.

Buffer Stock Facility

This facility was established in 1969 and its aim is to assist members in financing contributions to approved international buffer stocks. Repayments are made within 3–5 years or earlier, if contributions to a buffer stock are refunded or the borrowing country's balance of payments situation improves. Some of the agreements in which members have been assisted in joining include the Fourth, Fifth and Sixth International Tin Agreement, the 1979 International Sugar Agreement and the 1979 International Rubber Agreement. This facility is now hardly ever used. In fact, it has not been utilized since 1984.

Systemic Transformation Facility (STF)

The STF was created in April 1993 to provide assistance mainly to the so-called 'transition' states, namely, Russia, other states of the former Soviet Union as well as other economies in transition.

The STF will be open to members experiencing balance of payments needs resulting from severe disruptions in traditional trade and payments arrangements. Such needs could be manifested by (1) a sharp fall in total export receipts on account of a shift from a significant reliance on trading at non-market prices to multilateral, market-based trade; (2) a substantial and permanent increase in net import costs, due to a shift toward world market pricing, particularly for energy products; or (3) a combination of both.

The STF is intended to be of a temporary nature and access is limited to not more than 50 per cent of quota.

Facilities for low income countries

Structural Adjustment Facility (SAF)

This facility was adopted in March 1986. Resources are provided on concessional terms to low-income developing member countries facing protracted balance of payments problems, in support of medium-term macroeconomic and structural adjustment programmes. A member state seeking access to this facility develops and updates with assistance of the Fund and the World Bank, a medium-term policy framework for a three-year period, which is set out in a policy framework paper (PFP). Detailed annual programmes are formulated prior to disbursement of annual loans, and include quarterly bench marks to assess performance. Loans under this facility are made at an interest rate of 0.5 per cent per annum and are repayable in ten equal semi-annual installments over $5^1/_2$–10 years.

Enhanced Structural Adjustment Facility (ESAF)

This facility came into being in December 1987 and is intended to help the Fund's poorest member countries undertake strong macroeconomic and structural programmes to improve their balance of payments position and foster growth. This facility is aimed in particular at low income countries faced with high levels of indebtedness as well as those whose exports are concentrated in commodities whose prices have remained persistently weak in world markets.

Objectives, eligibility and basic programme features of this facility parallel those of the SAF; differences relate to provisions for access, monitoring, and funding. A policy framework paper and detailed annual programme are prepared each year. Arrangements include quarterly bench marks, semi-annual performance criteria, and in most cases a mid-year review. Adjustment measures are expected to be particularly strong, aiming to foster growth and to achieve a substantial strengthening of the balance of payments position. Loans are disbursed semi-annually and repayments are made in 51/2–10 years. Interest rate will be at 0.5 per cent – subject to the availability of the contributions of donor countries.

Besides the regular and special facilities just described the Fund provides technical assistance and financing to its members. It also provides *emergency assistance* in the form of purchase to help members meet payments problems arising from sudden and unforeseeable natural disasters. Such purchases do not involve performance criteria or the phasing of disbursements, and must be repurchased in $3^1/_4$–5 years.

Most of the Fund lending takes place through stand-by and extended arrangements. Of the 42.2 billion SDRs of Fund credit outstanding at the end of April 1996, 74 per cent fell into these two facilities (see Table 3.2).

Because of the way it is structured, the Fund argues that its ability to lend depends on the prompt repayment of loans within the agreed time frame. Table 3.3 shows that in overall context the net availability of resources tends to be far smaller than the gross disbursements would suggest.

Table 3.2   Outstanding fund credit by facility and policy at end of April 1996

Facilities and policies	mn SDRs	% of total
Standby arrangements[1]	20 700	48.2
Extended arrangements	9 982	23.7
Compensatory and contingency financing facility	1 602	3.8
Systemic transformation facility	3 984	9.5
Sub-total	36 268	86.2
SAF arrangements	1 208	2.9
ESAF arrangements[2]	4 469	10.7
Trust Fund	95	0.2
Total	42 040	100.0

[1] Includes outstanding first credit tranche and emergency purchases.
[2] Includes outstanding associated loans from the Saudi Fund for Development.

Source: IMF, Annual Report, 1996.

Table 3.3   Net annual flow of fund resources to member states 1887–1996
(in millions of SDRs)

Year ending 30 April	Total disbursements (1)	Repurchases and repayments (2)	Col. (1) Minus Col. (2) (3)	Total outstanding credit provided by the Fund (4)
1987	3 824	6 749	−2 925	33 443
1988	4 597	8 463	−3 866	29 543
1989	3 095	6 705	−3 610	25 520
1990	5329	6 398	−1 069	24 388
1991	7 530	5 608	1 922	25 603
1992	5 916	4 770	1 146	26 730
1993	9 058	4 119	4 939	28 496
1994	5 987	4 513	1 474	29 889
1995	11 175	4 231	6,944	36 837
1996	12 347	6 100	6 247	42 040

Source: IMF, Annual Report, 1996.

The IMF and its sister institution, the World Bank, are the world's two premier international financial institutions (IFIs) which together with the regional development banks (for example, the Inter-American Development Bank) are a major force in shaping global development policies. While financial institutions generally often come in for criticisms in various degrees because of the controls they exercise over their leading policies, the IMF is constantly in the spotlight not only as a lender, but perhaps more importantly as an influence in shaping the policies of its member states and of the position it occupies in the international financial community. In recent years, responding to challenges in member states the Fund is now engaged in both short and medium term lending and has added new facilities, so that it not only provides balance of payments support, but it is also involved in structural adjustment which is engaging the attention of an increasing number of its members, both old and new. The range of criticisms against the Fund has correspondingly widened, and with the fall in the standard of living in many countries these criticisms have become increasingly intense. Criticisms of the Fund and Fund expectations tend to centre over the following:

1. That the Fund seeks to exert its influence in areas outside its mandate;
2. That the Fund is dogmatic and adopts an 'ideology' biased in favour of free markets and free enterprise;
3. That it colludes with the World Bank and even with the commercial banks in pressuring developing countries to adopt Fund-conceived policies and strategies;
4. That it treats the circumstances of all countries as the same and therefore applies the same remedies everywhere;
5. That its 'solutions' or 'remedies' reflect the thinking of economists from the developed countries, who do not understand the problems of developing countries;
6. That it adheres (explicitly or implicitly) too rigidly to the 'monetarist' doctrines which are based on incorrect assumptions;
7. That the Fund-supported programs not only do not work, but harm the poor. In fact they may discourage growth and destroy long-term growth potential;
8. That it is insensitive to social concerns and places too much emphasis on 'getting the balances' right;
9. That it imposes onerous lending terms and austere conditions that often tend to perpetuate dependence on creditors and increase poverty;
10. That it places too great a share of the burden of international adjustment of deficit countries, a large number of which are developing countries;

11. That the time frame allowed for structural adjustment is often too short and the resources are generally too small to sustain a reform programme. As a result, countries falter, social conditions deteriorate and a social reaction can set in;

12. That it is a tool of imperialism used by the United States to destabilize countries and to cause the downfall of governments the United States does not like;

13. That it overrides the national sovereignty of member states;

14. That developing countries have little say in the policies and operations of the Fund.

In its various publications the Fund has tried to respond to some of these criticisms, and in the following section I shall try to summarize that response.

As indicated earlier, the fund's Charter permits it a great deal of discretion in how it fulfills its mandate. Article I requires the Fund not only 'to promote international monetary cooperation' and 'to promote exchange rate stability' but 'to facilitate the expansion and balanced growth of international trade' and 'to assist in the establishment of a multilateral system of payments in respect of current transactions between members'. For members experiencing balance of payments difficulties Fund resources are to be made temporarily available to them under adequate safeguards.

Initially, the Fund was established to provide short-term balance of payments assistance to member states thus providing them with the opportunity to correct maladjustments in their balance of payments without resorting to measures inimical to trade and development. The Fund has argued it is neither a charitable organization nor a development institution. Its funds are limited and revolving. In order to remain a lending institution it has to insist on repayment, and therefore attach conditions to its loans which ensures members' ability to repay. The resources (facilities) at the disposal of the Fund carry various levels of conditionality which are subject to Fund discretion within certain defined parameters, for example, the period for repayment.

But even though the Fund is not a 'development institution' in the normally accepted sense of the word, yet it has to support the development efforts of its members and its policies and operations must reflect this. Development is a broad process 'that encompass improving the efficiency with which economic resources are used, adapting social arrangements and institutions to foster growth, changing attitudes, providing incentives, and much else besides. In particular, it is a process that affects and, in turn, is influenced by a whole array of economic policies – regarding the budget, the amount of money in circulation, the value of the currency, and so on – that are the heart of the IMF's concerns in its relations with its member countries'.[20]

The Fund may draw a member's attention to the effect the budget deficit may be having on inflation, savings and investment, but may not make specific recommendations with respect to reducing that deficit. The tendency to base recommendations on broad aggregates focusing on certain selected variables often make all packages look the same. With respect to a budget deficit, for example, the number of measures available to a government for reducing or eliminating a deficit is limited and they all generate reactions of various kinds, depending on who is affected. On the revenue side the government can take action to improve tax collection, increase taxes or impose new taxes. On the expenditure side it can cut salaries, reduce the public sector work force, reduce or eliminate subsidies or sell off inefficient state enterprises. Reduction of subsidies to the utilities may lead to higher rates to consumers. A government may sustain a budget deficit by borrowing from the central bank (printing money) or by borrowing in the local market or from abroad. But there are limits to which it can do this. Sooner or later it would have to make adjustments which is not always politically easy to do. In the same way, there are limits on the extent to which a government can borrow to finance a persistent balance of payments deficit. The Fund frowns on controls and looks favourably upon market-oriented measures, for example, changes in the exchange rate. The Fund is inclined to the view that excess demand is a major cause of inflation and balance of payments disequilibrium.

The Fund argues that by the time a member comes to it for assistance the situation may have deteriorated to the point where 'strong medicine' is needed. The Fund is often used as a scapegoat for unpopular but necessary reform measures. Even without the Fund, adjustments are inevitable. Countries cannot live beyond their means for very long and what adjustment measures do is to bring them back within their means and this often entails a drop in the standard of living. Adjustment programs are not without cost.

There is great controversy over the effectiveness of Fund programs and their distributional impact. The Fund takes the position that while its programs may not have produced the initially envisaged results in all cases one has to view the situation in terms of what might have been in the absence of a program. It also may take some time before the fruits of a program is seen. Up front, critics tend to see the costs of budget and balance of payments adjustment. But these adjustments are necessary for long-term growth. Bringing inflation under control increases confidence in the local currency and encourage savings and investment. Reducing the budgetary deficit may be crucial to this process. The generation of savings on the current account will also enhance the government's capacity to undertake capital expenditure which can assist growth and create employment. Balance of payments difficulties are seen as posing 'a threat to growth because they affect the flow of financial resources and of imports, and this can disrupt development. Further, they undermine confidence in long-term prospects for the economy, discourage investment, and can result in a less efficient use of scarce resources'.[21] Adjustment programs may also not have the desired effect because national authorities are not paying enough attention to implementation.

Without adjustment, the Fund argues, the poor will also suffer. In fact they may suffer more and longer in the absence of adjustment. The Fund does not deny that adjustment may change existing patterns of income distribution, but it is up to governments to implement programs in a way which leads to a sharing of the burden of adjustment programs on the poor, which tends to affect both rich and poor. It is working more closely with the World Bank and the UN agencies in addressing the impact of adjustment on poverty. It is recognized that the poor generally are unable to protect themselves against the effects of inflation and that programs of adjustment can produce hardships which increasingly are being addressed through social amelioration programs funded by aid agencies and bilateral donors. Adjustment, however, is not simply about reducing public expenditure, but also about directing resources to more productive uses and increasing the country's competitiveness. With growth will come greater employment and an improvement in the standard of living.

With respect to its orientation the Fund argues that it does not have 'sociopolitical'[22] views that determines the way it operates, and it does not take a position on social and political issues but work within the existing sociopolitical system of its member countries. It is, however, guided by experience which shows that 'if economic activity is left relatively untrammeled, it is likely to be more efficient and to lead to greater prosperity than if it is restricted and controlled, especially as most countries lack the administrative capacity to control the economy effectively'.[23]

With respect to collusion with the World Bank, the Fund argues that while each has its own separate mandate there will be some inevitable overlapping in their operations. The Fund and the Bank also cooperate in certain areas, and not only share information but draw on each other's expertise. This cooperation has increased in recent years as both institutions have become increasingly involved in helping member coun tries to restructure their economies. On the issue that member states are forced by the Bank to accept the conditionality of the Fund as a precondition for financial support, the Fund argues that such cooperation that takes place is to avoid working at cross purposes.

With respect to the influence of the industrial countries on the Fund, the latter argues that this follows from their economic size and their importance in international trade. Their voting power is proportional to their quota contributions. Despite this, however, developing countries as a group still represent about 40 per cent of the vote. This is about the same as the combined share of the five largest shareholders. 'Not only is this enough to influence the Fund's decision making in important ways, it is also sufficient to give them veto power over those major decisions that must be approved by an 85 per cent or 70 per cent majority.'[24] In any event, it is argued, there is no formal voting on most issues. Decisions are generally arrived at by consensus.[25]

While the Fund may not be a 'popular' organization it provides a certain amount of order in the international economy. There is a view that if the IMF did not exist, it would have to be created. It is the institution that comes nearest to being an international central bank. As far as the technical approach to problem solving is concerned, the mixed results still give rise to many questions. While the performance of some countries may have improved with structural adjustment, some others long associated with Fund programs continue to flounder. The use of the exchange rate instrument in particular has raised questions about its appropriateness in a context where devaluations have produced improvement without necessarily correcting the balance of payments disequilibrium. One of the problems here is that while the Fund may pressure a state experiencing payments problems to become more competitive, it cannot ensure access to foreign markets, particularly in countries where the Fund does not exercise influence.

ISSUES IN THE REFORM OF THE INTERNATIONAL MONETARY SYSTEM

The United States had emerged from the war as the dominant global power, and committed itself to playing a key role in the post-war monetary system. The US not only pledged to buy its dollar liabilities for gold at US$35 per ounce (the 1934 price), but was to be the major source of international liquidity. As a store of value the dollar enjoyed the same status as gold. One of the main purposes for the creation of the IMF was to provide liquidity to encourage the expansion of international trade. In the early post-war years, however, the Fund was relatively insignificant as a source of international reserves. In 1951, for example, reserve position in the IMF amounted to only 3.4 per cent of world monetary reserves as compared to 68.8 per cent for gold and 27.8 per cent for foreign exchange.[26] At the time of the Agreement it was hoped that newly mined gold would play a significant part in expanding world reserves. This was not to be, and with the dollar quickly assuming the role of international money, liquidity came to depend on American spending abroad. American balance of payments deficits became critical to the functioning of the international monetary system. By 1970 foreign exchange accounted for 48.2 per cent of world monetary reserves.

The agreements adopted at Bretton Woods in 1944 provided the institutional framework for the post-war economic boom that lasted some 25 years. World production and trade expanded significantly in this period. Many new products and exporting nations were also to emerge. Within the two decades following the end of the Second World War both Japan and Germany (with American help) were well on the way to becoming major economic powers. By the late 1950s, however, with the declining ability of the US to redeem its dollar liabilities in gold, cracks had already began to appear in the system. With member countries of the Fund, pursuing different monetary policies and experiencing different rates of inflation, the fixed exchange rate system also started to come under pressure, and by the late 1960s/early 1970s could no longer be sustained.

The Bretton Woods system was not a perfect one, and in an attempt to reach a compromise between the American and British positions it left many questions hanging in the air. The adequacy of resources at the disposal of the IMF, the composition of reserves, a mechanism to create reserves, the role of gold, the conditions on which members could access IMF resources, the conditions under which members could change their exchange rates, the exchange rate system itself and the obligations of surplus and deficit countries in the adjustment process were questions that were not fully addressed. With the weakening of the United States and with the recovery of Western Europe and Japan from the ravages of the war these questions began to command more urgent attention. The decreasing dependence of Europe on the United States also introduced a new factor in the equation. Integration in Europe picked up momentum in the 1950s and took a serious turn in the 1960s, thus strengthening the European influence on international monetary cooperation.

In 1972 the Executive Directors to the Board of Governors set up a Committee (Committee of the Board of Governors of the IMF on the Reform of the International Monetary System and Related Issues) to advise and report on all aspects of international monetary reform.[27] The Committee of Twenty, as this Committee came to be known, submitted its final report in June 1974, and suggested that reform should centre around the following:

(a) an effective and symmetrical adjustment process, including better functioning of the exchange rate mechanism, with the exchange rate regime based on stable but adjustable par values and with floating rates recognized as providing a useful technique in particular situations;
(b) cooperation in dealing with disequilibrating capital flows;
(c) the introduction of an appropriate form of convertibility for the settlement of imbalances, with symmetrical obligations on all countries;
(d) better international management of global liquidity, with the SDR becoming the principal reserve asset and the role of gold and of reserve currencies being reduced;
(e) consistency between arrangement for adjustment, convertibility and global liquidity; and
(f) the promotion of the net flow of real resources to developing countries.

The Committee's work was overtaken by events. The creation of the SDR facility in the late 1960s made no impact. By early 1973 the major currencies went on float, and following the second amendment to the Fund's Articles in 1976, members were no longer obliged to maintain fixed exchange rates. A decision was also taken in 1976 to eliminate the official price of gold and to abolish the obligation of IMF members to use gold in transactions with the Fund. A commitment was also undertaken to make the SDR the principal reserve asset, but the ability of the major countries to raise resources in the capital markets has, for the time being, pushed this objective into the background. The question of linking development assistance to the SDR was and is still not supported by the industrial countries, who are of the view that the two things should be kept separate. With respect to exchange rates, developing countries were initially fearful of market-determined rates in the absence of sophisticated financial structures – such as forward and future markets. There was a concern that a free market for their currencies would not only lead to steep depreciations and price instability, but the floating of major currencies would also create uncertainties which would disrupt their efforts to diversity their trade flows and to manage their foreign debt. The international financial environment has changed radically since then, and developing countries are experimenting with a variety of arrangements. The issues relating to the exchange rate, however, remain far from settled, as we shall see in the next chapter.

THE IMF AND ADAPTATION TO CHANGING CIRCUMSTANCES

The founding fathers of the IMF could not foresee all the problems and challenges that would face it, and its evolution therefore has not been without controversy. From the very beginning there was disagreement over the uses to which IMF money could be put and about the conditions that should be attached to those uses. There was also concern about the authority of the Fund and the scope and frequency of consultations. As membership grew and new challenges emerge, the Fund has been innovative in introducing several new arrangements since the 1960s to deal with specific problems. These were discussed earlier. With increasing pressure on its resources the Fund created the General Arrangements to Borrow in 1962. Under this Agreement the Fund can borrow from the major industrial countries (the Group of Ten) if any of them drew from the IMF. In the late 1960s the SDR was created with a view to increasing international liquidity.

The 1970s was a tumultuous decade, requiring increased Fund activity. To deal with the oil crisis the Fund introduced two new oil facilities and the Extended Facility. The major development in the 1970s, however, was the collapse of the par value system in the early part of the decade, and the Second Amendment to the Fund's Charter in 1978 which allow member states to pursue more flexible exchange rate arrangements under IMF surveillance. The new Article IV calls on the Fund to exercise 'firm surveillance' over the exchange rate policies of members and to 'adopt specific principles for the guidance of all members with respect to those policies.'

In the 1980s the debt problems emerged as the major concern for the international financial system as defaults by debtor countries threatened the survival of the international banking system. While the financial assistance provided directly by the IMF to debtor countries themselves was not always significant in terms of amount, the Fund developed a critical role as a mediator and catalyst in negotiating rescheduling arrangements, mobilizing resources and evaluating and helping to put together structural adjustment programmes. In this period the Fund developed a close working relationship with both official and commercial creditors. To assist and encourage developing countries in undertaking policy reforms two structural adjustment facilities designed to lend on concessional terms were added to the Fund's arsenal in the 1980s

The entry of countries from the former Soviet Union and Eastern Europe into the IMF, increasing financial liberalization and the globalization and integration of money and capital markets continue to pose new challenges to the Fund. The growing interdependence in the world economy calls for quicker reaction, greater resources and the availability of up-to-date information on a more timely basis. The collapse of the Mexican peso as a result of speculation in December 1994, and the consequences generated, created a situation which neither the IMF nor the international community could easily deal with. For fear that the Mexican crisis would spread, both the United States and the IMF provided some US$37 billion in loans and loan guarantees to assist Mexico.

To avoid future Mexicos, the Interim Committee of the Fund sees the need for stronger surveillance over both countries that borrow and those that do not borrow. A set of recommendations calling for more continuous dialogue with member states and more regular and timely provisions of economic data were endorsed by the Group of Seven industrial countries meeting in Halifax, Canada in June of 1995. The IMF was also mandated to use its GAB (General Arrangements to Borrow) powers to set up a fund of US$58 million to meet currency crises, when these occur.[28]

CONCLUDING OBSERVATIONS

July 1944 marked the 50th anniversary of the Bretton Woods Conference, out of which grew the IMF, the World Bank and the General Agreement on Tariffs and Trade (now the World Trade Organization) – the three most important post-war international economic institutions. The discussions which had started long before 1944 clearly envisaged a more ambitious and a more complex system for managing the world economy and this included a world central bank and an international currency ('unitas' for the Americans and 'bancor' for the British). Given the time constraint imposed on the negotiators, the original agenda was aborted and a series of major compromises between the British and Americans (the major players) were made. The proposal for an international central bank issuing an international currency was reduced to the setting up of a 'fund' with far less resources than was originally envisaged, and with the US dollar as the centre-piece of the system. A European Reconstruction Fund earlier conceived as an investment fund for relief and reconstruction became the World Bank. The two other pillars that featured in the earlier part of the discussions, namely, a mechanism for channelling soft loans to developing countries and the International Trade Organization (ITO) which would have as one of its major objectives stabilizing the prices of primary commodities, were put on the back burner. 'Bretton Woods succeeded, at least in part, because it avoided the direct discussion of trade and the plans for the ITO and transferred the debate to the monetary level, where agreement could conceivably be reached.'[29] So that when the Americans later failed to ratify the ITO, the highly inadequate General Agreement on Tariffs and Trade (GATT) which was supposed to be a temporary organization remained to provide the framework for the conduct of international trade.

There is general agreement that these institutions brought a certain degree of order to international monetary and trade relations, particularly given the background against which they came into being. There is disagreement, however, on how well they have adapted to the changes taking place in the global environment since 1944 and how well they have responded to the special concerns of developing countries who are now the main clients of the IMF and World Bank.[30] Developing countries are generally of the view that these three major institutions have served mainly the interests of the industrialized nations, and the voting structure of the IMF and World Bank, which are seen as undemocratic, continue to ensure this. This situation has not changed notwithstanding the increasing membership of these institutions, which is now more international (universal) in character, and the concerns with poverty and underdevelopment which are put with increasing regularity on the agenda of international discussions.

The collapse of the par value system in the 1970s was a traumatic, but not an unexpected development, given the changes that have been taking place in the global economy. The United States share of world output dropped from 42 per cent in 1962 to 26 per cent in 1988. Its share of world trade has also been falling. With this development has come other changes in the international economy. The rise of Japan, Germany and other smaller industrial powers, increasing currency convertibility and capital mobility, the acceleration of the integration process in Europe and the globalization of goods, services and capital markets challenged fundamental premises of the Bretton Woods system. The mixture of fixed and floating exchange rate regimes now prevailing can be described as a non-system. When this is put in the context of the limited resources of the Fund and the negligible disbursements of funds on a net basis, increasing questions are being asked about the relevance of the IMF in the emerging environment. The Fund, for its part, now sees surveillance over members' exchange rate policies as being at the heart of its responsibilities.[31] Given the range of factors and variables that influence the exchange rate, this position would at one time easily have generated fears, particularly among developing countries, about erosion of national sovereignty. Debt problems, and persistent poor economic performance, however, have forced a large number of them to put themselves under the guidance of the IMF and World Bank which are now seen as the main sources of policy advice The risk of being a cynic over the unlimited benefits of economic liberalization, deregulation, and privatisation in the context of the free market paradigm appears to be too high – at least for the moment.

The criticisms of the Fund go far beyond its policies, its ideological framework, its decision-making machinery, its structure or its limited resources in the context of the role it desires to play in managing the world's monetary system. Critics point to its modus operandi, its inflexibility, its obsession with balancing the fiscal and external accounts, its apparent unconcern with the social costs, its secrecy, its lack of transparency, its lack of sensitivity, its arrogance, its failure to differentiate among countries in applying its strictures, the irrelevance of its policies in particular situations, the power often wielded by incompetent staff, and the list can go on. Behind all this lies a feeling on the part of a large number of developing countries that they are unable to influence the operations of the Fund and increase its sensitivity to their concerns. This raises basic questions about the governance of the Institution which is strongly influenced by the G-7 countries, namely Britain, Canada, France, Germany, Italy, Japan and the USA. What the post-war experience has shown is that both the Fund and the Bank tend to react, and react rather slowly to unfolding events and criticisms. In the absence of a more dynamic and creative role the pace and quality of change in the international economy may will undermine further the moral authority which an institution like the IMF should command, not to mention its effectiveness in a rapidly changing global environment.

Notes

1. J. B. Condliffe, *The Commerce of Nations* (London: George Allen & Unwin Ltd., 1951), p. 361.
2. *Ibid.*
3. See Timothy Green, *The History, the Lure, and the Power of Man's Most Precious Metal* (New York: Simon and Schuster, 1970), p. 19.
4. *Ibid.*, p. 23.
5. See Condliffe, *op. cit.*, p. 505.
6. *Ibid.*
7. T. Greene, *op. cit.*, p. 20.

8.   A. G. Kerwood and A. L. Longheed, *The Growth of the International Economy, 1820–1980* (London: George Allen & Unwin Ltd., 1983), p. 188.
9.   See R. F. Mikesell, *Financing World Trade* (New York: Thomas Y. Crowell Company, 1960), p. 34.
10. By 4 May 1992 the Board of Governors of the Fund had adopted membership resolutions for all 15 states of the former USSR. At 1 June 1992, seven former Soviet States – Armenia, Estonia, Georgia, Kyrghyzstan, Latvia, Lithunia, and Russia – had joined the Fund. Albania had joined in 1991.
11. IMF, *Annual Report*, 1992, p. 53.
12. *Ibid.*, p. 54.
13. *Ibid.*
14. This section draws heavily on publications of the International Monetary Fund, particularly its *Annual Reports*.
15. J. Gold, *The International Monetary Fund and International Law* (Washington, DC: IMF, 1965) p. 1.
16. IMF, *Annual Report*, 1992, p. 14.
17. *Ibid.*
18. *Ibid.*
19. *Ibid.*, p. 13.
20. Bahram Nowzad, *Promoting Development: The IMFs Contribution* (Washington, DC: IMF, undated), p. 1.
21. IMF, *Ten Common Misconceptions about the IMF* (Washington, DC: IMF, undated), p. 1.
22. *Ibid.*, p. 8.
23. *Ibid.*
24. *Ibid.*, p. 17.
25. *Ibid.*
26. Using 35 SDR per ounce as a valuation for gold.
27. *Reform of the International Monetary System*, (A Report by the Executive Directors to the Board of Governors of the IMF, Washington, DC, 1972), p. 80.
28. See IMF *Survey*, 8 May 1995.
29. See H. James, *International Monetary Cooperation Since Bretton Woods*, (New York: Oxford University Press, 1996), p. 33.
30. For an excellent discussion of these topics see Mahbub ul Haq *et al. The UN and the Bretton Woods Institutions* (London: Macmillan, 1995).
31. See IMF, *Annual Report*, 1995, p. 3.

Further Reading

Bretton Woods Commission, *Bretton Woods: Looking to the Future*, Washington, DC, 1994.
Eichengreen, B., *International Monetary Arrangements for the 21st Century*, The Brookings Institution, Washington, DC, 1994.
Guitan, M., 'The IMF as a Monetary Institution: The Challenge Ahead', *Finance and Development*, Vol. 31 (September, 1994), pp. 38–41.
James, H., *International Monetary Cooperation Since Bretton Woods*. Oxford University Press, New York, 1986.

Kenen, P. B., F. Papadia and F. Saccomanni (eds) *The International Monetary System*. Cambridge University Press, Cambridge, 1994.

Meyers, R. J., *The Political Morality of the International Monetary Fund: Ethic and Foreign Policy*, Vol. 3, Transaction Books, New Brunswick, 1987.

Michie, J. and J. G. Smith (eds) *Managing the Global Economy*, Oxford University Press, New York, 1995.

Muehring, K., 'Can they really build a new monetary order', *Institutional Investor*, Vol. XX (June, 1995), pp. 31-36.

Shelton, J., *Money Meltdown*, The Free Press, New York, 1994.

Solomon, R., *The International Monetary System 1946-1976*, Harper and Row, New York, 1977.

Ul Haq, Mahbub, Richard Jolly, Paul Streeten and Khadija Haq, *The UN and the Bretton Woods Institutions*, The Macmillan Press Ltd., Houndmills, Basingstoke, 1995.

United Nations Conference on Trade and Development, *International Monetary and Financial Issues for the 1990s*, Vols. I and II, New York, 1993.

Williamson, J. (ed.) *IMF Conditionality*, Institute for International Economics, Washington, DC, 1983.

Van Dormael, A., *Bretton Woods: Birth of a Monetary System*, Holmes and Meier Publishers, New York, 1978.

4 The Foreign Exchange Market, Exchange Rate Determination and Exchange Rate Systems

INTRODUCTION

There are almost as many currencies in the world as there are countries. Not all the latter, however, are independent and, therefore, not all are members of the United Nations, or the International Monetary Fund which had a membership of 181 at the end of April 1996. Two examples of countries which are not independent but have their own currencies are Hong Kong and the Cayman Islands.[1] At the same time there are several independent states that use the same currency. For example, the CFA franc is issued by the Central Bank of West African States (BCEAO) and is the common currency in Benin, Burkina Faso, Côte D'Ivoire, Mali, Niger, Senegal, and Togo. The Eastern Caribbean dollar which is issued by the Eastern Caribbean Central Bank is used in Anguilla, Antigua and Barbuda, Dominica, Grenada, Montserrat, St Kitts-Nevis, St Lucia and St Vincent and the Grenadines. Anguilla and Montserrat are not independent states. In certain countries (for example, Panama and the Bahamas) the US dollar circulates side by side with the local medium.

Most currencies are hardly known or used outside their home base. International transactions are carried out in only a few currencies, mainly those of the industrial countries. Countries whose currencies do not enjoy this status conduct their international business through one or more of the major currencies, that is, they make and demand payments in internationally acceptable currencies. Trading in the foreign exchange markets reflect the dominance of the major currencies. For example, a survey carried out in 1995 indicated that US dollar/Deutsche mark trading accounted for the largest share of foreign exchange transactions in London (22 per cent) and New York (30 per cent). The next largest share related to US dollar/yen transactions which accounted for 17 per cent in London, 20 per cent in New York, and 76 per cent in Tokyo. The US dollar/pound segment contributed 11 per cent in London and 8 per cent in New York.[2] (See Table 4.1).

Table 4.1   Relative shares of currencies traded in selected centres, 1995
(percentages of principals' overall turnover)

Currencies	London	New York	Tokyo	Singapore
US$/£	11	8		12
US$/DM	22	30	12	29
US$/Yen	17	20	76	27
US$/Sw Fr.	6	7	..	9
US$/other	25	21	6	..
DM/Yen	2	2	4	..
DM/other	14	11	..	23
Other	4	–	2	..

Note: Data are on a net basis, adjusted for double counting of domestic interbank business.
.. not available

Source: *Bank of England Quarterly,* November 1995.

International trade and investment differ from domestic trade and investment within any given country in that not only different laws and regulations come into play, but different currencies and practices may be involved. Trade, investment and speculative activities underlie the demand and supply of the various currencies. To pay exporters in a particular country, or to invest in that country, it is generally necessary for traders and investors to acquire the currency of that nation. Countries, however, whose currencies are not internationally acceptable tend to demand payment in one or more of the major currencies which can be put into the foreign reserves account to meet foreign obligations since their own currencies may not be accepted outside their home borders. Thus, while there may be a schedule for the supply of the local currency reflecting the demand for foreign goods and foreign investment, there is no direct demand from abroad for the local currency. The demand is for local goods, services and investment which are paid for or financed with foreign currency. As with all currencies, however, the difference between foreign exchange receipts and foreign payments which are reflected in movements in foreign reserves exert a major influence on the external value of the domestic currency at any point in time. To this question we now turn our attention.

THE FOREIGN EXCHANGE MARKET

Foreign exchange is simply the monetary unit of a foreign country, and the foreign exchange market is where foreign currencies are exchanged or traded for each other. The terms 'foreign exchange' and 'foreign currency' are used interchangeably, but the term 'currency' has a much broader usage when used in reference to foreign exchange which covers a range of different instruments denominated in foreign currencies. The exchange rate is the price of one country's currency in terms of another. It is common to express it in one of two ways. With respect to the relationship between, let us say, the US dollar (US$) and the German Deutsche mark (DM) it can be written as 1 DM = US$0.50 (the indirect quote) or US$1.00 = 2 DM (the direct quote) that is, units of foreign currency per unit of local currency. With respect to the Japanese yen it can be quoted as US$1.00 = 150 yen or US$0.006 = 1 yen. In practice quotations in terms of per US dollar are more common than the other way around. With respect to the pound sterling, however, Americans tend to prefer formulations that quote dollars per pound (for example, US$1.60 = £1). Foreign exchange dealers normally quote two prices, one for selling (an offer rate) and one for buying (a bid rate). The spread – the difference between the two rates is the margin which (together with the volume of business) determine the profit of the trader.

Under the Bretton Woods exchange rate arrangements which prevailed (legally) until 1976, member countries of the International Monetary Fund were required to declare a par value either in terms of gold or the US dollar. Since the second amendment to the Fund Articles, they are no longer required to do that. But a dwindling number of developing countries still opt to peg their currency to one of the major currencies. Barbados, for instance, currently pegs its dollar to the US dollar at the rate of B$2.00 = US$1.00 (B$1.00 = US$0.50). The dollar relationship with other currencies is determined through cross calculations. For instance, if B$2.00 = US$1.00 and US$1.00 = 150 yens, then B$2.00 = 150 yens or B$1.00 = 75 yens or 1 yen = B$0.01. In this kind of arrangement the Barbadian dollar floats with the US dollar, and may move in a direction not dictated by conditions in the Barbadian economy. For instance, if the US dollar were to depreciate *vis-à-vis* the yen from let us say US$1.00 = 150 yens to, let us say, US$1.00 = 120 yens (this is another way of saying the yen has appreciated *vis-à-vis* the dollar), while the Barbadian dollar is kept at B$2.00 = US$1.00, then the new cross rate will be B$2.00 = 120 yens or B$1.00 = 60 yens (B$0.02 = 1 yen). In other words Barbadian residents would now have to give up more local currency to obtain a yen.

Effectively, the Barbadian dollar would have been devalued without any action by the Barbadian government. Goods from Japan would cost more in terms of the local currency. To the extent that the US dollar retains its relationship with other currencies there would be no change between the latter and the Barbadian dollar.

The foreign exchange market is the world's largest market.[3] Its daily turnover is greater than that of any other market. The foreign exchange market, it should be noted, is not located in any particular building or place. The foreign exchange market for any currency is the network of companies, individuals and institutions (central banks, commercial banks, brokers) located in the various financial centres (for example, London, New York, Paris, Zurich, Hong Kong, Tokyo, Singapore, and so on) buying and selling that currency for other currencies. The international telex/telegraph/fax/computer network provides instant information to each centre and allows each to know what is happening in the other. By being able to buy in one centre and sell another instantly the price in one cannot diverge too far from the price in the others.

Without government intervention the exchange rate is determined by the interaction of supply and demand. The currency market, however, is not the same as other markets. The currencies traded today are mainly fiat currencies, that is, they are accepted as a means of payment by the decree of government who issue them. Fiat currencies are not generally demanded for their own sake, but for what they can buy. The demand for a particular currency is in a sense a derived demand. It reflects the demand for goods, services and investment. This means that exchange rates are determined by a wide variety of factors, for example, domestic and foreign prices of goods and services, trading and investment opportunities, capital movement, speculation, and so on.

It is important to note that not all currencies are traded freely. Developing countries generally impose a wide range of restrictions on foreign currency transactions, and as a result illegal markets in foreign exchange emerge to satisfy demand that cannot be met within formal markets. These illegal markets commonly referred to as 'parallel' or 'black markets' are generally found wherever there are restrictions on foreign exchange transactions. The 'black market' rate trends to give a better indication of the 'equilibrium rate' than the formal or legal rate.

International transactions, as indicated earlier, are carried out in only a few currencies, mainly those of the major industrial countries such as the United States, Japan, Germany, the United Kingdom. The prices of goods and services in international trade are quoted in one or more of the major currencies and payment is also effected in these same currencies. These currencies derive their quality and reputation not from the design of the bank notes, but from the strength of their respective economies and their role in the international economy. The term hard currency is used in reference to the currencies of the major industrial countries. In the gold standard days any currency convertible into gold at a fixed exchange rate would have been described as hard. A soft currency would have been one without any gold backing. Since gold no longer holds the pre-eminent position it once held in the international monetary system, this criterion is no longer relevant. The major feature of a hard currency in present day circumstances is the degree of free tradability. Tradability, of course, refers to the extent to which the monetary authority in any particular country allows the residents of that country to buy and sell that currency for foreign currencies. For various reasons, not many countries are in a position to allow their currencies to be freely traded. Under Article VIII, Section 2(a) of the IMF Charter, member states are prohibited from imposing restrictions on the making of payments and transfers for current international transactions. Recognizing the different circumstances affecting the various countries, Article XIV Section 2 provides a basis for exceptions, but countries are required to continually monitor such restrictions with a view to removing them. A few countries which had opted to restrict the tradability of their currencies when the Bretton Woods systems came into being, had returned to convertibility by the late 1950s. In the post-war period a large number of developing countries have used a combination of exchange controls and trade restrictions as part of their development policy centered around a strategy of import substitution. Increasingly, however, as part of the trade liberalization condition accompanying structural adjustment packages, many of these controls are being dismantled. The view is being taken that exchange controls are inconsistent with a process of trade liberalization and general economic reforms.

Let me begin the discussion on exchange rate determination by using two currencies that are widely used in international trade – the US dollar ($) and the German Deutsche mark (DM). The supply/demand interaction is shown in Diagram 4.1. The discussion takes place in a two-country world. German consumers and investors need US dollars to buy US goods and services, or to invest in the US. In order to get US dollars the Germans have to give up (supply) DMs. On the other hand, Americans need DMs to buy German goods or to invest in Germany. Put differently, the demand curve for DMs by Americans is in fact the supply curve of dollars to the Germans. On the other hand, the demand curve for dollars by the Germans represents the supply of DMs to the Americans. The vertical axis in Diagram 4.1(a) shows the American view of the exchange rate (the

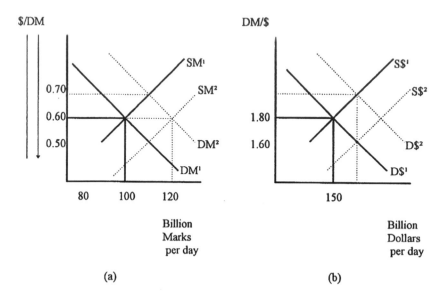

Diagram 4.1   A Supply and Demand Model of the Foreign Exchange Market.

average price of DM in terms of US dollars, $/DM) over the course of the day and the quantity of DM traded per time period is shown on the horizontal axis. In Diagram 4.1(b) the vertical axis shows the German view of the exchange rate (the price of dollars in terms of DM, DM/$) and the horizontal axis shows the quantity of dollars traded per time period.

The demand curve is downward sloping. Why? In the case of the Americans when the dollar price of DMs fall (that is, the dollar appreciates *vis-à-vis* the DM) German goods and services will become cheaper and Americans will demand more marks. The same would apply to the Germans. When the DM price of dollars falls, American goods and services will become cheaper and Germans will demand more dollars. The increased demand for dollars will, of course, increase the supply of DMs. When the DM depreciates *vis-à-vis* the dollar, this would stimulate the Americans' desire for German goods, services and assets. The increased demand for DMs would also be associated with an increased supply of dollars. We also assume that the supply schedule (curve) is upward sloping, that is, it has a positive slope. What this implies is that as the value of the foreign currency falls, there would be an increased demand for goods and assets in that country and this would increase the supply of local currency. Of course, the reverse is also assumed, that is, as the foreign currency appreciates it becomes more expensive to acquire goods, services and assets in that country, and therefore the supply of foreign exchange falls. The slope of the lines also has significance in that it gives an indication of elasticity, that is, the responsiveness of the demand for, and supply of, currencies to changes in the exchange rate.

In terms of the balance of payments, the Americans' demand for DMs would be reflected as credit items (export of goods and services and investment inflows) in the German accounts, while the Germans' demand for US dollars would show up as credit items on the Americans' side. The excess supply or demand for currencies reflects developments in the real economy. A deficit in the balance of payments means that the payments of foreign currency have exceeded the supply, while a surplus means that receipts have been greater than payments.

In Diagram 4.1(a) $0.60 is the equilibrium rate, that is, the price that clears the market and 100 billion marks is the equilibrium amount. If the price were below this value, demand for DM would exceed the supply, and this pressure (as in a commodity market) would force the price upwards. In the same way if the price were above $0.60 the supply of DM would be greater than the demand, and as in the goods market downward pressure would be exerted on this price. In Diagram 4.1(b) 1.60 DM is the (equilibrium) rate at which the Germans' demand for dollars is equal to the supply of dollars. The equilibrium amount is 150 billion dollars.

If the Americans wanted to maintain the rate at, let us say, $0.50 /1 DM, the authorities would have to be prepared to supply the excess demand for DMs. Alternatively, if they wished to maintain the rate at $0.70/1 DM, the authorities will have to buy up the excess supply of marks. Under the original Bretton Woods arrangements, IMF members had undertaken to defend declared exchange rates within agreed bands.

At this point it would be instructive to provide some clarification with respect to the use of the terms 'depreciation' and 'appreciation' which are used in relation to the effects of market forces on exchange rates. When Americans have to give up say $0.70 for a DM instead of say $0.50, the value of the dollar has in fact fallen (depreciated). On the other hand, if they had to give $0.30 instead of $0.50, the value of the dollar has in fact increased (appreciated). The same applies with respect to the DM. Where exchange rates are fixed, the term 'devaluation' is used to describe a reduction in the external value of the national currency by the government concerned. The effect is the same as what was described as a depreciation earlier. A revaluation is the opposite of a devaluation, that is, the external value of the national currency is increased by an official decision. Governments' actions, of course, need not be in accord with the dictates of market forces.

The curves (schedules) of Diagram 4.1 are drawn on the basis of certain conditions, and can shift upwards or downwards if the basic parameters change. For instance, if the Americans' taste for German goods increases or there is an increase in US incomes, or interest rates in Germany increases, the demand curve for DM in Diagram 4.1(a) could shift upward to DM^2. Developments in Germany (for example, an increase in productivity) which results in lower prices can also lead to increased American demand. German demand for American goods and services could be affected in the same way. In this case the demand curve for dollars could shift outwards to $D\$^2$ from $D\$^1$ for example. The supply curves can also shift in either direction in response to changes in basic conditions. For instance, increased German taste for American goods or a boom in Germany would result in a downward movement in the supply curve of Deutsch marks (SM^2) in Diagram 4.1(a) which will correspond with the upward movement in demand curve for dollars in Diagram 4.1(b). What this means is that for every price on the vertical axis in Diagram 4.1(a), Germans are prepared to offer more marks for a US dollar. This may result in a worsening of the balance of payments position of the Germans, and thus put increased pressure on the exchange rate. A depreciation of the mark is in fact an appreciation of the dollar. An appreciation of the US dollar will make German goods cheaper to Americans, and theoretically supply and demand forces in the absence of controls and restrictions would tend to provide a self-correcting mechanism.

As indicated earlier, the demand for a currency of a particular country basically reflects the demand for goods and services produced by that country or the desire to invest in that country. There are other factors, of course, which affect the demand for a particular currency. Some of these arise from the desire to speculate, or to make a gift or a loan in that currency. Foreign economic transactions are reflected in the currency markets, and this can again be easily demonstrated by referring back to Diagram 4.1. In Diagram 4.1(a) the equilibrium rate based on the SM^1 and the DM^1 functions is US\$0.60 = 1 DM and the equilibrium amount demanded and supplied at this rate is 100 billion DM. Let us assume as a result of increased incomes in the US or an enhanced taste for German goods the DM curve shifts outward to DM^2. This means that at the exchange rate of US\$0.60 = 1 DM the demand for DMs exceeds the supply by 20 billion DMs. This is an indication of a US balance of payments deficit (the equivalent of the German balance of payments surplus). The excess demand for DM over the supply of DM at the exchange rate of US$0.60 = 1 DM will put downward pressure on the US dollar and if left to market forces will depreciate (the DM appreciates) to the point where demand and supply for DM are once more equal at a new equilibrium rate – US$0.70 = 1 DM in Diagram 4.1(a). Note that the rate could also change as a result of movements in the supply curve.

To the extent that exchange rates are left to respond to market forces there can be great variability and unpredictability in this rate. Even in the context of the floating system now adopted by the major industrial countries, the monetary authorities still intervene to keep the rate within some desirable band – hence the term 'managed' or 'dirty floating'. Foreign exchange can be purchased or sold for immediate delivery (a spot transaction) at the prevailing rate (the spot rate) or can involve an agreement to buy or sell foreign exchange in the future at a rate agreed upon today. Buying or selling foreign exchange for future delivery constitutes a market (the forward market) and represents an attempt to hedge against the unpredictability of movements in the spot rate. Futures contracts are generally for less than one year. It should be pointed out that it is possible to hedge even in the spot market. For instance, if an American needs to make a payment in DM in the future, he can purchase the DMs in the present and hold them in a bank account.

As indicated earlier, under the fixed (but adjustable) par value system adopted in 1944, member states of the IMF were required to defend the declared par value within agreed margins. The monetary authorities in each country would intervene in the foreign exchange market to buy up surplus foreign exchange or to provide foreign currencies to meet excess demand. Shifts in the supply and demand for foreign exchange tended to result in changes in the country's international reserves rather than result in variations in the exchange rate. Every country needed to have a stock of reserves (foreign currencies) to intervene in the market when necessary. In the absence of such reserves crisis situations easily developed, particularly when governments tried to hold on to overvalued rates.

With the floating of the major currencies, exchange rate questions have become more complicated. The issues in the present day context arise not only from the question of whether to peg or not, but what to peg to. Developing countries in particular have found it necessary to experiment with various kinds of arrangements, given the fact that each arrangement is associated with different consequences.

The nominal exchange rate discussed above has its uses but there are some other concepts of the exchange rate which are important in discussions relating to trade and adjustment. One of these concepts is the *nominal effective exchange rate.* Before the advent of floating a 10 per cent devaluation of the peso (let us say) against the US dollar, meant a 10 per cent devaluation against other currencies that had a fixed relationship to the US dollar. A country normally has more than one trading partner, and therefore while its currency may appreciate against some currencies, it may depreciate against others. One also has to take into account the fact that some trading partners are more important than others. The nominal effective exchange rate is the trade-weighted average of bilateral nominal exchange rates. The approach taken is to construct an index by weighting each foreign currency by the country's share in the domestic country's foreign trade. But this is easier said than done, since trade takes place in a matrix kind of framework. Indices can vary from simple to very complex. The nominal effective exchange rate represents how much of a basket of foreign currencies a country can get for one unit of the domestic currency. A larger number measured relative to a base year, implies that you will get a larger basket of foreign currency than in the base year.[4]

A related concept is the *real exchange rate* which seeks to take account of the relative movement of prices in the home country and in trading partners. Even if the nominal exchange rate were to remain unchanged, different rates of inflation among trading partners would affect export and import prices. The real exchange rate is the price in real terms of a real dollar a country uses for its international transactions.[5] In general form, the real exchange rate can be defined as follows:[6]

$$E = \frac{En/Pd}{\$1/Pw}$$

E is the real exchange rate; *En* is the nominal exchange rate expressed in units of domestic currency per US dollar.; *Pd* is the appropriate price deflator for the domestic currency; and *Pw* is the appropriate price deflator for the US dollars.

There are many variants of the real exchange rate, depending on what one wants to emphasize.[7] Basically though, the concept gives an indication of movements in competitiveness by showing the number of units of foreign goods required to buy one unit of domestic goods. A real appreciation signals a loss of competitiveness, that is, it now takes more units of foreign goods to buy one unit of domestic goods.

Then there is the *real effective exchange rate* which is a multilateral version of the real exchange rate. 'Changes in bilateral real exchange rates are weighted by a foreign country's share of trade with the domestic country. So the real effective exchange rate measures how much of a basket of foreign goods you can get for one unit of domestic currency. A larger number relative to a base year implies you will get a larger basket of foreign goods with the domestic currency than in the base year.'[8]

Putting a value on a currency is not an easy matter. The 'equilibrium' rate, that is, the rate that would correct a trade deficit and even lead to a trade surplus can be elusive. Trying to find the 'equilibrium' rate is like trying to hit a moving target. The factors affecting the demand and supply for foreign exchange are unpredictable and complex. Countries have different economic structures and different production and consumption patterns. Different products are associated with different demand and supply elasticities.

An attractive concept in theoretical discussions of exchange values is the purchasing power parity (PPP) which uses the cost of a given basket of items in different countries to identify the equilibrium exchange rate.

PURCHASING POWER PARITY (PPP)

There are a number of theories on exchange rate determination. Some of the earliest explanations stressed external factors affecting the balance of payments. Perhaps the first to shift the emphasis was the purchasing power parity (PPP) doctrine (or hypothesis) which emphasizes the relationship between relative prices and the exchange rate. The basic assumption is that people value currencies for what they will buy. If 400 Japanese yens bought the same amount of goods and services as one US dollar, the equilibrium exchange rate in a free market should be in the region of 400 yens to US$1.00. A rate different from this would generate market forces that would eventually push the rate back toward the purchasing power parity level. The theory is often presented in three versions. One is the law of one price, which relates exchange rates to prices of individual homogeneous goods in different countries. Essentially, this version states that when there are no transaction costs or trade barriers (such as tariffs or quotas), the prices of identical goods sold in different countries should be the same when expressed in a common currency.[9] The second is the absolute or positive version which states that the exchange rate is simply the ratio of two countries' general price levels. In other words it compares the purchasing power of two different currency units at a given moment. The 'general price level' can be taken as a nationally weighted average of prices of all goods and services which are produced in each country.[10] There are three main problems with this version. It not only assumes that goods are similar across countries, but that nations produce and consume identical bundles of these goods. Another deficiency is that it does not take into account the significance of transportation costs and trade barriers, both of which can have a substantial effect on prices. A third difficulty arises from the fact that the general price level covers both tradable and non-tradable goods. Non-tradable goods prices, however, cannot be eliminated directly through commodity arbitrage as is the case for tradable goods. This is one possible explanation for the difference often observed between official exchange rates and purchasing power parities.

Because of the calculation difficulties involved, a third version of the PPP emerged. This has come to be known as the relative or comparative version, and seeks to relate the current parity change rate to changes in the purchasing powers of two currencies from a base period where the exchange rate was in equilibrium to a more recent period. It argues that 'the percentage change in the exchange rate from a given base period equals the difference between the percentage change in the domestic price level and the percentage change in the foreign price level'.[11] Let us assume that between 1980 and 1990 the US average price level rose by 50 per cent and Japanese prices by 45 per cent; then the US dollar value of a yen would have risen by 5 per cent. Put more simply, the depreciation or appreciation of a nation's currency is equal to the difference between the rise in the nation's price level and the rise in foreign prices. This proposition is known as purchasing power parity. A currency maintains its purchasing power parity if it depreciates by an amount equal to the excess of domestic inflation over foreign inflation.

PPP relates exchange rates and price levels without saying anything about cause and effect.[12] In some countries domestic factors are the major influence on the inflationary process, while in others it is external considerations. One of the key issues in the adjustment process would depend on the speed with which residents adjust to purchasing power changes.

The relative version is not altogether free from difficulties of its own. While any price index can be used, any errors in these indexes will be reflected in the calculation of the parity change. For the exchange rate to adjust exactly to changes in the difference between national price indexes, the base period must be one of equilibrium. It is also worth noting that disturbances in the balance of payments can be brought about by factors other than changes in the price level. The theory also does not pay attention to the effect of capital movements on exchange rates. In other words, it concentrates on the current account of the balance of payments, and in this sense, it differs from the so-called 'balance of payments theory' of exchange rate determination which takes account of all items giving rise to the demand and supply of foreign exchange. The purchasing power parity is not a complete theory of exchange rate determination. It simply emphasizes the relationship between national prices and the exchange rate. Financial tests have provided conflicting results. While it is a long-run theory, there are doubts that it holds in the long run, not to mention the short run. Increasingly the exchange market is being treated as a financial asset market and portfolio decision-making theory is being used to explain movements in exchange rates. In most financial assets approaches, explanations related to international trade in goods are not completely excluded.

THE 'BIG MAC' APPROACH

Given the recent interest in the undervaluation or overvaluation of currencies in the context of greater flexibility in exchange rate arrangements, the *Economist* magazine has since 1986 been publishing a 'Big Mac' index which has enjoyed a great deal of popularity. The index is intended to provide 'a light-hearted guide to whether currencies are at a "correct" level. It is not a precise predictor of currencies, simply a tool to make exchange-rate theory a bit more digestible.'[13]

'Big Mac' is a Mac Donald's product – the well-known American fast-food chain which operates in over 75 countries. It is assumed that the 'Big Mac' is made to more or less the same recipe everywhere. The 'Big Mac' PPP is the exchange rate that would leave hamburgers costing the same in America as abroad. Table 4.2 shows the result of the most recent exercise. To understand how the index is constructed let us take a hypothetical example. If at the end of 1995 (to take a random date) the price of a Big Mac hamburger was, say, US$4 in the US and ten Barbadian dollars in Barbados; to get the Big Mac PPP we have to divide the Barbados dollar price by the US dollar price, and this gives us 1 US$=B$2.50. If at that particular point in time (end of 1995 in this hypothetical example), the actual exchange rate was B$2.00=US$1.00 the implication using PPP arguments is that the Barbadian dollar was 25 per cent overvalued against the US dollar. From the other point of view the US dollar was 20 per cent undervalued against the Barbadian dollar. Even if the actual nominal exchange rate does not move, PPP exchange rate (that is, the rate that

Table 4.2　The hamburger standard

Country	Big Mac prices		Implied PPP* of the dollar	Actual $ exchange rate 7/4/95	Local Currency under (-) over(+) valuation, %
	In local currency	In dollars			
UNITED STATES[ø]	$2.32	2.32	–	–	–
Argentina	Peso 3.00	3.00	1.29	1.00	+29
Australia	A$2.45	1.82	1.06	1.35	–
Austria	Sch 39.0	4.01	16.8	9.72	+73
Belgium	Bfr 109	3.84	47.0	28.4	+66
Brazil	Real 2.42	2.69	1.04	0.90	+16
Britain	£1.74	2.80	1.33**	1.61**	+21
Canada	C$2.77	1.99	1.19	1.39	–14
Chile	Peso 9.50	2.40	409	395	+4
China	Yuan 9.00	1.05	3.88	8.54	–55
Czech Republic	CKr. 50.0	1.91	21.6	26.2	–18
Denmark	DKr 26.75	4.92	11.5	5.43	+112
France	Fr 18.5	3.85	7.97	4.80	+66
Germany	DM 4.80	3.48	2.07	1.38	+50
Holland	F I5.45	3.53	2.35	1.55	+52
Hong Kong	HK$9.50	1.23	4.09	7.73	–47
Hungary	Forint 191	1.58	82.3	121	–32
Indonesia	Rupiah 3 900	1.75	1 681	2 231	–25
Israel	Shekel 8.90	3.01	3.84	2.95	+30
Italy	Lire 4 500	2.64	1 940	1 702	+14
Japan	Y391	4.65	169	84.2	+100
Malaysia	M$3.76	1.51	1.62	2.49	–35
Mexico	Peso 10.9	1.71	4.70	6.37	–26
New Zealand	NZ$2.95	1.96	1.27	1.51	–16
Poland	Zloty 3.40	1.45	1.47	2.34	–37
Russia	Rouble 8 100	1.62	3 491	4 985	–30
Singapore	S$2.95	2.10	1.27	1.40	–9
South Korea	Won 2,300	2.99	991	769	+29
Spain	Ptas 355	2.86	153	124	+23
Sweden	SKr 26.0	3.54	11.2	7.34	+53
Switzerland	SFr 5.90	5.20	2.54	1.13	+124
Taiwan	NT$65.0	2.53	28.0	25.7	+9
Thailand	Baht 48.0	1.95	20.7	24.6	–16

*　Purchasing power parity: local price divided by price in the United States.
ø　Average of New York, Chicago, San Francisco and Atlanta.
**　Dollars per pound

Source: *The Economist*, 15 April 1995.

leaves hamburgers costing the same in each country) will change as the domestic price of hamburgers change.

While the Big Mac index is simple and interesting, it is worth noting that it is confined to one good (rather than a basket) and draws on short-term movements in prices and exchange rates. Its major shortcoming, however, is that while 'the theory of PPP relates only to traded goods, the 'Big Mac' is not shipped across borders, and rents (which account for a large share of total costs) vary enormously across countries. Local prices may also be distorted by taxes and trade barriers (for example, tariffs on beef).'[14] It is also worth keeping in mind that PPP is a long-run theory since it argues that in the long run the exchange rate of two currencies should move towards the rate that would equalize the prices of an identical basket of goods and services in each country.[15]

EXCHANGE RATE REGIME

Exchange rate regimes fall basically into two categories, fixed and floating. Between these two extremes there is a continuum of arrangements reflecting varying degrees of government intervention. It is worth noting that what countries claim to operate and what takes place in practice may be two entirely different things. A country, for example, may peg its rate, but change the parity frequently. On the other hand, another country may declare a floating regime, but intervene in the foreign exchange market so frequently that the rate hardly changes in the short term. As the most important price in an open economy, governments find themselves unable to leave the exchange rate entirely to market forces, particularly since some of the earlier assumptions that adjustment would be automatic under a floating system has not been borne out by practice.

The debate over fixed versus flexible exchange rate regimes has a long history. Under the gold standard each country would fix the price of gold in terms of its own currency, and since gold was a homogeneous commodity a set of exchange rates was a natural result. For example, if the US dollar price of gold, were set at US$ 4 per ounce, the German DM at 8 marks per ounce, and Pound Sterling at £2 per ounce then the rate of exchange between these three currencies would have been US$4 = 8 DM = £2 or US$1 = 2DM = £0.5.

For exchange rates to be maintained at a fixed level over time the monetary authorities would have to be prepared to buy and sell gold at the official price in unlimited quantities, or the rates would come under pressure if the authorities could not supply the public demand for gold.

Countries needed to have a stock of gold, and because of this the availability of gold placed a constraint on the supply of currency. Under the gold-exchange standard established after the Second World War a different kind of fixed-rate system was adopted. Under the Bretton Woods system member countries agreed to peg their currencies to the US dollar or gold. As indicated before, having declared a par value the monetary authorities were required to defend this rate within a margin of plus or minus 1 per cent on either side of par. It was necessary to keep a stock of reserves (gold and foreign currencies), to defend the declared exchange rate. When reserves were low, crises developed, since the ability of the monetary authorities to maintain the existing rate would come under suspicion. Speculators often increased this pressure in an effort to make a profit.

It was possible under this system to maintain exchange rates that were not equilibrium rates, that is, rates that would equate the supply of and the demand for foreign currency. Even when reserves were low, direct controls on the flow of foreign exchange and the use of tariffs, subsidies, and quotas could be used to eliminate excess demand for foreign currency. Additional 'weapons' to reduce demand could take the form of monetary and fiscal policy. A change in the exchange rate was often resorted to as an extreme measure, even though the system was conceived as a fixed, but adjustable one.

When the Bretton Woods system collapsed in the early 1970s, it was widely feared that the chaotic situation of the 1930s would once more emerge. Increasingly, however, more flexible exchange rates regimes are being adopted as part of the economic liberalization process. Despite the large fluctuations, world trade has continued to grow at a faster rate than world output. The arguments for and against a fixed exchange rate standard, however, have not gone away.

The arguments

The appropriateness of an exchange rate regime is determined by the structural characteristics of an economy and by policy objectives. The exchange rate links the domestic economy to the international economy, and therefore it plays a critical role in determining the ultimate impact of internal or external stocks. Two areas where the exchange rate is particularly relevant as a policy instrument are the maintenance of domestic price stability and achieving internal and external balance. The relevance of the different exchange rate regimes in terms of attaining particular objectives rests on the existence of certain conditions, for example, the share of tradeable goods in total output.

The most important argument in favour of a system of fixed exchange rates is the degree of certainty it brings to the conduct of international business. Exchange rates can have a critical bearing on profits and costs. The other advantage stems from the constraint it places on governments wishing to pursue expansionary monetary and fiscal policy which will eventually bring pressure to bear on the exchange rate. In the absence of reserves which could be used to defend a particular rate, a devaluation of the currency may become inevitable. So that if the aim is to avoid a change in the exchange rate, governments would have to be careful with adopting policies that lead to increased demands for foreign goods, which translate into greater need for foreign exchange. Higher domestic prices would not only encourage residents to seek cheaper foreign goods, but would also discourage foreign buyers from buying local goods. A trade deficit would therefore get worse or an existing surplus could be reduced. Of course, under a floating system the market would adjust through a depreciation of the domestic currency which would make foreign currencies more expensive to residents while reducing the price of local goods in foreign exchange to external buyers. Supporters of a fixed-rate system have traditionally associated speculation and volatility with floating rates. Their major argument is that this volatility would tend to make international trade and investment more risky and would therefore impede international integration.[16] The monetary discipline called for under a fixed-rate system is needed to discourage political leaders from using inflationary finance to finance their activities.

Proponents of floating rates argue that such a system not only has the advantage of leaving the country with greater freedom in the use of monetary policy, but is likely to be less crisis-prone. A major argument is that flexible rates are better capable of insulating the economy from shocks. Excessive monetary expansion, for example, would quickly be reflected in the exchange rate and on domestic inflation, and it would be up to the authorities to decide the tolerable limits of price changes. Those opposed to a fixed rate system also argue that with the use of the forward markets for foreign exchange by both importers and exporters, a great deal of the uncertainty associated with a flexible exchange rate system could be removed. As for the other major criticism that a flexible regime is subject to large unpredictable and destabilizing swings, it is argued that this is not borne out by experience. The intervention by monetary authorities in the foreign exchange markets can keep rates from fluctuating too wildly. Additionally, it cannot be argued that a fixed rate system, particularly in the light of past experience is free of speculation. Once rates are allowed to become overvalued, speculation over a possible change leads to behaviour which puts further pressure on an already beleaguered currency. The argument that a fixed exchange rate places a constraint on inflationary policies is not borne out by experience. It is not easy for governments to sacrifice growth and employment as a way of relieving pressure on the exchange rate. The tendency has been to restrict imports in order to deal with the balance of payments problems through tariffs, quotas, devaluations, exchange controls, and so on. Far from encouraging trade a fixed exchange rate system could discourage it, since the imposition of restrictions invites retaliation.

Choosing an exchange rate regime

The decision by the United States in December 1971 to cut the link between the US dollar and gold marked the end of an era. A major plank from the Bretton Woods system was removed. Between 1971 and 1973 the major currencies went on float in flagrant violation of the IMF Charter. Between 1973 and 1 April 1978 when the Second Amendment to the Fund Articles came into effect, an illegal regime prevailed. Under the Second Amendment member states are allowed a great deal more freedom in the choice of exchange rate arrangements. They can float or peg to any denominator except gold. They are also free to enter cooperative arrangements by which members maintain the value of their currencies in relation to the value of the currency or currencies of other members. The Fund's responsibility is to exercise firm surveillance over the exchange rate policies of members, and to adopt specific principles for the guidance of all members with respect to those policies. Table 4.3 shows the exchange rate arrangements adopted by member states of the IMF at the end of 1978, at the end of 1984, and at the end of June 1996. The table shows that some countries still choose to peg to a single currency. The number of countries pegging to the US dollar has been declining, as is the number pegging to a currency basket of their own choosing. The number of currencies pegged to the US dollar declined from 42 at the end of 1978 to 34 at the end of 1984 and to 20 at the end of June 1996. Those pegging to the French franc (largely former African colonies) have continued to do so. Countries pegging to the SDR have also declined in number. Countries described as 'managed floating' or 'independently floating' have increased significantly in recent years.

As indicated earlier, the exchange rate option available to member states of the IMF are quite varied. A great deal of experimentation is currently taking place, as members search for a regime that is internationally workable.

Table 4.3 Exchange rate arrangements adopted by member states of the IMF, 1978, 1984 and 1996

Arrangement	1978 (end)	1984 (end)	1996 (end of June)
Currency pegged to			
US dollar	42	34	20
French franc	14	14	14
Other currency	8	5	9
SDR	12	11	2
Other currency composite	20	31	20
Flexibility limited vis-à-vis a single currency	...	7	4
Cooperative arrangements	5	8	10
Adjusted according to a set of indicators	5	6	2
Managed floating	26[a]	20	45
Independently floating	[b]	12	55
Total	132	148	181

... not available.

[a] includes countries with other arrangements.

[b] included in 'managed floating'.

Source: IMF, *International Financial Statistics*, various issues.

COOPERATIVE ARRANGEMENTS IN THE EUROPEAN UNION (EU)

Political developments in the former Soviet Union and Eastern Europe have led to the dismantling of a number of economic and currency alignments and the emergence of a number of new currencies and arrangements. While this is taking place, some regions in the world are attempting to strengthen their economic integration efforts in the field of trade by pursuing monetary union as well. In Western Europe, for example, the third and final stage of Economic and Monetary Union is scheduled to begin on 1 January 1999 with the irrevocable fixing of exchange rates among the currencies of participating countries and against the new single currency, to be called the 'Euro' which will replace the European Currency Unit (ECU). Western Europe, of course, has been on this road for some time.

The European Monetary System (EMS) was set up on 1 January 1979 with the aim of creating a 'zone of monetary stability' in Europe. The European Currency Unit (ECU) and the exchange rate arrangements constitute the exchange rate mechanism (ERM) which is the centerpiece of the system.[17] The ERM is an attempt to blend the advantages of fixed and flexible exchange rate systems. A central rate expressed in ECUs is fixed for each currency in the EMS. These ECU-related rates which cannot be changed unilaterally are used to establish a grid of bilateral exchange rates between EMS participants, with allowance made for the fluctuation of these rates within a defined narrow band. Central banks are obliged to intervene in the foreign exchange markets to keep the rates stable, and a credit mechanism was set up to assist them in doing so. Until August 1993, fluctuation margins of ±2.25 per cent (±6 per cent in the case of Spain and the United Kingdom) were permitted around these central parities. Additionally, there is a 'divergence indicator' the aim of which is to gauge the relative extent of each currency's divergence from its central ECU parity. An ECU basket formula is used as an indicator to detect divergences between Community currencies. The 'threshold of divergence' is fixed at 75 per cent of the maximum spread for each currency, and any movement of a currency beyond this 75 per cent of its maximum permitted divergence against the ECU carries a presumption that appropriate action will be taken. Intervention to support bilateral parities is obligatory at the margins with 'unlimited' accounts of credit coming from the 'very short-term facility' (VSTF).

When the EMS was inaugurated in 1979, all the Community member states were participants, but the United Kingdom opted to stay out of the ERM arrangements until October 1990 when it decided to become a participant. The ERM was rocked by a series of crises in 1992 and 1993 which witnessed several devaluations of certain member currencies and the withdrawal of the British pound and Italian lira from the arrangement. In August 1993, the bilateral bands were increased from ±2.25 per cent to ±15 per cent for all pairs of currencies with the exception of the Dutch Guilder and the German Deutsche mark.

While the EMS was a step forward in achieving monetary union, it did not quite achieve all that its creators had intended. Certainly, with the aim of achieving greater stability, there has been more deliberate efforts to co-ordinate monetary and fiscal policies and this has had a favourable effect on exchange rate fluctuations. The commitment to a fixed exchange rate arrangement, however, can have costs in that members may have to adopt interest rate policies that are inconsistent with the needs of the domestic economy. Policy divergences have resulted in several realignments, particularly in the early years, in order to ease the tensions that have risen from time to time.

Originally, the ERM intended to have the ECU (as a weighted basked of the participating currencies) act as the *numéraire* of the system, with the parity grid defined relative to ECU parities. In practice, however, the system has evolved around the Deutsche mark which, as the most stable currency, is the *de facto* nominal anchor. This has placed great responsibility on Germany whose economic and monetary policies underlie the stability of the system.

The ECU evolved from the need for a unit of account in the EU, and succeeded the European Unit of Account (EUA) in 1979 when the European Monetary System was inaugurated. All Community currencies are represented in the ECU and since the original basket was created new ones have been added as the Community has expanded. The amounts of national currencies chosen are intended to give each currency a weight that would reflect the relative economic size of the country. The weights are determined by a combination of economic criteria and even subjective considerations. The official economic criteria are[18]: the share of the country in the GDP of the Community, its share in intra-Community trade and its share in the EMS financial support system. The criteria serve only as broad indicators. In practice the actual shares of weights of particular currencies may be greater or less than that dictated by economic criteria. In order to take account of relative changes in the importance of member economies, the weights are reviewed every five years or may also be reviewed (on request) in the event that the value of any one of the currencies varies by more than 25 per cent (that is if a change in weight exceeds 25 per cent). The ECU can also be revised to accommodate new members. At the last revision in 1989, the Portuguese Escudo and the Spanish Peseta were included. With the entry into force of the Treaty on European Union on 1 November 1993, the ECU 'basket' of currencies was frozen. Austria, Finland and Sweden are not represented.

The current composition of the ECU which was agreed to in September 1989, is shown in Table 4.4. As can be seen, the Deutsche mark carries the greatest weight, 30.1 per cent, followed by the French franc with 19.0 per cent. The 'weight' of a currency in the ECU is the ratio, in percentage terms between the number of units of that currency in the ECU and the value (rate) of the ECU in terms of that currency. If, for example, on 16 August the ECU was worth 2.1158 Dutch guilders and since there were 0.2198 guilders in the ECU's basket, the guilder's weight in the ECU on that day would have been 10.39 per cent, that is 0.2198 divided by 2.1158. If we wished to find out how much the ECU is worth against another currency, say the US dollar, it would be necessary to find the value of each of

Table 4.4   Currency composition and weights of the ECU at 21 September 1989

ECU component currencies	Amount	Weight %
Belgian franc	3.301	7.6
Danish krone	0.1976	2.45
Deutsche mark	0.6242	30.1
Greek drachma	1.440	0.8
Portuguese escudo	1.393	0.8
French franc	1.332	19.0
Dutch guilder	0.2198	9.4
Irish pound	0.008552	1.1
Luxembourg franc	0.130	0.3
Italian lira	151.8	10.15
Spanish peseta	6.885	5.3
British pound	0.08784	*13.0*
		100.0

the components (using the prevailing exchange rates) and add them together, in similar fashion to the SDR. The ECU's value in national currencies is calculated and published daily by the European Commission. The movements in the weights of the respective currencies, it should be noted, reflect movements in exchange rates, rather than shifts of relative economic importance.

At present the ECU plays three main roles. The main purpose for which the ECU was created was to provide an accounting unit for the official sector. It acts as the denominator of the Community's transactions. The Community's budget is specified in terms of ECUs. Secondly, when the EMS was created in 1979, the ECU was the centerpiece of the system. It was the *numéraire* for the exchange rate mechanism, the basis for the divergence indicator, the unit of account for the operations of the European Monetary Cooperation Fund (EMCF) and the means of settlement for operations arising through the system. In practice, however, the ECU's role in the EMS has been limited largely to settling transactions among EMS central banks. Thirdly, the ECU is being increasingly used in private transactions.[19] One hears about the private ECU. Technically, the 'private' ECU is no different from the 'official' ECU. The private ECU is simply a contract in which the contracting parties have denominated payment obligation in ECU and have accepted its official definition. This is an agreement to accept the value of ECU arising from official changes in its composition – the so-called 'open basket'. An alternative arrangement is one that defines the ECU as the sum of the currencies in the basket at the time the contract is concluded – the 'closed basket' approach.

The ECU is not a national currency in the sense that it is represented in the form of notes and coins.[20] It can, however, be used for international financial and commercial transactions as any national currency. It is bought and sold on the foreign exchange markets against most national currencies. ECU bonds are floated on the international capital markets and traders also invoice in ECUs.

To have an accounting device to which member states in a grouping could relate is one thing. A decision to establish a common currency to replace existing national currencies raises very complex questions both in theory and practice. A national currency is not only an emblem of sovereignty, but also provides the issuing government with the benefits of seigniorage and as an instrument of management. A currency union involves costs and benefits and these are usually discussed within what is called 'optimum' or 'optimal' currency area theory.

Over time a number of criteria have emerged in the literature against which a country's suitability for participation in a monetary union is discussed.[21] To begin with, not all writers use the term 'optimal' or 'optimum' in the same way, or in the same sense, and there are also variations in the questions they seek to answer. Some writers, for example, seek to establish 'a perfect economic region' for a currency area. An 'economic region' is defined as an 'optimal currency area' when it exhibits characteristics which lead to an automatic removal of unemployment and payments' disequilibria; automatic in the sense that no interference is required from monetary and fiscal policies to restore equilibria. This, of course, is a difficult question from one which seeks to determine whether or not a given group of countries should form a currency or exchange rate union.[22] While the adoption of a single currency and a situation involving irrevocably fixed exchange rates are commonly proposed as having the same implication, the single currency arrangement tends to convey a feeling of stronger commitment to union since it is more difficult to get out of.

The main criteria around which discussions on optimal currency areas centre are factor mobility, financial integration, openness and diversification. It is argued that where factor mobility exist there is no need for an exchange rate as an adjustment mechanism. A high degree of financial integration will also assist the movement of capital. Highly open economies, it is argued, are susceptible to price instability and given the high costs of adjustment associated with exchange rates, countries highly dependent on trade should benefit from joining a currency union. The criterion of diversification revolves around the argument that a diversified economy will tend to have a more stable balance of payments, and therefore there should be less reliance on the need for adjustment through the exchange rate.

These criteria are not without controversy. In practice the desire for a single currency may be based both on economic and political arguments. In Europe monetary union is seen by some not only as a way of strengthening the integration process, but perhaps as a step towards political union. A single European currency is also no doubt perceived by some as a counterweight to the US dollar. The European monetary union accounts for about 40 per cent of world export and encompass a region of over 400 million people and a total GDP of over US$7000 billion.

PRACTICE IN DEVELOPING COUNTRIES

Several developing countries have continued to peg their currencies to an intervention currency, though pegging to a major currency within an internationally agreed system of fixed exchange rates is not the same as pegging to one in a framework where the major currencies are floating. The major attraction to pegging to a single currency is undoubtedly its administrative simplicity. This is one way of getting around the problem of continuous decision-making that is required under managed floating. It also allows a fair amount of stability, particularly when the peg is to the currency of a country with whom there are strong trading and financial ties. To the extent that other countries also peg to the same currency, the cross rates may also be relatively stable. By pegging to the currency of a major trading partner, a country can minimize changes in the prices of imports and exports that stem from changes in the adopted exchange rate. Activities can be planned with greater certainty having a favourable effect on output and employment. A major disadvantage of pegging in a world of floating is that the pegging currency would float with the intervention currency against the rest of the world.

As nations try to diversify their external economic relationships, the single currency peg is becoming less attractive. Countries with more than one major trading partners may opt to peg to a group or basket of currencies. The objective is the same, that is, to reduce variations in the average price of imports or exports caused by exchange rate fluctuations. Basically, the basket would consist of prescribed quantities of foreign currencies in proportion to the different shares of trade the country carries on with its different trading partners. Once the basket is defined, the domestic currency value is derived using the exchange rates of the foreign currencies in the basket. A declining number of countries has been using the SDR basket. Most countries pegging to a basket use currency composites of their own. Among the basket peggers are Poland, Papua New Guineau, Cape Verde and Burundi. Countries which decide to peg, whether to a single currency or to a basket, can adjust the rate from time to time in response to movements in certain indicators. Hungary, for instance, defines the value of its currency (the forint) in terms of a basket comprising US dollars (50 per cent) and the Deutsche mark (50 per cent), but this value is adjusted at irregular intervals principally in light of the difference between the domestic and foreign rates of inflation.

Even to countries that are floating, a fixed exchange rate regime continues to hold certain attractions. Since 1979, most members of the European Union have participated in an arrangement called the exchange rate mechanism (ERM) which is a compromise between floating and completely fixed exchange rates. While maintaining flexibility with third currencies, participating currencies in the ERM are required to establish a central parity against the European Currency Unit (ECU), from which a bilateral parity grid of exchange rates between member countries can be derived. Fluctuation margins for each currency around those central parities are defined, and central banks are required to defend the fixed rates. Such target zones systems are seen as a way of reducing exchange rate volatility which can hinder trade and investment. The ERM arrangement has experienced several crisis in recent years, and is still evolving in the context of the efforts to have greater monetary integration in Europe.

Because of domestic inflation and the adoption of market oriented policies, the number of countries which have adopted more flexible exchange rate arrangements has increased significantly in recent years. These arrangements, however, are not all the same. While the rates are generally influenced by supply and demand conditions, there are different kinds of interventions and institutional frameworks. In no case is the rate left completely to market forces. The monetary authorities in the industrial countries intervene when necessary to counter disorderly conditions in the exchange markets, or when otherwise deemed appropriate. In developing countries the floating mechanism and method of official intervention differ widely. For example, in Trinidad and Tobago, the Trinidad and Tobago dollar is determined in the interbank market on the basis of supply and demand conditions. Banks are allowed to conduct foreign exchange transactions, both spot and forward, with the public without limitations. Commercial banks must notify the Central Bank of Trinidad and Tobago in advance of any planned significant adjustment to the exchange rate. In

Guyana, the external value of the Guyana dollar is determined freely by market forces in the cambio market. The Bank of Guyana (the central bank), conducts certain transactions on the basis of the cambio rate by averaging quotations of the three largest dealers in the cambio market on the date the transaction takes place. In Tanzania, the Bank of Tanzania, (the Central Bank), holds a weekly auction of foreign exchange at which foreign exchange is sold to foreign exchange bureaus and commercial banks. The weighted average of bids emerging from the auction is the official rate. The arrangements by some other developing countries are more explicitly 'managed'. In Pakistan, for instance, the State Bank of Pakistan sets the rate at which it will purchase and sell US dollars in transactions with authorized dealers.

As indicated earlier, a floating exchange rate is one whose equilibrium value is determined by supply and demand conditions (market forces, and not by the intervention of monetary authorities in the foreign exchange markets). Despite the many theoretical arguments against floating by developing countries, since the early 1980s a number of them, faced with persistent balance of payments problems have experimented with various forms of floating. This often came as part of Fund supported structural adjustment programmes, and after the failure of extensive foreign exchange controls to correct balance of payments difficulties. Inadequate financial resources to defend fixed exchange rate was also a factor. Floating was seen as the best way to determine the equilibrium exchange rate. There are basically two forms of market arrangements facing developing countries desiring to float. One is to adopt a system with a market that is operated within the private sector by commercial banks and licensed foreign exchange dealers. In the other the authorities tend to use an auction system to ensure a sufficiently competitive market. Foreign exchange is surrendered to the central bank for auction to the highest bidders. The bank conducts the market and serves as the channel for the auction process. Certain countries use a combination of both forms.[23]

There are economic characteristics which set developing countries apart from the developed ones, and therefore arrangements which may be appropriate for the latter would not necessarily serve the interest of the former. Some of these characteristics include an undiversified production structure with heavy dependence on a narrow range of agricultural or mineral exports for export earnings, a high ratio of trade to production, critical reliance on foreign sources for food, drugs, raw materials, producer and consumer goods, and an undeveloped money and capital market. Persistent adverse movements in the terms of trade is a major source of pressure on exchange rates in developing countries.

In the developed countries with their more diversified production structure and developed capital markets changes in exchange and interest rates can be expected to affect the balance of payments even in the short term. For reasons stated earlier, developing countries have to rely less on these instruments. Up until the 1970s, it was felt that free floating was not a realistic option for most of them in the absence of well-functioning foreign exchange and financial markets. In many of them the fact that markets for common stocks, bills, securities, and so on, were still in the infancy stage raised questions about feasibility. Government controls over current transactions and capital movements existed in most developing countries. For most currencies forward exchange facilities did not and still do not exist.

What has been the experience? Since the early 1980s an increasing number of developing countries and economies in transition have allowed their currencies to float with varying results. According to studies done by the IMF[24] the following conclusions have emerged.

1. *Do parallel market rates closely follow the money supply?*
   To answer this question, the IMF looked at the relationship between parallel market rates and broad money (lagged one period) for a sample of 13 major developing countries over the period 1977-89. 'This suggests that while official rates have been held by governments at often inappropriate levels, exchange markets took account of the strengths and weaknesses of monetary policy'.[25]

2. *Will currencies go into a free fall, that is, would the exchange rate tumble thus aggravating inflationary forces?*
   Here the results were mixed. 'In many countries, the initiation of floating arrangements continued a process of real effective depreciation and improving competitiveness that was already underway'.[26] In certain countries (for example, Brazil and Peru) inflation was rapid. In El Salvador and Guatemala a small appreciation followed floating and the strengthening of economic policies.

3. *What will happen to major economic indicators?*
   The Fund study found that economies generally performed better after floating and the adoption of comprehensive stabilization programs. Of the twelve countries surveyed for the period 1985–92, inflation declined in six following floating and accelerated in one. In other cases inflation was broadly unchanged. With respect to output, of the eleven countries surveyed for the period 1985–92 six experienced faster GDP growth after floating (with a one-year lag) and in two growth deteriorated.

4. *General conclusion*
'After a decade of experimenting with flexible rates, the evidence is
building that developing countries with diverse economic structures
can satisfactorily operate floating rate systems, even if they have relatively simple financial systems. The key is to support the floating
arrangements with conservative monetary and fiscal policies to ensure
macro-economic stability.'[27]

THE DEVALUATION CONTROVERSY

During the period when the Bretton Woods fixed exchange rate system
was in force, the exchange rate had come to be regarded as a kind of
'sacred cow', not to be touched, except in extreme circumstances. Fear of
initiating a process of competitive devaluations which characterized the
period just prior to the Second World War, exerted a major influence on
the approach to external adjustment in the post-1945 period. The system,
in practice, came to be much more rigid than the founding fathers of the
Bretton Woods system had intended. With the changes taking place in
the global economy, the fixed-rate system could not adequately adapt,
and by the early 1970s, it gave way to more flexible arrangements in an
atmosphere of great uncertainty. The resort to floating by the industrial
countries was a response to the pressures that had emerged, and even
though the system had long had a substantial academic following not
many policy-makers were willing to openly embrace floating as a better
alternative.

As indicated earlier, an increasing number of countries are adopting
some form of flexible exchange rate arrangement. Some have found out,
however, that there are limits to what the exchange rate can do, and that
domestic macroeconomic policies and the external environment have
crucial roles to play in the adjustment and growth processes. Some countries still prefer to peg to a single currency or to a basket of currencies, and
to them the devaluation question still has a great deal of relevance. To this
issue we now turn.

The use of currency devaluation to correct a balance of payments
problem in developing countries has long been surrounded by controversy.
While devaluation is a major element in most IMF/World Bank supported
structural adjustment programmes, many critics feel it tends to create more
problems than it solves in non-industrial countries. One of the major
difficulties arises from the fact that all the information required to make a
decision on the exchange rate may not be available. A devaluation may

also be undertaken for the wrong reasons, or the authorities may be unwilling or unable to put in place the necessary supporting policies to make the exchange rate change effective. To appreciate these comments it is necessary to understand how a devaluation works.

Let us start from the point where say, the Jamaican dollar (J$) is pegged to the US dollar (US$) at a rate of say, J$4.00 = US$1.00 (J$1.00 = US$0.25). If the Jamaican Government were to devalue the Jamaican dollar by 100 per cent the rate would move to J$8.00 = US$1.00 (J$1.00 = US$0.12). For people wanting to acquire Jamaican dollars, this means that instead of having to give up 25 US cents to acquire one unit of the local currency, they now only have to give up approximately 12 US cents. For Jamaican goods and services quoted in US dollars (and assuming no change in the quotes) the devaluation would not make these goods and services any cheaper to foreign buyers. For goods and services quoted in Jamaican dollars, and assuming that the local prices did not increase by the same percentage as the devaluation, then Jamaican goods would become cheaper to foreign buyers. The assumption is that lower prices to foreigners would stimulate exports of local goods and services. A devaluation can also affect the profitability of local exporters and the revenue of government. In cases where income or revenue in foreign exchange has fallen, a devaluation could restore all or part of this loss in terms of local currency, since a devaluation means that the price of foreign currency has increased.

A good reason for devaluation occurs when local prices have risen (for whatever reason) faster than prices in competing countries. A devaluation may restore back an element of competitiveness assuming that competitors do not offset the devaluation by changing their own exchange rates. It is worth remembering that devaluation is not the only way to reduce the price of local goods and services. Increasing productivity could have the same effect. This could come about through improved management, training of workers, adoption of modern technology, and so on. But this can take longer and is not always easy to accomplish.

A devaluation also affects imports. Since local residents have to give up more local currency to acquire a unit of foreign currency, and prices of imports are fixed in terms of foreign currency, it is assumed this would lead to reduced demand for foreign goods and a switch to local goods. Basically, the effect on the balance of trade or the balance of payments depends on the responsiveness of exports and imports to the change in the exchange rate.

Because 'responsiveness' is dependent on a wide range of factors, the effect on the trade balance is not always predictable. Let us first look at the effect on exports. The underlying assumption is that the devaluing country has unemployed resources and produces a range of exports, demand for which is price elastic. There is an export base in place. In other words, as prices are reduced in terms of foreign currency, foreign demand would increase by enough to more than offset the loss of foreign currency earnings resulting from the change in exchange rates. The assumption is also that domestic prices do not increase. But even if they increase this increase should not be by the same extent of the devaluation. Even if there were no export platform in place, the assumption is that the change in the exchange rate can trigger a reallocation of resources in favour of the tradable sector fairly quickly.

As indicated earlier, a large number of developing countries are critically dependent on a narrow range of exports for foreign exchange earnings. For many of these products these countries are price takers, that is, they are unable to influence world prices (which generally are quoted in foreign currency) by their own actions. Several of these products are characterized by what is called an 'inelastic demand'. This means that even if the exporting countries were able to reduce their prices by devaluation or other means, foreign demand would not necessarily increase. For instance, if the price of sugar or bananas were reduced it does not mean that people would consume more of these products. Some products, of course, are more price elastic than others. It is worth pointing out that even if demand does not increase and earnings remain the same, profitability would be enhanced since the local currency equivalent would be greater as a result of the devaluation. This should serve as an incentive for exporters to sell more abroad. Because of this effect exporters may find themselves in a position to reduce the prices of products quoted in the buyers' currencies.

A devaluation is also expected to affect imports. Since residents have to give up more local currency to acquire a unit of foreign currency, imports become more expensive and this should lead to a switch from foreign (traded) goods to local (non-traded) goods. It is assumed that the devaluing country produce goods and services that can replace imports or at least has the capacity to do so at fairly short notice. If the devaluing country is unable to do so the higher import prices would be reflected in higher domestic prices. The increased demand for local products will also help to push up prices. To the extent that domestic producers depend on foreign inputs and capital goods, export prices will increase, thus offsetting some of the advantage from devaluation. Consumer goods, medicines, food, and so on, coming from abroad will also be associated with higher prices which would lead to an increased cost of living. This in turn will encourage trade unions to seek higher salaries and wages for their members to offset part or all of the cost of living increases. Increased production cost will lead to increased prices and a 'wage-price' spiral could easily develop. This could put further pressure on the exchange rate, thus reinforcing the inflationary process. There is an argument related to the monetary approach to the balance of payments that this sequence of events does not in fact take place. The increase in prices associated with the initial devaluation (depreciation) will be of a temporary nature, if the money supply does not change. However, real money balances will be reflected in decreased spending on goods and services, and this will have a dampening effect on prices. Whatever validity there may be in this contention, there is considerable evidence of devaluations (depreciation) followed by an increase in the inflation rate, leading to more exchange rate adjustment, resulting in more inflation, and so on.

Depending on the demand and supply elasticities for imports and exports, a devaluation can in fact worsen the terms of trade and widen rather than narrow or remove a trade deficit. For a devaluation to correct a trade balance what is called the Marshall-Lerner condition in the literature must be present. This condition states that absolute values of the two demand elasticities (that is, the demand elasticity) for the country's exports plus its demand elasticity for imports must be greater than one. Countries which are capable of meeting a significant part of their needs from domestic production would appear to be in a better position to make a devaluation work than one which is not. When a country is dependent for critical supplies (medicine, food, raw materials, capital goods) on foreign sources, a devaluation would inevitably lead to an increase in local prices, sometimes by much more than what is warranted by the devaluation. In the absence of price control measures, labour organizations will insist on increased remuneration to offset the increase in the cost of living. Increased wages and salaries are likely to be reflected in higher production costs, and unless producers are willing to accept lower profit margins, they will increase the quotations for their goods. If the government were persuaded to take action to keep wages and salaries from increasing in the face of rising prices, the result will be a lower standard of living. Such a policy, of course, would lead to a redistribution of income in favour of profits, and this may be deliberate if the view is taken that an unequal distribution of income is necessary to encourage saving and investment. Certain social implications also flow from this situation. One option is to control both prices and wages within the framework of a prices and incomes policy so that increasing domestic costs are not allowed to offset the benefits of a devaluation, and the standard of living is kept at some acceptable level. A prices and incomes policy can be a difficult thing to implement. In certain countries wage agreements contain a cost of living allowance provision which is linked to movements in the price index, so that as prices increase, so does the allowance. Price control can also lead to the scarcity of goods, if suppliers are not satisfied with their profit margins.

If the prices of exports remain the same while import prices increase as a result of the devaluation, the effect is a deterioration in the terms of trade (the price of exports divided by the price of imports) and a loss in real income. Even if the Marshall-Lerner condition holds and net export earnings increase with the positive impact on national income, there is another factor which will determine the ultimate effect on the trade balance, and this is the marginal propensity to absorb. If this is less than one, the effect will be positive; if it is more than one the increased income could lead to a greater absorption with negative consequences for the balance of payments.

A devaluation will not work if the conditions are not right or if the required supporting policies are not implemented. There is a great deal of exchange rate pessimism in developing countries. An equilibrium rate is a moving target dependent on a range of conditions outside national control. One of the attractions of exchange rate policy, however, is that it does not require the kind of bureaucracy that import and exchange controls require. The latter have the additional disadvantage of often leading to resource misallocation and inefficiency which in turn impact on the competitiveness of the economy.

In the context of the structural adjustment programmes being championed by aid institutions like the IMF and the World Bank, increasing attention is being focussed not just on the level of the exchange rate, but on the exchange rate regime. The increasing adoption of flexible exchange rate regimes has put greater importance on the exchange rate as an adjustment mechanism. Despite what the Fund studies show, the controversy over the advantages and disadvantages of a fixed but adjustable system versus a more flexible system has not vanished. Both regimes have their adherents, and the final verdict is not yet in. The exchange rate not only serves as an anchor to domestic prices, but its movements also helps to influence international competitiveness, The exchange rate, therefore, is an important policy instrument, but its relative role in the adjustment process is controversial. In situations where there are market imperfections, its effectiveness in bringing about the desired resource allocation would be limited.

CONCLUDING OBSERVATIONS

We often use terms like 'undervaluation', over-valuation', 'real exchange rates' and 'equilibrium rates' as if these terms have clear theoretical and operational meanings. Exchange rate analysis is a challenging exercise, given the range of factors that influence exchange rate behaviour. Expectations, inflation, interest rates, capital mobility, speculation provide only some of the explanation. In an open economy the exchange rate is an important policy instrument, but the growing importance of private capital markets, has made it difficult for governments to exercise the desired degree of control over this price.

The fixed exchange rate system associated with the Bretton Woods agreement broke down in the 1970s because of the changes in the international economy.[28] Even if there were the political will to reinstitute this system on a worldwide basis, this may not be feasible given the fact that the sums now traded in the foreign exchange market far outweigh the resources available to central banks for intervention purposes.

One of the major complaints about the par value system was that the rates were not adjusted as often as they should, and the resultant overvaluations were a major impediment to external adjustment. While flexible arrangements have relieved the pressures on the exchange rates, there have been disappointments in certain areas. The insulation against external disturbances has not always been as strong as desired. In many cases external imbalances have persisted notwithstanding the adoption of a flexible exchange rate regime. Because of this 'ineffectiveness', the demand for international reserves remain high. Nations are not always prepared to leave their fortunes to the market. In 1995, for example, when the yen appreciated against the US dollar, Japanese exporters responded by slashing export prices and shifting production to high-value goods.

Despite the unexpected large variability in exchange rates as a result of floating, the fears that global trade and investment would be adversely affected have not proven correct. We have a long way to go, however, in understanding and explaining exchange rate behaviour. The assumption of the floating system that the exchange rate would be as stable as macroeconomic fundamentals has not been proven correct. In the case of developing countries which have adopted flexible arrangements, the continuous depreciation in most cases, even where the fundamentals appear to be sound, indicate the issue of the exchange rate regime is even less settled. Open import policies and fluctuations in foreign exchange earnings associated with skewed production structures continually create crises, and this further aggravates the confidence problem which seems to underlie the currencies of most developing countries. Residents in these countries tend to switch their savings to foreign currency, through both legal and illegal channels, not only to avoid the effects of domestic inflation or in search of higher returns, but perhaps even more importantly to guard against future depreciation or devaluations. The process of flight, however, often hastens the very event they may be trying to guard against.

Notes

1. The practice, as far as the IMF is concerned, is for the colonial power (in this case the United Kingdom), to accept the Fund's Articles in respect of its colonies.
2. See D. Thomas, 'The Foreign Exchange Market in London,' *Bank of England Quarterly Bulletin* Vol. 35 (December 1995), pp. 361–9.
3. London is the world's largest centre for foreign exchange business. Total average daily turnover during April 1995 was US$464 billion – 60% higher than in April 1992. See D. Thomas, *op. cit.*
4. See J. O. Grabbe, *International Financial Markets* (New York: Elsevier, 1986), p. 173
5. R. Dornbusch, F.L.C.H. Helmers (eds) *The Open Economy* (New York: Oxford University Press, 1988), p. 393.
6. *Ibid.*
7. *Ibid.*
8. Grabbe, *op. cit.*, p. 176.
9. See L. Bartolini, 'Purchasing Power Parity Measures of Competitiveness,' *Finance and Development*, Vol. 32 (March 1995), pp. 46–9.
10. See J. H. Bergstrand, 'Selected Views of Exchange Rates Determination after a Decade of Floating', *New England Economic Review*, May/June, 1983. This article provides an excellent discussion of the purchasing power parity doctrine.
11. *Ibid.*
12. See W. Ethier, *Modern International Economics* (New York: W. W. Norton & Company, 1983), p. 353.
13. See the *Economist* magazine of 15 April 1995.
14. *Ibid.*
15. *Ibid.*
16. See J. Williamson, *The Open Economy and the World Economy* (New York: Basic Books, Inc., 1983), p. 238.
17. See A. G. Haldane, 'The Exchange Rate Mechanism of the European Monetary System: A Review of the Literature,' *Bank of England Quarterly Bulletin*, Vol. 31 (March 1991), pp. 73–82.
18. See D. Gros and W. Thygesen, *European Monetary Integration: From the European Monetary System to Monetary Union* (London: Longman, 1992), p. 204.
19. D. Gros and W. Thygesen, *op. cit.*, p. 208.

20. ECU coins have been issued by some member countries in limited denominations. However, the metal (silver or gold) content of these coins is worth much more than their face value. These coins are more collector's items than transaction money.
21. An excellent discussion of currency area theory is to be found in J. R. Presley and G. E. J. Denis, *Currency Areas* (London: The Macmillan Press Ltd., 1976).
22. *Ibid.*, p. 10.
23. P. J. Quirk, B. Christensen, K. Huh and T. Sasaki, *Floating Exchange Rates in Developing Countries: Experience with Auction and Interbank Markets* (Washington, DC, IMF: 1987). Occasional Paper No. 53, pp. 4–8.
24. P. J. Quirk and H. C. Cortés-Douglas, 'The Experience with Floating Rates', *Finance and Development*, Vol. 30 (June 1993), pp. 28–31.
25. *Ibid.*
26. *Ibid.*
27. *Ibid.*
28. See H. James, *International Monetary Cooperation Since Bretton Woods* (New York: IMF and Oxford University Press, 1996), p. 234.

Further Reading

Aghevli, B. B., M. S. Khan and P. J. Monteil, *Exchange Rate Policy in Developing Countries: Some Analytical Issues*, IMF, Washington, DC, 1991.
Bartolini, L., 'Purchasing Power Parity Measures of Competitiveness', *Finance and Development*, Vol. 32 (September 1995), pp. 46–49.
Burton, D. and M. Gilman, 'Exchange Rate Policy and the IMF', *Finance and Development*, Vol. 28 (September 1991), pp. 18–21.
Claessens, S., 'How Can Developing Countries Hedge their Bets', *Finance and Development*, Vol. 29 (September 1992), pp. 13–15.
Cooper, R. N., *Currency Devaluation in Developing Countries. Essays in International Finance*, No. 86, Princeton University Press, Princeton, 1971.
Diaz-Alejandro, C. *Exchange Rate Devaluation in a Semi-Industrialized Country: The Experience of Argentina, 1955–61*, MIT Press, Cambridge, MA, 1966.
Dornbusch, R. and F. L. C. H. Helmers (eds), *The Open Economy*, Oxford University Press, New York, 1988.
Edwards S., *Real Exchange Rates, Devaluation, Adjustment and Exchange Rate Policy in Developing Countries*, MIT Press, Cambridge, MA, 1989.
Flight, H. and B. Lee-Swan, *All You Need to Know About Exchange Rates*. Sidgwick & Jackson, London, 1989.
Frankel, J. A., *On Exchange Rates*. MIT Press, Cambridge MA, 1993.
Ghatak, S., *Monetary Economics in Developing Countries*, St Martin's Press, New York, 1995.
IMF, *The Exchange Rate System: Lessons of the Past and Options for the Future*, IMF, Washington, DC, 1984.
Kaldor, N., 'Devaluation and Adjustment in Developing Countries', *Finance and Development*, Vol. 20 (June 1983), pp. 35–37.
Kenen, P. B., *Managing Exchange Rates*, Routledge, London, 1988.

Llewellyn, D. T. and C. Miller, *Current Issues in International Monetary Economics*, The Macmillan Press Ltd., London, 1990.

Maciejewski, E. B., 'Real Effective Exchange Rates Indices', *IMF Staff papers*, Vol. 30 (March 1983), pp. 491–541.

Mansur, A. H., 'Determining the Appropriate Levels of Exchange Rates for Developing Countries', *IMF Staff Papers*, Vol. 30 (December 1983), pp. 784–818.

Marrinan, J., 'Exchange Rates Determination: Sorting Out Theory and Evidence', *New England Economic Review* (November/December 1989), pp. 39–50.

Ohr, R., 'Exchange-rate Strategies in Developing Countries', *Inter-economics*, Vol. 26 (September 1991), pp. 115–21.

Quirk, P. J. and H. C. Cortés-Douglas. 'The Experience with Floating Rates', *Finance and Development*, Vol. 30 (June 1993), pp. 28–31.

Spencer, G. and A. Cheasty. 'The Ruble Area: A Breaking of Old Ties?' *Finance and Development*, Vol. 30 (June 1993), pp. 2–5.

UNDP/SAATA. *Aspects of Exchange Rate Determination*, United Nations, New York, 1991.

Williamson, J., *The Open Economy and the World Economy*, Basic Books Inc., New York, 1983.

Williamson, J., *The Exchange Rate System*, Institute of International Economics, Washington, DC, 1985.

5 International Banking

INTRODUCTION

International banking is not a new phenomenon.[1] International lending by means of letters of credit and bills of exchange can be retraced as far back as the 21st century BC. Florentine banking houses of the 14th and 15th centuries had branches and subsidiaries through Europe. British and European bankers were deeply involved in the development of the 'new world'. The breakdown of the gold standard, the decline of sterling as the world's major currency, and the emergence of foreign exchange and trade restrictions in the inter-war period were to have a major influence on the growth and evolution of the international banking business. What distinguishes recent spurts in international banking from earlier periods is the size and scope of the business.

With the return to convertibility of major currencies in the later part of the 1950s and the removal of foreign exchange restrictions, the framework for international operations changed radically. The rapid recovery of Europe and Japan and the coming into being of the European Community created enormous opportunities for trade and investment which in turn opened up increased business for banks, nationally and internationally. With the introduction of controls in the United States in the early 1960s restricting lending abroad, an increasing number of American banks found it necessary to go abroad to meet the needs of their clients seeking foreign markets and investment opportunities. Overall, US bank branches abroad increased from 117 in 1957 to 457 in 1969. In Europe the number increased from 16 to 104 over the period, and in Latin America from 76 to 265. European and Japanese banks themselves started to move abroad to meet the challenge of their competitors. One effect of the post-war globalization of the world economy was the qualitative change in the international banking business. With the emergence of transnational business, companies were not only getting larger, but the range of services they required was also growing. Mergers, take-overs, the need to finance large projects, and so on, not only called for investment funds beyond the capacity of individual banks, but for consultancy and other business services which the banks increasingly found themselves obliged to provide. The changing international environment and developments in technology created challenges which the banks were quick to recognize and to turn

127

into profitable opportunities. The surpluses experienced by oil exporting countries in the 1970s, the emergence of huge payments deficits for many countries and the pressures brought on the international monetary system created a situation for the banks to play a larger role in the international intermediation process.

Banking operations have changed enormously in the last three decades as banks have tried to meet the needs of both borrowers and investors. While up to the early sixties 'the bulk of international banking operations was accounted for by home based transactions conducted predominantly in connection with foreign exchange and trade related operations, recent years have witnessed a spectacular rise of Euro-currency business and, concurrently, of activities carried out through offshoots located in foreign financial centres ('multinational banking')'.[2] Not only have new instruments come into being, but many banks have sought to increase the share of their foreign business in total operations. This has often involved not only more offices abroad, but a strategic presence in major financial centres and the forging of relationships with other financial institutions.

The international capital markets, like national ones, encompass the operations of a wide range of financial intermediaries providing various kinds of financial services. Essentially, they collect surplus funds for relending rather than for non-financial outlays. Among them are investment banking houses, securities brokers, commercial banks, savings and loan institutions, insurance companies, and so on. Commercial banks, however, are the major players. Financial intermediaries are distinguished by the various kinds of debt instruments they issue and/or the forms of credit they extend. By specializing in various kinds of financial services they meet the preferences of savers and the needs of borrowers. Essentially what a bank does is to accept deposits from savers (governments, corporations, or individuals) and then relend these savings to borrowers (governments, corporations or individuals) for various purposes and for varying lengths of time. While a bank may use its own capital for lending, deposits provide the major source of a bank's resources. Until the early 1960s banks were largely engaged in what is known as retail banking, that is, collecting small deposits and making small short-term loans. A wholesale or parallel market has since emerged in a number of countries both with respect to the local and foreign currency business. Transactions in the wholesale market involve relatively larger deposits and also larger loans.

To protect depositors, some regulatory authorities stipulate a relationship between the bank's capital and the bank's assets, particularly loans.

Borrowers (that is those who wish to spend more than their current resources permit) may borrow for current spending, for working capital or investment. The interest spread, that is, the difference between what the bank pays its depositors and what it charges its borrowers largely determines its income. Interest rates are generally lower on short-term loans. Borrowing takes place through a range of instruments that may involve a short-term draft, a medium-term or long-term loan or a bond. In recent years Certificates of Deposits (CDs) have emerged as a major instrument both in domestic markets, and in the international system. Essentially a CD is a receipt for a large deposit, which is negotiable and is therefore associated with a greater degree of flexibility than fixed deposits. CDs can be issued in different amounts and in different maturities. Most deposits in the Euro-currency markets are denominated in US dollars. While the interbank deposit market has been growing in many countries it plays a major role in the international financial system as a source of funds. In fact the interbank relationship is at the heart of the Euro-currency system.

Since the major part of a bank's liabilities (deposits) are short term, their lending tends to be short term. To overcome the handicap of small size, or the short-term nature of liabilities, a range of new techniques has emerged involving joint ventures, syndicate lending, consortiums, rollover credit, and so on. The rollover technique involves the commitment of a bank 'to provide funds for a given period of time, which may run to 10–12 years, on the basis of an interest rate which is adjusted at regular intervals. It thus enables a bank to extend longer term finance whilst minimising its interest-rate risk inherent in the traditional form of fixed-rate financing.'[3]

In the same way that financial intermediaries within countries bring savers and borrowers together, they perform the same function at the global level by moving funds from surplus areas to deficit areas. Transactions, however, may be more complex since more than one currency will be involved and different countries have different regulations governing borrowing and lending activities. Essentially, capital movements describe the movements of funds from one country to another for any number of purposes, including speculation, purchase of financial instruments (debt and equity) or investment in real assets. Currencies that are convertible allow easy movements into other currencies. Most of the currencies of developing countries are not fully convertible, that is, there are trade restrictions and foreign exchange regulations governing the conversion of the local currency into foreign currencies. Besides 'normal' capital outflows, 'capital flight' has become a widespread phenomena in developing countries where high inflation rates and expected changes in the exchange rate often drive holders of funds to seek a save haven in more stable environments. Such flights may also reflect a desire to hide gains from illegal transactions.

THE GROWTH AND NATURE OF INTERNATIONAL BANKING

The outbreak of the international debt crisis in the early 1980s quickly drew attention to the plight and role of the money centre banks in the international financial system. Quietly and almost unobstrusively over the previous two decades the banks had been transforming the banking business both in national markets and internationally. With the developments in technology and the deregulation of financial markets, a revolution in banking had been taking place. The range of innovations is reflected in

the rise of wholesale banking, liability management, multinational banking, Euro-banking, the Asian Currency market, international banking facilities (IBFs), rollover credits, multiple currency loans, 'securitised' lending, collateralised mortgages, note issuances facilities, interest rates and currency options and swaps and financial futures. Credit cards, debt cards, automated teller machines, cash management accounts, electronic fund transfers, point of sale terminals and also part of this worldwide process of change which began in the 1960s, has been sustained over two decades, and continues to reshape the nature of banking and financial markets.[4]

As indicated earlier, with clients becoming increasingly involved in international activities, banks found themselves not only having to provide a wider range of services, but to seek out new sources of funds to finance increasingly larger projects and to exploit new techniques. Not only was there innovation in domestic markets, but international banking activities were becoming increasingly sophisticated, and specialization diminished. Commercial banking which has normally been associated with retail banking became increasingly less important in the business of a number of banks seeking to mobilize funds for large scale lending and for longer periods. Growth meant stepping out of national boundaries and constraints.

With business becoming increasingly international, banks sought to rationalize their presence overseas to meet the new challenges. Banks use a variety of devices for maintaining a presence in particular centres. This may range from a simple correspondent relationship or representative's office or affiliate to a full service branch or subsidiary. The definition of a transnational bank is not easy to pin down. Banks have long maintained correspondent relationships with other banks abroad to conduct their normal operations, particularly those related to trade financing. Transnational banking activities, however, have to be defined in more functional terms that are associated with a stronger presence overseas. At one end of the spectrum a transnational bank can be viewed as one that operates in, and is subject to the laws of, at least two countries.[5] At the other end the definition may involve not only geographical spread, but the range of services provided including commercial banking, merchant banking, leasing, factoring, consulting, and so on.[6] Based on a definition that a transnational bank was a deposit-taking bank with branches or majority-owned subsidiaries in five or more different countries and/or territories, 84 were identified in 1975.[7] Of this 84, seven were based in the United States, ten in the United Kingdom, ten in Japan, seven in France, five in Canada and five in Germany. A 'global bank' can also be measured in terms of the proportion of its assets domiciled abroad. Of the 50 largest banks in the world only ten had more than 50 per cent of their assets abroad.[8] While there is a broad correlation between size and the volume of international banking undertaken, the largest banks in the world are not necessarily the banks with the highest proportion of overseas assets.

Size based on assets does not tell how international a bank is. A recent survey carried out by *The Banker* magazine[9] sought to rank 'global banks' on the basis of the proportion of assets domiciled overseas. At the top of the list was the Standard Chartered Bank (based in the UK) with 73.2 per cent of its assets overseas in 1995. Standard Chartered's total assets, however, was only US$ 60.4 million. On the other hand, the Sumitomo Bank (Japan), the largest bank in the world in 1995 based on assets (see Table 5.1) had only 30 per cent of its business overseas. One can also classify banks on the basis of the share of income generated overseas or the percentage of employees in foreign offices. The international profits of banks vary widely, and the income generated from overseas business may not correspond with the share of total business done abroad.

The ten largest corporations in the world are banks, with assets ranging between US$380 billion and US$525 billion in 1995. Eight of these are Japanese. Citicorp which was ranked 30th (with assets of US$ 295 billion) was ahead of companies like General Motors, Ford Motors, General Electric, Toyota Motors, Exxon and the Royal Dutch/Shell Group.[10]

To carry out its international activities a bank can choose from among at least six different types of representation.[11] They are the correspondent banking connection, a representative office, minority participation in an

Table 5.1 The world's 25 largest banks in 1995 (ranked by shareholders' equity)

Rank 1995	Rank 1994	Bank	Fiscal period	Shareholders' equity US ($m)	Total assets US ($m)	Net profit US ($m)	Return on average equity
1	1	Sumitomo Bank	1994	22 239	527 717	310	1.40
2	8	HSBC Holdings	1994	22 225	314 872	3 208	15.22
3	2	Dai-Ichi Kangyo Bank	1994	19 942	531 216	116	0.58
4	4	Sanwa Bank	1994	19 671	521 060	446	2.28
5	3	Fuji Bank	1994	19 622	534 074	339	1.73
6	5	Bank America	1994	18 891	215 475	2 176	12.08
7	6	Sakura Bank	1994	18 711	519 675	174	0.96
8	11	Citicorp	1994	17 824	250 489	3 366	21.19
9	9	Caisse Nationale de Credit Agricole	1994	17 676	328 159	1 130	6.89
10	7	Mitsubishi Bank	1994	17 064	456 399	368	2.15
11	13	Deutsche bank	1994	15 430	369 977	878	5.71
12	–	Industrial & Commercial Bank of China	1993	15 155	337 487	1 416	10.38
13	12	Industrial Bank of Japan	1994	13 692	411 709	213	1.65
14	10	Union bank of Switzerland	1994	13 362	179 690	931	7.46
15	33	Barclays	1994	13 233	253 755	1 342	14.37
16	19	ABN Amro Holding	1994	11 923	290 837	1 318	11.19

Table 5.1 (Continued)

Rank 1995	Rank 1994	Bank	Fiscal period	Shareholders' equity US ($m)	Total assets US ($m)	Net profit US ($m)	Return on average equity
17	39	Westdeutsche Landesbank Girozentrale	1994	11 165	244 429	276	3.10
18	16	NationsBank	1994	11 011	169 604	1 690	16.10
19	22	Swiss Bank Corporation	1994	10 987	161 808	618	6.07
20	24	Long-Term Credit Bank of Japan	1994	10 940	312 590	320	2.95
21	17	Tokai Bank	1994	10 901	326 136	320	2.97
22	15	Chemical Banking Corporation	1994	10 775	171 423	1 294	11.80
23	34	Bank of Tokyo	1994	10 659	271 766	494	4.74
24	23	Caisse d'Epargne et de Prévoyance (CEP)	1994	10 544	187 415	291	2.81
25	14	Bank of China	1994	10 482	245 742	991	10.67

Source: Euro-money, June 1995.

affiliated bank, a subsidiary company, a branch establishment, or a joint venture. Traditionally banks have tended to hold balances with banks in other centres to settle payments transactions in foreign currency involving residents and other transactors. The correspondent relationship does not represent any direct investment abroad. A stronger presence could take the form of a representative office which does not do banking business (that is take deposits or extend credit) but serves as a point of contact to gather information and make new business connections. It can be used to provide counsel to clients of the home office, and also keep the latter abreast of developments in a particular market. In the case of a 'participation' relationship the bank takes a small share in an existing organization and thus become associated with an indigenous institution not only in possession of knowledge and experience in a particular market but one which may already have an existing banking network. This is one way of penetrating a market where the host government may insist on local majority holding of financial institutions. Affiliation could take the form of a joint venture arrangement where two banks share ownership on a 50-50 basis. It is worth pointing out that the term joint venture is sometimes used to describe an arrangement in which two or more banks agree to cooperate in a particular undertaking that may involve the provision of technical and other services to each other, or to explore new areas or operations together.[12] To carry out special functions a bank may opt to establish a majority of a fully owned subsidiary which will be a separate company with its own legal personality and subject to the laws of the host country. Unlike the case of an affiliate, the subsidiary's parent company has full control over the affairs of the subsidiary. Establishment of a branch office is one of the most common forms of doing business abroad, even though it may involve substantial investment and manpower requirements. Branches do not have their own legal entity and are an integral part of the head office and the assets of the parent company stand fully behind the branch office. The parent bank has direct responsibility for all the commitments of its branches and this tends to be a major advantage in the wholesale market. 'Other things being equal branches offer the best opportunities in terms of referral and new business whilst, at the same time, providing the parent bank with ample scope for in-house supervision and control over foreign business.'[13] A modified form of the branch relationship is the agency which is not allowed to take deposits but can lend resources brought in from outside. A bank may also decide to get together with one or more other banks to establish a new bank with all the partners holding equal shares in the capital. These cooperative undertakings which are often put together to handle large risks are commonly referred to as joint ventures or consortium banks. Without collaborating in the establishment of a new institution, banks often get together to contribute to a large loan which individually they could not make. The lending institutions may not all contribute the same amount. Such an arrangement known as syndicated lending is now common both in international and domestic markets. One observer describes a syndicated loan as one 'made by two or more lending institutions, on similar terms and conditions using common documentation and administered by a common agent.'[14] 'Similar' does not mean identical, since there can be variation within the overall structure of the loan, for example tranches of different maturities may be incorporated within a syndicated loan each funded by a different group of leaders. The essential point is that 'the vast majority of terms and conditions are similar for each of the participating lending institutions or banks.'[15] For one thing the borrower pays a single and common rate of interest to all the lending institutions in the syndicate. Syndication not only allows small and medium sized banks to meet the needs of clients, but at the same time offers an avenue for reducing risk.

In the inter-war period American banks were generally content to explore the opportunities available in the large and growing domestic market. International banking was confined to the large New York city banks. The banks of European colonial powers such as Britain and France found it profitable and simple to develop branch networks throughout the Empires in which the laws of the *'mother country'* prevailed and financial and currency arrangements were essentially extensions of those at home. This made the movement of funds fairly straightforward. Banking in the Empire was the same as banking at home. In the colonial days even the local currencies were versions of the *'mother'* currency to which they were closely tied. Following independence, the banking connections continued to prevail, even though the adoption of 'independent' currencies and changes in the foreign exchange regulations had implications for the movement of funds. In some cases economic nationalism in host countries forced branch and subsidiary operations to be turned into affiliate organizations. Canadian banks also developed a branch network in the Caribbean and certain parts of the British Commonwealth. Even immediately after the Second World War few American banks showed any interest in going abroad. By the early 1960s, however, a depressed American economy and the imposition of restrictions prohibiting lending abroad forced an increasing number to establish foreign offices. The budding Euro-currency market in Europe with its freedom from controls offered a way out of the myriad restrictions hampering their growth at home. In 1960 US banks operated 124 banks in 33 countries; by 1971 these numbers had grown to 577 branches in 67 countries.[16] The number of banks with branches abroad increased from 8 in 1961 to 136 in 1978. In the 1960s a number of other countries had also began to expand or rationalize their overseas banking operations in response to a variety of factors including the growth in other markets and changes in host countries policies.[17] The number of branches abroad operated by British and French banks actually fell between 1961 and 1978 though the number of banks doing overseas business increased as was the case with most other countries. German branches actually increased from 2 to 47 over the period, while Japanese grew from 27 to 122, and Swiss from 3 to 33. While only 6 Japanese banks were engaged in international banking in 1961 this had increased to 23 in 1978. Overall the number of banks engaged in international banking is estimated to have increased from 112 in 1961 to 387 in 1978.

The obvious question here is why has this growth in international banking taken place. Earlier, reference was made to some of the factors. Basically the major motivation guiding any privately owned enterprise is profit. The activities in which banks are preoccupied at the domestic level, that is, relending or investing funds taken on deposit or borrowed, form the major plank of their global business as well. Banks may enter foreign markets to compete in the domestic market or participate in the international currency markets or both. Sometimes foreign markets may offer better profit margins, but this is not always the case.[18] While the search of corporate-finance fees is a motivation, some are attracted by the profits in global securities trading; some see the need to diversify their assets in traditional fund management. For others, overseas expansion is undertaken not only for growth but the accompanying geographical diversification is seen as a strategy for reducing risks. While the banks' initiatives have played a part in the globalization of banking and finance, certain crucial developments also helped. These were summed up in a recent survey as follows.[19]

a. The progressive removal in recent decades of the post-1914 restrictions on the flow of capital internationally as well as in local markets;
b. rapid developments in information technology and telecommunications;
c. the increasingly international scale on which many corporate customers now operate;
d. global markets for debt, and increasingly for equity;
e. twenty-four hour trading;
f. securitization;
g. financial innovation.

Certainly, a major factor for going international has been the internationalization of production which forced banks to rethink their functional specialization and forms of operation. Hampered by regulations in the home market and faced with the possibility of losing corporate clients to competitors, going international was inevitable.

The international banking industry is poised for even greater changes with removal of restrictions in the domestic markets of a large number of countries and the growing competitiveness among banks. In the US, for example, the Glass-Steagall Act of 1933 which separates banking from the securities business is likely to go. The barriers against interstate banking are already crumbling. In a number of countries the distinctions between various kinds of financial institutions are becoming increasingly difficult to discern as financial companies compete for each others' business. While insurance operators are trying to get into the banking and securities business, many banks are already offering insurance products and taking steps to participate in the wholesale banking business.

The decisions over where banks locate their offices and the form of presence chosen are influenced by a variety of factors. London is Europe's oldest financial centre and still the world's leading centre.[20] Every transnational bank is represented there. The percentage of foreign companies listed in its stock market is higher than that of any other exchange, including New York or Tokyo. It is the largest centre of Euro-currency operations and the focal point of the Euro-bond market. While there are several factors which have contributed to London as the world's premier financial centre, perhaps the two most important are the range of skills developed over the years, and the regulatory environment which allows banks considerable flexibility in their international operations. 'Unlike the position in some other countries, insurance, commodities trading, markets, stockbroking, bond trading and legal services in the U.K. are all concentrated around the city.'[21]

While New York does not rank with London as an international financial centre, it is an important link in international banking. Not only are the large American international banks headquartered in New York, but the fact that the US dollar market is the largest component of the Euro-currency system, put this centre in a critical position. About 60 per cent of Euro-bonds are now issued in US dollars and 90 per cent of syndicated bank loans are denominated in US dollars. New York commercial and investment bankers are prominent as lead managers of both Euro-bond and Euro-loan syndicates. They also dominate the arrangement of Euro-note facilities, Euro-commercial paper distribution and trading in swaps.[22] The majority of the international banking facilities (IBFs) which have been permitted since 1981 are also located in New York. The IBFs came into being as a result of a change in the regulations which now allow existing banking institutions to conduct offshore wholesale banking business, that is business with non-residents. They are often described as onshore 'offshore centres', even though they are merely a separate set of books maintained by institutions engaged in banking. The hope was that the IBFs would have attracted back some of the business that went to London and other offshore centres. This has not materialized, partly because of the restrictions with which IBFs operations are circumscribed.[23] Since 1986 Japanese banks have also been allowed to carry out operations similar to those of the American IBFs.

Tokyo's growth as an international centre coincided with the emergence of Japan as a major trading nation and as an exporter of capital. In recent years some Japanese banks now rank among the biggest in the world, and have become increasingly active overseas. Of the ten largest banks in the world in 1995, eight were Japanese. For several reasons Tokyo does not enjoy the status of London or New York as an international financial centre. One is the restrictions placed on foreign banks in Japan. Another relates to the role of the yen in international trade and finance. While the importance of the yen as a borrowing currency has been increasing, it is still not greatly used as a reserve currency. Only a small part of world trade is priced in yen. Though Tokyo's stock market is second only to New York's the listing of foreign companies is insignificant.[24]

Unlike London, New York, Paris, Tokyo and Switzerland which are international financial centres, Hong Kong and Singapore are more regionally oriented. The latter is the centre of the so-called Asian Dollar Market which, it should be noted, is not a separate segment of the Euro-currency markets, but a part of the London centred external markets in foreign currencies. Since Euro-dollars are dollars placed in Europe, Asian dollars can be seen as dollars placed in Asia.[25] The time zone difference between London and Asia is a major factor behind the emergence of this market. 'When the London market is closed, the Asian dollar market is open; when the Asian market is about to be closed in late afternoon, the London market has just opened.'[26]

Besides the 'functional' centres a number of countries (not all of them sovereign states) offer facilities which banks have been able to use profitably without necessarily having a physical presence there. Various names have been used to describe these centres. Among them 'booking', 'shell' and 'brassplates'. Leading examples of such centres are the Bahamas and Cayman Islands. As these countries become more sophisticated however, an increasing number of institutions are finding it necessary to have a physical presence. In the Cayman Islands there are about 550 banks and/or trust companies registered. Forty-seven of the 50 largest banks in the world are reportedly among them. In the Bahamas[27] there were 431 banks and trust companies registered at the end of June 1996. Of these, 300 had licences to deal with the public, and of this 91 were identified as Euro-currency branches of foreign banks and trusts. Forty-eight had US parents. Of the 300 banks and/or trust companies 117 were subsidiaries of Banks and Trusts based outside the Bahamas. Twenty-three were of Swiss origin and nine American. The 'paper' or 'shell' centres are so called because to do business there, it is not necessary to have a physical presence, that is, an office where business is actually transacted. A brass plate in the office of a local agent (usually a lawyer) and a set of ledgers are enough to satisfy the legal requirements for company registration. The actual banking is done from head office The shell centres generally do not levy income and corporation taxes, but benefit from registration fees and the employment created for lawyers, accountants, typists, and so on. Thus, for a small cost a bank can set up a device in an environment free of regulations, currency restrictions and taxes which can be used not only to access the Euro-currency market but to minimize or escape taxes on its global operations. For the small and medium sized American banks the use of 'shell' centres enhanced their ability to compete, since many could not afford to set up full service branches in major centres like London.

Reputable financial institutions are not the only ones who see advantages in establishing an 'office' in a 'booking' centre. 'Paper' banks can be set up for a wide range of purposes, not all of them honest. To meet the demand there has been a proliferation of offshore banking centres, though most of them are unable to match the Bahamas or the Cayman Islands which play an important role in the Euro-currency market. With the establishment of the IBFs it was thought that the offshore centres would disappear, but this has not happened, indicating that they serve a function which banks deem useful. One of the strategies used by the offshore centres to ensure their survival is to diversify the range of services they effect. The Cayman Islands, for example, are not only a haven for banks, but also host 'captive' insurance companies, which now number more than 400.[28] This offshore insurance business was once monopolized by Bermuda. They also promote themselves as centres for ship registration.

Every financial centre has its own laws, its own peculiarities and its own attractions. Each has developed a reputation for offering a particular service, though increasingly some have moved to diversify their appeal through changes in regulations and in tax and secrecy laws. There are some centres which do not even enjoy full political independence and whose currencies are not reserve or trading currencies. The so-called 'shell' or 'paper' centres attract institutions not because of the volume of domestic savings, but because of their location and regulatory environment. These features permit them to provide a service to financial institutions which the more established centres could not provide. The range of services provided by offshore centres such as the Bahamas and the Cayman Islands is broad, and includes Euro-currency borrowing and lending, deposit placing and taking, bond and floating rate note issue, consortium lending and group financing, trust and insurance business, international financing and corporate services and financial services for private clients. It is estimated that as much 'as half of the world's stock of money either resides in, or is passing through tax, havens making them an essential catalyst for world trade.'[29] The offshore bank deposit business and the offshore based mutual fund industry involve billions of dollars.

The increasing integration of the world's financial system and the ease with which funds can be transferred from one centre to another has often raised questions about the monitoring of this system. The debt crisis in the early 1980s gave a clear indication of the kind of problems that could arise in the absence of guidelines to inform the international operations of banks. Of great concern, too, has been the use of banks to 'launder' money. 'Money laundering is the process by which criminals attempt to conceal the true origin and ownership of the proceeds of their criminal activities.'[30] In 1982 it was estimated by one observer that as much as US$85 billion per year could be available for laundering from the proceeds of the sales of drugs alone in the United States and Europe.[31] More recent estimates put the proceeds from drug trafficking in the US and Europe at around US$122 billion a year – US$85 billion after production, distribution and 'enforcement' expenses.[32]

Money launderers have adopted increasingly sophisticated techniques and a number of governments have taken action either as a group or individually to curb the practice. In 1989 the G7 group of nations set up the Financial Action Task Force (FATF) which now operates independently and reports to its members' finance ministries from Paris. Money laundering, like drug trafficking normally involves more than one country and therefore requires a co-ordinated approach that calls for agreement on guidelines and the exchange of information on a regular basis. In this context a large number of countries have ratified the 1988 United Nations Convention of the Illicit Traffic in Narcotic Drugs and Psychotropic Substance. Some countries (among them the Bahamas and the Cayman Islands) have signed the Mutual Legal Assistance Treaty with the United

States which provides for the mutual exchange of information where there is *prima facie* evidence of criminal activity. It needs to be noted that money laundering takes place not only through banks, but also through non-bank financial institutions and other business entities. The action taken so far, however, which includes the exchange of information, the closer monitoring of cash transactions and the seizure of assets, have had some effect. The measures adopted by western countries are forcing launderers to move to Eastern Europe, the former Soviet Republics, the Middle East and South-east Asia, and particularly to emerging offshore centres such as Tangier and Malta which are trying to attract legitimate business. The cost of laundering money has also risen. Accountants, lawyers and financiers are demanding more money for hiding and laundering ill-gotten gains in their legitimate businesses. Drug lords are reportedly paying 20 per cent plus to well-educated money-brokers to infiltrate the money in the system as compared to 5–7 per cent of few years ago.[33] The wholesale price of currency notes has declined in a number of centres as launderers now find it more difficult to get rid of them. However, as some avenues become closed, launderers continue to discover new conduits through which illegal money is legitimized.

Essentially, laundering involves moving cash from one place to another to disguise its source or the conversion of the ill-gotten gains into another asset which can later be resold. Cash can be moved physically, through wire transfer, through money transmission services provided outside the formal financial sector or through travellers cheques. Wittingly and unwittingly banks have been an integral part of the laundering process. In normal circumstances the owner of a deposit should be easy to trace, but banks' operations are shrouded in secrecy. Obtaining such information may involve a legal process. In tax havens which rely on secrecy for their business, governments often resist intrusion.

Unfortunately, there is no supranational body or set of international laws to which transnational banks are subject. National regulations often conflict with each other and are not always enforced with the same tenacity. Mechanisms through which national regulatory authorities can collaborate by the exchange of information and which can be used to refine or update regulations are also lacking. In fact the competition among financial centres would appear to preclude this to some extent. Some simply lack the resources. With banks' behaviour undergoing constant change and as they explore new ways of doing international business, existing regulations always appear to be outdated. International supervision has become increasingly difficult and some banks have not hesitated to exploit this. The experience with the Bank of Credit and

Commerce International (BCCI) is a classic example of the difficulties raised for international supervision. BCCI was formed in 1972 and built its business largely on the deposits of small unsophisticated customers. When it was closed in 1991 for an assortment of irregularities including fraud, some US$20 billion could not be accounted for.

BCCI had no natural home base and operated in some 70 countries. It was not under the supervision of any single regulator. Funded by Arab capital, BCCI had an unregulated parent holding company in Luxembourg, conducted the bulk of its business through banks incorporated in Luxembourg and the Cayman Islands and was run from London by expatriate Palestinians.[34] No one was sure which supervisory authority was responsible for BCCI which exploited all the loopholes in the existing arrangements.

INTERNATIONAL BANKING AND REGULATION

The failure of a number of banks, some operating wholly in domestic markets and some doing both domestic and international business, has raised questions about bank safety, and the adequacy of existing regulatory frameworks. Banks have failed both in developed and developing countries. The causes of failure vary widely, but mismanagement and fraud rank highly among them. The collapse of Barings (a UK investment bank) in 1995 raised fresh concerns about the risks posed by the bourgeoning derivatives market.

The failure of even one bank can undermine confidence and destabilize an entire banking system, as happened with Banco Latino in Venezuela in 1994. A banking system, too, may be affected not by the action or policy of a particular bank, but by the general macro and financial policies of a government. The Mexican debacle in December 1994, following the 40 per cent devaluation of the peso was not the consequence of the action of any single bank, but the result of the conjucture of a number of factors and developments with which the policies adopted could not adequately deal.

Supervisory authorities have adopted a number of approaches in trying to protect depositors. An increasing number of countries are providing deposit insurance schemes, some of which have come into being following a major banking crisis. The schemes are intended to boost depositor confidence and discourage bank runs. They all have different features. Some are compulsory, while others are not. In most cases the cover carries a limit. Norway and Yugoslavia provide unlimited coverage. While countries like Belgium, Spain, Canada and India offer cover for local currency deposits only, a number of other states (for example, Germany, Luxembourg, Netherlands) provide insurance for all currency deposits. The provision of deposit insurance schemes has not been without controversy. Since it involves a cost, the stronger financial institutions tend to argue that they are being asked to subsidize the existence of the weaker institutions. Financial institutions that compete with the banks, but are not members of the scheme are placed in an advantageous position by not having to contribute financially. It could be argued, however, that not being members of a scheme could also work against them. The more general argument against deposit insurance scheme is that covering the liabilities of banks could lead to irresponsible management, since managers may take the view that since depositors are protected, they can afford to take greater risks.

Another approach taken to protect the public is the stipulation of capital adequacy standards, but defining capital for regulation purposes is not an easy task. Capital is often measured in relation to assets, but not all assets carry the same risk. Some banks make loans and are exposed to what is called credit risk (default), while securities firms are exposed to market risk (asset price movements, interest rate fluctuation and movements in exchange rates). The supervising of banks operating across several borders raises even more complex issues, not least of which is the resources available to supervisory authorities and the relationship between the authorities of the various countries. In Europe the Basel Committee Concordat[35] drawn up in 1974, has undergone several revisions, but establishing a capital adequacy standard satisfactory to everyone has proved particularly difficult.

It is recognized that while good supervision can reduce bank failure, it cannot completely prevent them. With increasing competition from non-bank financial institutions, and with many businesses borrowing directly from the markets, banks are likely to take increasingly greater risks.

COMMERCIAL BANKS AND THE DEBT CRISIS

Commercial banks are major financial intermediaries, not only at the domestic level, but also in the international financial system. While the domestic business, however, is largely a 'retail' one confined to dealing in relatively small amounts, international banking activities, dominated by institutions from Europe, North America and Japan, have become increasingly sophisticated and innovative as they try to meet the needs of an expanding world economy.

The leading banks are present in all major money centres. While some institutions operate exclusively in foreign currencies, others take deposit and make loans both in the currency of the country where they are located and also in the currencies of other countries. In other words, they have both resident and non-resident clients. The growth of the Euro-currency markets in the 1960s and 1970s permitted them to considerably expand their international activities. With the establishment of the Euro-currency system, the banks have been able to circumvent national regulations and thereby forge a more integrated international capital market. The Euro-currency market is a wholesale market in which the banks not only take large deposits, but also deal in large loans, mainly to corporations and governments.

The two oil shocks of the 1970s were a significant factor in the emergence of commercial banks as a major provider of finance to developing countries. The large surpluses of the oil exporting countries were deposited with the money centre banks which provided the mechanism for recycling these funds to oil importing countries to finance their balance of payments deficits and investment plans. The governments of the industrial countries did little to discourage this development, since borrowing allowed debtor countries to continue to import. In fact to boost their exports as a means of stimulating domestic industrial recovery they provided export credits and/or guarantees on generous terms.[36] The availability of funds was only one factor in the debt accumulation of the 1970s and early 1980s. The banks appeared to be able to earn much higher spreads on their lending to LDCs than they could obtain elsewhere. Low or even negative (in real terms) interest rates was a major incentive to borrow. Rather than make domestic adjustment consistent with lower exports earnings and revenues, a large number of developing countries resorted to borrowing to maintain high levels of expenditures. When oil prices fell, even some oil exporting countries chose to become major borrowers. Despite the generally 'harder' terms associated with commercial bank finance, developing countries saw it as a way of circumventing the policy conditionality of institutions like the IMF and the World Bank. In any event, the traditional official lending institutions did not possess the volume of resources needed when measured against the balance of payments deficits that had emerged and the capital needs of borrowing countries.

Flushed with liquidity in the 1970s the banks adopted an aggressive lending policy that initially concentrated on the oil importing countries, but also soon encompassed the oil exporting countries themselves. Banks that had done little international lending became increasingly involved in the wholesale global business which seemed to offer greater opportunities for growth than domestic retail banking concerned with mobilizing small deposits and making small short and medium term loans. In the 1950s and 1960s the wholesale banking business dealing in large deposits and large loans had already taken shape. 'By the 1970s worldwide corporate lending would evolve into one of the slickest, most competitive of businesses, as the top banks fought for the accounts of large, successful companies, and began to expand quickly across state and national boundaries.'[37] Some banks had limited experience with international lending and also lacked the skilled personnel capable of making proper assessment of risks. Prudent banking practices were abandoned in a context where salesmen's performance was measured by the number of loans made. No upper limit was placed on the amount any country or company could borrow from the banking system.[38] Thus while 'the bank's (American) legal lending limits ranged between 10 and 15 per cent of their capital and reserves to a single borrower, and while this limited an individual bank's exposure to an individual borrower, it said nothing about how much a country could borrow in aggregate.'[39] Not all countries require their banks to publish figures relating to outstanding loans in relation to their risk capital. In the case of the United States the figures available at the end of 1982 indicate that 'the top ten US banks held credits with five most heavily indebted Latin American nations (Argentina, Brazil, Chile, Mexico and Venezuela) of US$43.8 billion. For the banks themselves, the ratio between credit outstanding and risk capital ranged from a minimum of 64 per cent for Interstate to a maximum of 245 per cent for Manufacturer's Hanover. On the average, it stood at 175 per cent.'[40]

In the early 1980s, it became evident that a number of developing countries could not service their debt, a large part of which was owed to commercial banks in the various money centres. In 1982, the outstanding public debt of developing countries was estimated by the IMF to be US$836.1 billion. Of this US$428 billion (more than half) was owed to banks. In some regions the proportion was higher; for example in Latin America it was 68 per cent. 'At the end of 1985 commercial banks from all over the world had lent to Latin America around US$ 217 billion. United States banks held 41.7 per cent of such an exposure, European banks 37 per cent, and Canadian banks 7.6 per cent.'[41]

The response of the banks to the debt crisis took several forms. One was a sharp contraction in new loans. Bank lending to developing countries is estimated to have declined from US$52.3 billion (70.5 per cent of private flows) in 1981 to US$7.0 billion 20 per cent of private flows) in 1988 (see Table 5.2). Some sought to call in outstanding loans in an effort to reduce their exposure. Others strengthened their capital base or

Table 5.2   The magnitude of commercial bank lending to developing
countries 1985–95

Year	(1) Total private flows US$ billion	(2) International bank lending[1] US$ billion	(3) (2) as a % of (1)	(4) Total outst. debt of developing countries US$ billion	(5) Outst. debt[2] owed to commercial banks US$ billion	(6) (4) as a % of Total outst. debt[2]
1981	74.3	52.3	70.5	n.a.	n.a.	n.a.
1982	58.2	37.9	65.1	836.9	427.9	51.2
1983	47.9	35.0	73.0	886.9	458.0	51.6
1984	31.7	17.2	54.2	926.3	470.4	50.8
1985	31.4	15.2	48.4	940.2	484.5	48.5
1986	25.3	7.0	27.7	1 033.8	507.2	46.3
1987	30.7	7.0	22.8	1 145.7	542.1	44.7
1988	39.1	7.8	19.9	1 147.2	438.4	38.2
1989	45.3	10.5	23.2	1 176.0	431.0	36.6
1990	51.8	15.0	28.9	1 255.0	411.7	32.8
1991	50.8	11.0	21.6	1 340.7	432.9	32.3
1992	76.8	31.0	40.4	1 409.9	446.7	31.7
1993	94.1	9.0	9.6	1 525.1	464.2	30.4
1994	110.4	21.0	19.0	1 654.7	543.1	27.4
1995[p]	n.a.	n.a.	n.a.	1 790.2	498.9	27.9

[1] Excluding bond lending by banks.
[2] Public and publicly guaranteed.
n.a. not available.
[p] Provisional.

Source: OECD, *Development Cooperation,* various issues; IMF, *World Economic
Outlook,* various issues.

increased reserves normally put aside in the event that some loans are not
repaid. The impact of these measures was a decline in the claims to capital
ratio for some of the major banks, and this removed part of the threat
posed to the international banking system. Banks also got rid of some bad
loans by selling them at a discount in the secondary markets. The
increased use of rescheduling not only helped to ease the debt servicing
burden of debtor countries, but the fact that rescheduling was often linked
to an IMF/World Bank Programme of adjustment gave the banks a greater
measure of security. As can be seen in Table 5.2 by the late 1980s /early
1990s bank lending had resumed, but other sources of funds assumed

greater significance. Debt owed to banks by developing countries as a proportion of total outstanding debt declined from over 50 per cent in the early 1980s to 27.4 per cent in 1994.

By the mid to late 1980s there was a strong consensus at the international level that if highly indebted countries were to resume growth new measures were needed for investment, and in this scenario banks were seen as playing a catalytic role. In 1985, amidst growing concern over the debt crisis, the then US Treasury Secretary James Baker, put forward a plan designed not only to 'bail out' the banks but to encourage new flows to debtor countries. The Plan's target group consisted of 15 middle income heavily indebted countries, most of them in Latin America. In a situation where the banks were already having difficulties with repayment of existing loans, the Baker Plan called not only on the World Bank and other multilateral development banks to increase their lending but on the commercial banks to provide some US$20 billion of 'new money' in the following three years. This was rationalized as being in the banks' own interest because the policy changes the debtor countries were being induced to make 'will enhance the value of their (the banks') existing assets, and the small amount of money will finance extra economic growth to allow countries to service their debts effectively.'[42] The Baker Plan failed to evoke the kind of response expected, and a new Plan was put forward by Baker's successor Nicholas Brady following the widely reported riots in Venezuela and growing fears of political instability, particularly in Latin America. A major element in the Brady Plan was the recognition that there was a need for credit institutions to forego part of their claims or interest payments. At the same time they were being asked to lend new money. The Plan was not specific on incentives for debt write off. For example, could claims written off by American banks be used to reduce tax liability. It also failed to deal with the consequences of debt cancellation for banking supervision in the countries concerned.[43]

THE EURO-CURRENCY MARKET

It is a widely held view that the emergence of the Euro-currency market played an important part in the breakdown of the Bretton Woods monetary system. There is also a strongly held view that if this international market in major trading currencies did not exist, it would have had to be created. Certainly, the Euro-currency market by facilitating the rapid movement of funds on a large scale put the par value system (which served world trade and payments well for more than two decades) under enormous pressure to which it eventually succumbed. The fact of its rapid growth and survival through a number of crises reflects to a significant extent the functional value it has come to acquire within the dynamics of the rapidly changing world economy. The Euro-currency market is not just a passive outgrowth of changes in the world economic system, but by adapting and responding to these changes, it has not only challenged existing financial and monetary structures, but critically influenced the pace and extent of 'real' development. In the process, countries both in the developed and the developing world have been affected, directly and indirectly.

What is this Euro-currency market? Theoretically any national currency can become a 'Euro-currency' or be used in Euro-operations. In practice (and for obvious reasons) the currencies around which Euro-markets have developed are those of the major trading nations. Thus, one speaks about the Euro-dollar, the Euro-franc, Euro-mark, and so on. The US dollar component is by far the largest of the markets, and this explains why the whole system is often spoken of as the Euro-dollar market. It needs to be noted that the Euro-dollar (or Euro-any currency) is not some special currency or type of money with characteristics different from the national currency. Euro-currencies are essentially claims denominated in particular currencies. In the same way a 'Euro-bank' is not necessarily some special bank set up to engage exclusively in Euro-currency operations. The institutions that participate are essentially the normal financial institutions engaged in domestic and international financial activities.

In 1964 the Bank for International Settlements (BIS) in its *23rd Annual Report* defined a Euro-dollar as 'a dollar that has been acquired by a bank outside the United States and used directly or after conversion into another currency, for lending to a non-bank customer, perhaps after one or more re-deposits from one bank to another.'[44] It should be pointed out, however, that Euro-currency operations are not confined to Europe. Even though the market is centred in London, other centres have been springing up in various parts of the globe responding to such factors like time zone advantages, liberal tax regulations and absence of restrictions on foreign operatons, and so on. Transactions take place through the international telephone/telex system. In its *36th Annual Report* the BIS put forward another definition indicating that it saw Euro-dollars as 'acquisition of dollars by banks located outside the United States mostly through the taking of deposits but also to some extent through swapping other currencies into dollars, and the relending of these dollars, often after redepositing with other banks, to non-bank borrowers anywhere in the world.'[45] Einzig later pointed out that the BIS definitions were too restrictive 'as they exclude a very high proportion of the foreign deposits which have been lent to some non-resident banks but which have not been relent to non-banking customers.'[46]

Traditionally, banks held deposits in the currency of the country where they were located. Increasingly, after the Second World War, European banks began to accept deposits denominated in currencies (particularly US dollars) other than that of the country where they were located, and the development of the Euro-currency market has developed largely around this phenomenon. The normal practice would have been to place the deposits in the United States, but now the banks began to lend these dollars to other banks to finance international trade. Higher returns from this activity was a major incentive. Fuelled by the United States' balance of payments deficits a market for dollars outside the United States began to take serious shape. It should be noted that while commercial banks in Europe had at various times prior to the late 1950s (the period which observers cite as the starting point of the Euro-currency markets) had accepted foreign currency deposits, such transactions never constituted an international market, or possessed the scale and systematic nature which how characterize present day dealings in foreign currencies.

In general, any deposit located at a bank in one country but denominated in the currency of another is called a Euro-currency deposit. Euro-currency activity has a great deal to do with the creation and utilization of bank liabilities.[47] It has do do with changes in claims, which may not involve the physical movement of cash out of national systems. For instance, an investor having a US$5 million deposit in a US located bank (Bank A) may be attracted by higher interest rates in the Euro-dollar market. He instructs Bank A to transfer his US$5 million to Bank B in London, with which he wants to hold a dollar denominated deposit. Bank A debits the investor's account and credits that of Bank B who now has a US$5 million dollar liability which is matched by a corresponding asset in the form of a dollar deposit. While the American investor's claim is now with a foreign bank instead of a US bank, there is no reduction in total deposits in the US, but Euro-dollar deposits have increased by US$5 million. Higher interest rates in the Euro-currency market is the major incentive for this kind of transaction. It should be noted that since Bank B has to pay interest on this deposit, it has to onlend the newly-received dollar funds to another bank or borrower, and this sets off a multiplier process.

The origin of the term 'Euro' is not certain, though the fact that the most important segment of the market is located in Europe may have something to do with it. The origin of the practice is commonly attributed to the desire by the Moscow Narodny Bank in London and the Banque

Commerciale pour l'Europe du Monde in Paris (the Paris affiliate of the State Bank of the USSR) to safeguard their dollar balances by holding them in Europe. The international cable code for this latter bank was 'Euro-bank', and according to one source[48] foreign exchange traders and banks began to refer to dollar deposits obtained from the bank as Euro-dollars. This practice soon spread to other major currencies. With the problems faced by sterling in the late 1950s there was an increased demand for dollars by British banks to finance trade.[49] The move to convertibility and the reduction of exchange controls in the late 1950s were important contributory factors to the creation of the environment in which the Euro-dollar market emerged.

Most observers agree on one thing, and it is that restrictions on the movement of funds in domestic markets played a major role in the growth of Euro-currency operations which, unfettered by national regulations and traditions relating to interest rates, reserve requirements, maturity of loans, and so on, allowed banks to become more innovative. The introduction of measures by the United States Government in the 1960s to protect its balance of payments provided a major fillip for US banks to go abroad in search of funds to meet the demands of US corporations interested in investing abroad. The need for long-term funds helped to fuel the growth of the Euro-currency market in this period. At first, only the larger American banks were interested in a European presence. A full service branch of subsidiary, particularly in London however, is an expensive undertaking and many of the small and medium-sized banks began to set up 'shells' in tax havens like the Bahamas and the Cayman Islands to conduct their Euro-currency business. The establishment of these shell or paper companies did not call for a physical presence and their operations which were conducted from head office involved minimum cost.

The growth of overseas business by transnational corporations in the post-war period has been accompanied by an equally rapid expansion of international banking. European (particularly the French and British and Canadian banks have long operated overseas branch networks that were closely linked to the finance of colonial trade and investment. Prior to the Second World War few United States banks were interested in international banking, and even so their presence was confined to the major financial countries. The growing interdependence in the world economy, technological strides, removal of many forms of controls and restrictions have encouraged banks to go into the international business.

As international financial intermediaries, the banks' stature has grown since the early 1970s, despite their slipshod lending practices in the oil boom period. The major banks operate very closely with the IMF and their importance as financing agents are not lost upon the governments of the industrial countries. Agreements by banks to reschedule the loans owed by a debtor country in most cases depends on a programme with the Fund, since rescheduling is seen as part of an effort to reduce the debt service burden and restore growth. This is a far cry from the mid-1970s when the Fund viewed the banks as working against its objectives which required a certain degree of discipline on the part of the member countries. Very often the latter preferred the hard terms of the banks to the policy conditionalities of the Fund and the Word Bank. The debt crisis changed the relationship between the latter two institutions and the commercial banks.

CONCLUDING OBSERVATIONS

Technology has not only revolutionized the operations of banks, but has changed the whole environment in which these institutions function. With a blip, large sums of money can be moved across national frontiers destabilizing financial systems and undermining central banks' ability to manage domestic monetary situations. In practice regulations never really catch up, and increasingly the desire to regain monetary autonomy is being sought through cooperative arrangements, regionally and internationally. The question of management and control is complicated by the growth of the underground economy which is threatening to dwarf the 'legal' economy. The annual turnover by the drugs trade alone is estimated by some sources to be in the region of US$ 250-300 billion[50] which exceeds the combined yearly turnover for copper, gold and iron-ore mining. By the early 1990s just two of the main criminal syndicates – Cosa Nostra and the Medellin Cartel – were laundering US$ 500 billion a year.[51]

There are a number of developments which have contributed to making the banking business a more competitive one. Among them are privatization of state-owned banks, deregulation, removal of exchange controls and the opening up of national markets to foreign banks. In this competitive setting, banks not only seek to provide an increasingly wide range of services, but enter profitable alliances and also place themselves in strategic locations. It would be a mistake to think that the institutions located in tax havens like the Bahamas, the Cayman Islands and Panama are confined only to little known fly-by-night organizations. Among them are the biggest and most reputable financial institutions in the world. The Cayman Islands alone reportedly manage some US$ 600 billion.[52] As the competition among banks and centres increases, the question of distinguishing 'legal' from 'illegal' money will become an increasingly challenging task in a globalized economy.

Notes

1. See M. K. Lewis and K. T. Davis, *Domestic and International Banking* (New York: Philip Alan, 1987), p. 216.
2. R. M. Pecchioli, *The Internationalization of Banking, The Policy Issues* (Paris: OECD, 1983), p. 9
3. *Ibid.*, p. 32.
4. M. K., Lewis and K. T. Davis, *op. cit.*, pp. 1–2.
5. See UNCTC, *Transnational Bank: Operations, Strategies and their Effects in developing Countries* (New York: UN, 1981), p. 3.
6. *Ibid.*
7. *Ibid.*
8. See *The Banker*, February 1997, pp. 71–73.
9. See *The Banker*, February 1997, pp. 16–17.
10. See *Fortune* Magazine, 5 August 1996, pp. 76–85.
11. See U. Steuber, *International Banking* (Leyden: A. W. Sijthoff, 1976), Chapter 2. See also S. W. Robinson, *Multinational Banking* (Leyden: A. W. Sijthoff, 1972), Chapter 2.
12. Robinson, *op. cit.*, p. 62.
13. Pecchioli, *op. cit.*, p. 62.
14. S. Hurn, *Syndicated Loans* (New York: Wodhead-Faulkner, 1990), p. 1.
15. *Ibid.*
16. See F. Heldring, 'The International Banking Function of U.S. Commercial Banks' in H. V. Prochnow and H. V. Prochnow Jr. The Changing World of Banking (New York: Harper & Row Publishers, 1974).
17. See R. M. Pecchioli, *op. cit.*, p. 59.
18. See The Banker, February 1992, p. 8.
19. *Ibid.*, p. 11.
20. See M. K. Lewis and K. T., Davis, *op. cit.*, pp. 234–6.
21. *Ibid.*, p. 236.
22. *Ibid.*, p. 239.
23. *Ibid.*, pp. 238–42.
24. *Ibid.*, p. 243.
25. See A. K. Bhattacharya, *The Asian Dollar Market: International Offshore Financing* (New York: Praeger Publishers, 1977), p. 3.
26. *Ibid.*
27. For an indepth discussion on the functioning of this centre, see R. Ramsaran, *The Monetary and Financial System of the Bahamas* (Mona, Jamaica, Institute of Social and Economic Research, University of West Indies, 1984).
28. For a discussion of this device, see Ramsaran, *op. cit.*
29. See *Euro-money*, April 1991.
30. See J. Drage, 'Countering Money Laundering', *The Bank of England Quarterly Bulletin*, Vol. 32 (November 1992), pp. 418–26.

31. *Ibid.*
32. See *The Banker*, 15 January 1993, pp. 15–17.
33. *Ibid.*
34. See *Institutional Investor*, November 1991.
35. For a further discussion on this agreement see M. Goldstein et. al., *International Capital Markets (Part II): Systematic Issues in International Finance* (Washington, DC: IMF, August 1993), p. 37; and also M. Goldstein *et al. International Capital Prospects and Policy Issues* (Washington, DC: IMF, September 1994), pp. 56–64.
36. See IMF, *World Economic Outlook* (Washington, DC, IMF, May 1995), p. 189.
37. See M. J., Dicks, 'The LDC Debt Crisis', *Bank of England Quarterly Bulletin*, Vol. 31 (November 1991), pp. 498–507.
38. S. C. Gwynn, *Selling Money* (New York: Penguin Book, 1986), p. 30.
39. *Ibid.*, p. 62.
40. See C. Johnson, 'Fleshing Out the Baker Plan for Third World Debt', *The Banker* (December 1985), pp. 15–19.
41. D. Carreau and M. N. Shaw, (eds), *The External Debt* (London: Martinus Nijhoff Publishers, 1995), p. 141.
42. See, G. Maier, 'The Brady Plan – a Vicious Circle or a Way Out of the Debt Crisis', *Intereconomics*, Vol. 24 (May/June 1989), pp. 116–19.
43. *Ibid.*
44. BIS *34th Annual Report*, p. 127.
45. BIS, *36th Annual Report*, pp. 145–6.
46. P. Einzig, *The Practice and Theory of International Interest Rates, the Euro-dollar System, 5th ed.* (New York: St Martin's Press, 1973), p. 207.
47. See G. W., McKenzie, *The Economics of the Euro-currency System* (London: The Macmillan Press Ltd, 1976), p. 13.
48. *Ibid.*, p. 13.
49. See G. Bell, *The Euro-dollar Market and the International Financial System* (London: The Macmillan Press Ltd, 1973), pp. 8–9.
50. See *The Banker*, July 1996, p. 46.
51. *Ibid.*
52. *Ibid.*

Further Reading

Aliber, R. Z., *The International Money Game* (2nd ed.) Basic Books, New York, 1973.

Anderson, T. J., *Euromarket Investments*, New York Institute of Finance, New York, 1990.

Baccus, D. J., *The Banks of Canada in the Commonwealth Caribbean: Economic Nationalism and Multinational Enterprises of a Medium Power*, Praeger Publishers, New York, 1974.

Banfield, C. E., *International Financial Markets*, The American Enterprise Institute Press, Washington, DC, 1996.

Bell, G., *The Eurodollar Market and the International Finance System*, Macmillan, London, 1973.

Bhattacharya, A. K., *The Asian Dollar Market, International Offshore Financing*, Praeger Publishers, New York, 1977.

Gwynne, S. C., *Selling Money*, Viking Penguin Inc., New York, 1986.

Hultman, C. W., 'International Banking, Competitive Advantage and Global Marketing Strategy', *Journal of World Trade Law*, June 1995.

Hurn, S., *Syndicated Loans: A Handbook for Banker and Borrower*, Woodhead Faulkner, New York, 1990.

Khoury, S. J., *The Deregulation of the World Financial Markets: Myths, Realities and Impact*, Pinter Publishers, London, 1990.

Lassard, D. R. and J. Williamson, *Capital Flight and Third World Debt*, Institute for International Economics, Washington, DC, 1987.

Lewis, M. K., and K. T. Davis, *Domestic and International Banking*, Philip Allan, New York, 1987.

Little, J. S., *Euro-dollars, The Money Market Gypsies*, Harper & Row Publishers, New York, 1975.

Mayer, M., *The Money Bazaars*, New American Library, New York, 1985.

McKenzie, G. W., *The Economics of the Euro-Currency System*, The Macmillan Press Ltd, London, 1976.

Naylor, R. T., *Hot Money*, Simon and Schuster, New York, 1987.

Odle, M. A., *Multinational Banks and Underdevelopment*, Pergamon Press, New York, 1981.

Pecchioli, R., *The Internationalisation of Banking: The Policy Issues*, OECD, Paris, 1983.

Quinn, B. S., *The New Euro-markets*, Macmillan, London, 1975.

Robinson, J. S. W., *Multinational Banking*, A. W. Sijthoff, Leiden, 1972.

Steuber, U., *International Banking*, A. W. Sijthoff, Leiden, 1976.

Sundararajan, V. and T. Balino (eds), *Banking Crises: Cases and Issues*, International Monetary Fund, Washington DC, 1991.

United Nations Centre on Transnational Corporations, *Transnational Banks: Operations, Strategies and their Effects in Developing Countries*, UN, New York, 1981.

United Nations Centre on Transnational Corporations, *Transnational Banks and the External Indebtedness of Developing Countries: Impact of Regulatory Changes*, UN, New York, 1992.

Walter, I., *Secret Money*, London: Unwin Hyman Limited, London, 1985.

6 The Debt Crisis and the International Financial System

INTRODUCTION

The Polish debt crisis of 1981 and the Mexican declaration in August of 1982 that it was unable to meet its external debt obligations brought to the fore the contemporary debt crisis. Brazil and a number of other countries soon followed Mexico. This was not the first debt crisis the world has faced, and it is unlikely to be the last. Lessons learnt are quickly forgotten. Similar situations arose in the 1870s, 1920s and 1930s. Even in the 1960s and 1970s a number of countries had difficulties servicing their debt and had to seek relief of one kind or another from creditor nations and institutions. While initially there were fears that the international financial system might collapse, both debtors and creditors have developed a variety of techniques and approaches which have enabled them to live with the crisis. In the middle of the 1990s decade the threat of collapse has receded somewhat, but the debt crisis is far from resolved.

Some countries, particularly those in Africa are still in crisis. Certain highly indebted countries because of improved debt-burden indicators have been able to re-enter the financial markets to a limited degree, but debt servicing remains a serious problem. Many creditors are still adjusting to the failure of borrowers to meet scheduled debt obligations, while recognizing the need to undertake new lending. In the interest of world monetary and financial order creditor governments and international financial institutions like the IMF and World Bank have become increasingly involved in defusing the crisis, and have explicitly linked debt assistance with policy reforms designed to make debtor countries more efficient and competitive. Since the early 1980s most debtor nations have entered structural adjustment programs with the IMF or World Bank. Other lending agencies like the IDB have often found it necessary to 'piggy-back' on these programs to pool resources and co-ordinate policies. Though structural adjustment programs (SAPs) have been the subject of a great deal of controversy with respect to their effectiveness and the social conditions they often create, many countries enter them because commercial banks and official creditors tend to insist on a SAP as a prerequisite for debt rescheduling. New resources associated with those programs are not generally of great significance in terms of the amount provided.

With the countries of the former Soviet Union and Eastern Europe being increasingly integrated in the world economy, the competition for finance will increase. The external debt of those countries is estimated to have grown from US$48.3 billion in 1983 to US$292.2 billion in 1995.[1] Some debtors, it should be noted, are also creditors. For example, debt owed by Sub-Saharan Africa to the Russian Federation amounted to some US$16.8 billion in 1994. Russia is reportedly owed by its debtors some US$173 billion, a large part of which may not be recoverable.[2]

Both in the 'transition' economies and in most developing countries, the level of domestic savings is not adequate to finance the desired level of investment. Foreign savings (in the form of loans, private investment, gifts, and so on) is seen as an essential complement to the domestic savings effort, particularly in the context of private-sector led economies which are now widely accepted as the critical development strategy. International lending and borrowing satisfies a need in the same way these activities do at the domestic level. International intermediation has become increasingly sophisticated as it responds to some of the challenges that have arisen in the context of the increased scale of lending and borrowing since the 1970s.

In this chapter we look at the present state of the 1980s external debt problem and some of the approaches and techniques that have grown out of it.

THE MAGNITUDE OF THE CRISIS

Among the major institutions providing data on the external debt of developing countries are the World Bank, the International Monetary Fund (IMF), the Organization for Economic Cooperation and Development (OECD), and the United Nations. Since the geographical coverage is not always the same, and since some types of debt may be excluded, the figures from the various sources are not always comparable. According to United Nations' figures the outstanding external debt of developing countries was estimated to be around US$1603 billion in 1994 as compared to US$926 billion in 1983 (see Table 6.1). This represents an increase of 73 per cent in the period. According to IMF projections the debt will continue to grow reaching around US$1991 billion in 1997. The IMF's estimate for 1994 was US$1655 million and for 1995, US$1790 billion.[3]

Of the total debt outstanding, over 80 per cent in recent years is classified as long term and the rest as short term. With respect to type of

Table 6.1   External debt of capital-importing developing countries, 1983–94
(in US$ billion)

	1983	1990	1994
All countries[a]			
Total external debt	926.1	1 284.3	1 603.1
Long-term debt	750.9	1 080.4	1 307.3
Concessional	135.4	307.1	394.5
Bilateral	101.4	231.9	283.5
Multilateral[b]	34.0	75.2	111.1
Official, non-concessional	179.3	271.7	312.0
Bilateral	102.5	114.1	136.3
Multilateral	47.1	127.3	149.6
IMF	29.8	30.3	26.1
Private creditors[c]	436.2	501.6	600.8
Bonds of which	27.7	103.7	209.8
Commercial banks	210.0	210.6	141.6
Short-term debt	175.2	–	295.6
Memo items			
Principal arrears on long-term debt	5.7	–	90.8
Interest arrears on long-term debt	3.2	4–1.5	34.9

[a] Debt of 122 countries, drawn primarily from the data of the Debtor Reporting System of the World Bank (107 countries). For non-reporting countries, data are drawn from OECD (15 countries), excluding, however, non-guaranteed bank debt of offshore financial centres much of which is not the debt of the local economies.
[b] Including concessional facilities.
[c] Including private non-guaranteed debt.

Source: UN, *World Economic and Social Survey*, various issues.

creditors, the simplest classification is 'official' and 'private'. Official debt can be divided into two parts, 'concessional' and 'non-concessional' and these can arise from loans made bilaterally (governments including their agencies to other governments and their agencies) or through multilateral channels (for example, IMF, World Bank, IDB, and so on). The UN figures for 1994, suggest that some 37 per cent of the long-term debt was owed to private creditors, mainly commercial banks and other institutional lenders as compared to 47 per cent in 1983. The share of official lenders has increased in recent years.

The distribution in terms of sources would vary from one debtor country to another. Middle income countries tend to have a higher proportion of commercial debt than lower income countries who find it more difficult to borrow on commercial terms. The latter tends to be more eligible for concessional loans (that is, loans made on less than strict market terms) from other governments and international aid agencies. Such loans which carry less onerous repayment terms with respect to grace period, interest rates and period of repayment are often referred to as 'soft' loans. Put another way, they carry a grant element, which varies from one loan to another. At one extreme there is a transaction called a 'grant' which does not have to be repaid, and at the other there is a commercial loan made on strict market terms. In between these two extremes, there are loans characterized by differing degrees of concession. A 'hard' or 'soft' loan tends to be assessed in terms of grace period, period of repayment, interest rate, and perhaps currency of repayment.

In order to get some indication of the contributions of the various regions of the world to the total debt we draw on the IMF data (Table 6.2) which for reasons indicated earlier, may not be strictly comparable with the UN data. In Table 6.2 it can be seen that in 1983 the western hemisphere (essentially Latin America and the Caribbean) was the largest contributor to the total debt. In 1995, however, this group was second to the Asian developing countries. Africa's share increased only slightly. Together the countries in Asia and Latin America account for over 60 per cent of the total external debt of developing countries. Sub-Saharan Africa accounts for more than half of Africa's debt. It is worth noting that despite

Table 6.2   Outstanding external debt[1] of developing countries by region, 1983 and 1995

Region	1983		1995	
	US$ billion	%	US$ billion	%
Africa	126.9	14.3	271.1	15.1
Asia	207.5	23.3	636.2	35.5
Middle East and Europe	210.2	23.6	288.3	16.1
Western Hemisphere	344.5	38.8	594.6	33.3
Total	889.1	100.0	1,790.2	100.0

[1] Excludes liabilities to the Fund.
Source: IMF, *World Economic Outlook,* various issues.

measures taken at the international level to mitigate the debt problem, the external debt of most developing countries has been increasing. Mexico's disbursed outstanding debt, for example, increased from US$100 billion in 1986 to an estimated US$158 billion in 1995. Over the same period Brazil's increased from US$111 billion to US$157 billion.

In terms of absolute amount, the outstanding external debt varies widely from country to country. The outstanding debt, however, is highly skewed. Brazil and Mexico alone account for more than half of the outstanding external debt of the Latin American/Caribbean region. These two countries with Argentina, Chile, Colombia, Peru and Venezuela account for almost 90 per cent.

A commonly used term in discussions relating to debt is 'highly indebted countries' (HICs), which may refer to those countries that not only have a large debt in absolute terms, but those that have high debt service ratios and are finding it difficult to service their loans or to raise new money. Jamaica's external debt, for example, is less than US$5 billion, but in per capita terms and as a percentage of GNP, it is one of the most highly indebted countries in the world. In 1995, the debt/GDP, ratio was in the region of 130 per cent. Guyana with a debt of around US$2 billion had a ratio of over 400 per cent and Nicaragua with an outstanding debt of US$10 billion had a ratio of over 500 per cent compared to 33 per cent for Brazil and 56 per cent for Mexico. With the help of rescheduling, debt conversion and debt write off, a debt service ratio of over 40 per cent for a large number of countries in the early 1980s have come down, but for many states whose debt does not appear large in absolute terms, debt servicing remains burdensome.

There are a number of indices which are commonly used to measure the 'burden' of debt. One is to express it as a percentage of annual Gross Domestic Product (GDP) or annual Gross National Product (GNP). This gives an indication of the significance of what is owed creditors in terms of total production (output) over a given period. Another commonly used index is the ratio of the outstanding debt to exports of goods and services – a relationship that gives an indication of the ability to service debt. Perhaps the most commonly used index is the debt service ratio, that is, debt service payments (interest and principal) during a given period (usually a year) expressed as a percentage of earnings from exports of goods and services over the same period. A high ratio tends to reflect a tight external debt situation, and this can affect a country's creditworthiness or its ability to raise new loans. While the ratio is widely used in describing any country's debt situation in the context of risk assessment, it has major shortcomings, particularly when used in isolation from other indicators.

By definition the debt service ratio is derived from two numbers: debt service payments (interest and principal) is the numerator and earnings from the exports of goods and services is the denominator. Note that not all foreign exchange inflows (for example, proceeds from loans and investments) are included in the denominator since these are highly unpredictable. However, even within the limited definition of the concept it is dangerous to aim at a particular ratio as a guide to borrowing or lending, since that ratio can change quickly in response to a variety of factors. For example, if the price of a major export commodity were to fall as a result of market developments the ratio would increase. A poor harvest resulting from pests or adverse weather conditions could also have the same effect. A sudden rise in interest rates could also increase the ratio. A rise in the cost of essential imports could also suddenly make a 'comfortable' ratio quite 'uncomfortable'. It is worth pointing out that a lower ratio may reflect not a change in fundamental conditions, but rescheduling of loans (inability to pay) which stretches repayment and servicing over a longer period. It is also worth noting that a given ratio (say 15 per cent) may have different implications for different countries. Certainly, a country with a good history of debt servicing, or one that has a good stock of foreign reserves, or one that has a diversified export base with good export prospects, or one that is part of an arrangement which permits ready access to liquidity, would be assessed quite differently from one which does not enjoy any of these assets. What is a 'high' or 'low' ratio cannot be prejudged, without looking at a variety of factors, including, of course, the structure of the debt itself. A low ratio may suddenly jump if debt service payments are 'bunched', that is, they may be small in the initial years, but they all may come due within a short space of time.

From the debtor country's point of view, the proportion of its foreign exchange earnings going to service debt can have critical implications for its long-term growth and development. The higher this proportion, the less foreign exchange will be available for other purposes such as paying for food, medicine, spare parts, raw materials and capital goods. Import compression which normally accompanies debt problems lead not only to social hardships, but to economic contraction and unemployment. This in turn further reduces the country's ability to service debt. To prevent countries falling into this situation debt alleviation often has to be accompanied by new resource flows. Measures like 'debt rescheduling' do not reduce debt, but simply postpones it to a later time. In cases where this takes place and new loans are also provided a country may find itself facing a more difficult situation further down the road, if the economy does not start growing. Structural adjustment programmes which are now integrally related to the debt problems are aimed at bringing back economies on course. It is now increasingly recognized that debtor countries should not be forced to service debt at any cost. Economic contraction may make a country less able to service its debt in the medium to long term, and creditors themselves may end up as losers. Contracting economies will also tend to reduce their imports from abroad, and this, of course, would affect supplier countries and unemployment could also increase.

Table 6.3 shows recent trends in selected debt indicators of developing countries. With respect to the outstanding debt/GDP ratio the all-countries

Table 6.3 Developing countries: selected debt indicators, 1983–95

Year	All countries	Africa	Asia	Middle East and Europe	Western hemisphere
Ratio of external debt to GDP[1]					
1983	33.0	36.8	23.1	30.3	46.8
1987	41.0	61.9	26.8	39.6	55.0
1991	34.3	65.2	23.3	36.7	40.0
1992	32.6	62.0	22.9	33.6	38.4
1993	32.0	66.6	22.4	34.3	37.0
1994	32.0	70.5	24.1	32.0	35.1
1995	30.8	65.3	28.2		
Ratio of external debt to exports[1]					
1983	135.6	166.5	95.3	108.2	290.5
1987	175.6	256.2	93.7	167.3	371.6
1991	128.8	243.8	68.4	131.0	279.9
1992	122.6	241.5	66.1	124.9	276.8
1993	124.2	259.0	65.9	141.0	277.9
1994	117.5	266.6	63.5	137.3	263.8
1995	107.0	252.4	58.1	127.7	242.9
Ratio of debt service[2] to exports[3]					
1983	18.4	22.7	12.2	14.1	42.5
1987	20.0	25.9	13.2	14.2	43.1
1991	15.4	31.3	7.9	10.5	39.1
1992	15.9	30.4	8.1	11.6	43.5
1993	15.8	27.2	8.1	12.5	45.1
1994	15.3	23.4	7.5	16.6	43.6
1995	16.0	30.7	7.8	14.5	47.5

[1] Debt at year-end in per cent of GDP or exports of goods and services in year indicated.
[2] Debt-service payments refer to actual payments of interest on total debt plus actual amortization payments on long-term debt.
[3] Exports of goods and services.

Source: IMF, *World Economic Outlook*, various issues.

figure seems to have declined since the early 1980s. But this clearly has not been the case for all countries. There was a sharp rise in the African ratio which moved from less than 40 per cent in 1983 to over 60 per cent in 1995. For Sub-Saharan Africa, the decline was worse with the ratio moving from 50.6 per cent in 1983 to over 100.0 per cent in 1995. With respect to the debt/exports ratio the all-countries figure also seem to be on a declining trend, reflecting developments particularly in Asia and in Latin America. Again here, the African trend has not improved with the ratio eventually exceeding that of Latin America in 1995. In the case of the debt service ratio the trend is generally a declining one, with Africa as the exception. As indicated earlier, the actual debt service could fall for any number of reasons, including inability to service debt. For any particular country in this position, the debt service ratio may be declining, while arrears are being built up.

These general trends (which incidentally can be influenced by the largest debtors) tend to hide the plight of a large number of countries which have continued to experience debt servicing problem in the 1980s and 1990s, particularly since debt problems tended to have a negative impact on capital flows. In the mid-1980s Argentina's debt service ratio exceeded 70 per cent, but in the last five years (1991–95), has averaged around 34 per cent. In the period 1986 to 1995, the ratio for Bolivia averaged 36.6 per cent, for Jamaica 32.0 per cent, for Mexico 31.5 per cent, for Guyana 34.6 per cent and for Venezuela 27.5 per cent.[3] The actual ratios, which we have described are in many cases lower than what they would have been in the absence of debt rescheduling and debt forgiveness.

The transition economies of the Russian Federation and of Central and Eastern Europe, tend to be associated with lower debt burden indicators than developing countries, but the situations varies widely from country to country. The ratio of debt service to exports in 1994, for example, varied from 8 per cent for Romania to 52.2 per cent for Hungary. The debt to GNP ratio in the same year varied from 18.3 per cent for Romania to 105.7 per cent for Bulgaria.[4]

Despite the slow down in international lending to developing countries during most of the 1980s, the accumulated debt of previous years led to heavy debt servicing outflows. Between 1983 and 1995, it is estimated that total debt service payments (interest and amortization) by developing countries amounted to some US$1892 billion of which US$894 billion represented interest payments.[5] In a number of cases debt servicing payments exceeded new borrowings. It is also interesting to note that for some of the regional and international financial institutions repayments of past loans have tended to exceed disbursements. For instance, in the case of the

IMF net lending to developing countries between 1984 and 1994 was minus US$21.1 billion. In other words repayments exceeded disbursements by this amount for the period as a whole. In 1995, however, there was a reversal of this trend when lending from the regular facilities increased sharply.

CAUSES OF THE DEBT CRISIS

For at least three years before Mexico announced in August 1982 that it could not meet its debt obligations, the signs of a serious world debt problem had already become apparent. But even before this, there were certain clear trends: 'In 1955, when debt data were fragmentary, the total medium-term and long term external debt of developing countries was about US$8 billion. By 1960, however, it had almost doubled as new countries became independent and lending began to replace colonial transfers.'[6] The process of decolonization continued in the 1960s and 1970s. Independence brought with it new commitments, expanded bureaucracies and rising expectations. Many of the developing countries which had long enjoyed independence as well as many of the newly independent states found it increasingly difficult to generate enough savings to finance the desired level of current and capital expenditure. 'The average annual growth rate of borrowing accelerated in the early 1960s, and by 1977 the external debt of the developing countries had reached a level of US$36 billion.'[7] The favourable international environment of the 1960s allowed a number of developing countries to achieve reasonable rates of growth, and this further enhanced their ability to borrow. By the late 1960s borrowing from private sources was already growing at a faster rate than borrowing from official sources, and this trend was to continue in the 1970s. The first oil shock of 1973–74 enhanced the foreign exchange earnings of oil exporting countries, but increased the amount spent on oil by importing nations. A number of countries found themselves borrowing not only to finance capital programmes, but also deficits in the current account of the balance of payments. By the time of the second oil shock in 1979 growth had not only slowed for some countries, but had become negative for a large number of others. Recession in the industrial countries in the mid-1970s did not help matters. This was compounded by further recession in the early 1980s. The drop in commodity prices in the 1980s increased the dependence of developing countries on the loan market.

Following the first oil shock, the situation in the capital markets had began to undergo radical change.

The euro-currency market had become established in the 1960s, and the surpluses put at its disposal by the oil exporting countries were to provide further fuel to the growth of this market. The money centre banks became a major mechanism for recycling funds from surplus to deficit countries. In the 1970s the financial needs of the developing countries had grown beyond what traditional sources of funds could meet, and governments turned increasingly towards private lenders. There was another reason for avoiding institutions like the IMF and the World Bank. Commercial bank credit may have entailed harder terms than official loans, but the latter were associated with conditionalities which borrowing countries did not relish. At the end of 1972, about two-thirds of the outstanding external debt of non-oil developing countries was owed to official lenders. By the end of 1980, however, private creditors accounted for about half of the outstanding medium-term and long-term public debt.[8]

A major consequence of the increased reliance on commercial bank loans was a greater servicing burden for debtor countries. Many commercial loans are based on variable interest rates linked to the London Interbank Offer Rate (LIBOR). When the latter increases the interest rates on old loans also increase resulting in heavier debt service payments. Between 1972 and 1980 Euro-dollar interest rates in London rose from about 5.5 per cent in 1972 to about 13.75 per cent in 1980, and averaged nearly 17 per cent during the first half of 1981. At the same time, however, the interest rates on loans from official lenders rose only slightly from about 4.5 per cent to a little over 5 per cent.[9]

When a government decides to borrow, it not only has to decide how much to borrow, but from whom and on what terms. Interest rate, grace period, length of repayment, currency, policy conditionalities are relevant considerations in the decision. It also has to look at the effects of new loans on its debt servicing capacity and the repayment schedule of existing loans, some of which will be short-term, some medium-term and some long-term. Also of relevance are projections relating to government revenue, the growth of the economy and foreign exchange earnings. Borrowing has to be a carefully thought out process, or a government could find itself facing debt service problems of a magnitude it did not anticipate, and which could force it to take drastic action of a kind that could affect both the social situation and the growth prospects of the economy. Faced with large and persistent fiscal deficits in the 1970s as well as balance of payments problems, many governments chose to borrow rather than reduce expenditure. In the absence of government savings to finance development programmes, dependence on foreign savings increased. Even in cases like Trinidad and Tobago and Venezuela which had large foreign exchange reserves, these reserves were quickly used up. Borrowing was undertaken not only to finance investment, but consumption and balance of payments deficits as well. During the 1970s even countries that had a good stock of reserves, and these include the oil exporting nations, borrowed to finance large scale projects which they hoped in time would expand foreign exchange earnings capacity. Some governments claimed their borrowing activities were partly aimed at getting themselves known in the international capital market. The orgy of borrowing that took place in the 1970s was made possible by the highly liquid position of the money centre banks. In this situation the quality of country risk assessment took a sharp downward turn that was to have disastrous consequences for the banks themselves, and the international financial situation.

It has long been argued that the use of foreign savings (be it through loans, grants or investment) can contribute to a higher growth rate in the domestic economy than would not be possible if investment were solely dependent on domestic savings. This is predicated, however, on the efficient use of these resources. In many cases, foreign resources were misused or mismanaged and did not contribute to an expansion of the productive capacity of the economy. Capital flight related to corruption, or stemming from inept macroeconomic policies would also have reduced the total volume of savings with repercussions on production, employment and servicing capacity.

APPROACHES TO THE RESOLUTION OF THE DEBT PROBLEM

Between the outbreak of the debt crisis in 1982 and 1985, there was no coherent or global programme for tackling the problem. The general attitude was that the debt question was more a liquidity than a solvency problem, and therefore was of a temporary nature. Structural adjustment programmes aimed primarily at balance of payments adjustment under IMF surveillance took on a greater degree of urgency. Commercial banks undertook little new lending and had little choice but to roll over or reschedule some loans. Increasing gloom over the resolution of the debt problem led Peru in July of 1985 to declare that it would limit debt payments to 10 per cent of export revenue. Other Latin American countries were calling for the linking of debt service payments to the growth of their export earnings.

By 1985 it had become clear that the issues relating to debt went far beyond the question of liquidity and that a concerted and deliberate effort was needed. The threat to the stability of the international financial system had become more widely appreciated, and the large exposure of the American banks was of particular interest to the American government. The Americans took the view that while the servicing of debt was impor tant, there was need to create conditions and adopt policies which could strengthen the indebted countries. The first major initiative from the Americans in this direction took the form of the Baker Plan.

The Baker Plan

The Plan was named after James Baker (then US Treasury Secretary) who first presented it at the joint annual meeting of the International Monetary Fund and the World Bank in Seoul, South Korea in 1985. It was put forward not simply as a debt relief plan, but as a 'Program for Sustained Growth' for indebted countries. According to Baker, the Plan (which targeted 15 heavily indebted countries) had three 'essential and mutually reinforcing' elements:

1. The adoption by principal debtor nations of comprehensive macro-economic and market-oriented structural adjustment policies to promote growth, reduce inflation, increase domestic savings and investment, induce repatriation of domestic flight capital and attract foreign capital flow.
2. A 50 per cent increase (US$9 billion) over the following three years in World Bank and Inter-American Development Bank lending to 15 key debtor countries in support of the countries' structural adjustment programmes.
3. Increased new lending (US$20 billion over the following three years) by commercial banks to those key debtor countries that commit themselves to policies consistent with the Plan.

The Baker Plan was intended to become operational by the beginning of 1986, but from the very start there was skepticism about the Plan. The proposals were not well developed. Some of the larger commercial banks were of the view that an infusion of new funds might prevent default, and therefore expressed guarded support. Many of the smaller banks, however, were more cautious in the absence of any clear incentives. One of the problems that arose was the question of guarantee for new loans. Given the problems being faced by debtor countries, many of the banks wanted to know whether the Reagan administration would compensate them in the event the loans were not repaid, or would come to their aid in the event that they encountered difficulties. In the absence of such a guarantee the banks showed little willingness to undertake new lending. It was also not clear how the additional lending was to be distributed among debtor countries.

By 1987 it was evident that the Baker Plan was not being implemented and official focus shifted to the so-called Menu Approach.

The Menu concept essentially supplemented new concerted lending packages by the banks with other financing options. On the one hand, the Menu proposed the use of alternative new money instruments such as trade and project loans, international bond placements and limited capitalisation of interest payments. On the other, it introduced for the first time in the management of the debt problem the possibility of financing the debtor countries through debt reduction techniques such as debt-equity swaps, debt bond exchanges, and buy-backs.[10]

Even before US policy in the form of the Brady proposals recognized the need for debt reduction, a number of mechanisms had already emerged with this objective in mind. It would be helpful at this point to describe some of the major ones. Rescheduling it should be noted, does not reduce debt. It stretches out principal repayments and debt service charges over a longer period than initially agreed, and so eases the immediate debt service burden. It is a short-term measure. The fact that interest continues to be paid over the extended period means that at the end of the repayment period a greater transfer of resources from the debtor country would have taken place. Instead of simply rescheduling one loan at a time, a country may seek to reschedule all loans falling due for payment within a given time span. This is called multi-year rescheduling. It should be noted that loans rescheduled are essentially commercial bank loans and official credit. The major multilateral financial institutions (for example, IMF, the World Bank) do not reschedule their loans. Between 1985 and 1995 developing countries had a total of 185 restructuring agreements (involving US$161.0 billion) with official creditors. Low income countries were responsible for 87 of these agreements. Over the same period the agreements with commercial banks numbered 67 and involved US$258 billion.[11]

The emergence of the secondary market in the 1980s provided the framework for a range of innovative financial transactions, including the conversion of existing debt obligations which had lost their face value into some other asset. While the banks were interested in cutting their losses, debtors were interested in returning external debt levels to manageable proportions and in restoring their credibility. They were also interested in attracting back flight capital and new investment.

The following section discusses some recent innovations in the capital markets, specifically related to debt reduction.[12]

Debt forgiveness

This refers to a situation where a creditor government may decide to cancel repayment of a loan. Highly indebted Sub-Saharan African countries have been the main beneficiaries of debt forgiveness. These countries are among the poorest in the world.

Debt for export swaps

Under this arrangement an importer will buy bank debt of the country he wants to import from in the secondary market at a discount, redeems the debt at a rate closer to the face value with the debtor's central bank, and use the local currency proceeds to pay the exporter.

Debt for nature swaps

Bank debt is bought in the secondary market at a discount by environmental organizations or other interested parties, and donated directly to the debtor country's government in exchange for policy commitments concerning the environment or exchanged for domestic currency to be used for environmental protection. An additional incentive for such swaps was provided by the US Treasury in 1987 when it ruled that lenders may deduct for tax purposes the full face value of developing country debt donated to fund charitable activities in debtor nations.

Debt for nature swaps have inspired some creditors to exchange foreign currency debt owed by extremely poor countries for local currency which is then donated to agencies like UNICEF to improve social services in the indebted country.

Exchange

These involve the exchange of existing debt instruments for new debt instruments denominated in domestic or foreign currency. The terms of the two claims nominally differ substantially. For example, the face value of the new claim may reflect a discount from the face value of the old claim; or the face value may remain unchanged while the contractual interest rate on the new claim is lower than on the old claim.

Buy-backs

As the name implies debtor countries buy back or repurchase their debt at a discount either directly from the lender or in the secondary market. A country may use its international reserves, or resources from bilateral or multilateral sources to make the purchase.

Debt-equity swaps

Faced with the possibility of not recovering their funds either fully or in part, many creditors have shown an increasing willingness to sell off their claims on debtor countries at a discount. A foreign investor desiring to capitalize on this situation buys the debt paper at a percentage of its face value and then presents it to the debtor country for exchange into national currency at its nominal value. The local currency equivalent can then be used to repay domestic debt, to purchase equity or to undertake other forms of investment. From the debtor's point of view, its foreign currency debt is reduced, while the creditor is relieved of what it may have considered a bad or irretrievable loan. The debtor country may also see this as a technique for encouraging foreign investment and attracting technology.

In a number of countries, particularly in Latin America, debt equity conversion programmes have been established. Not all operate in the same way.[13] In Brazil selective cases of debt equity conversion have been authorized only where the investor was the original creditor. In Argentina, debt equity conversions are permitted provided the local currency is invested in investor oriented activities and the investor matches the converted debt with an equal amount of new foreign money, both of which are converted at the official rate. The Chilean programme does not restrict opportunities to local investors. In almost all cases there are restrictions on the type of investment for which conversions may be used, so that the programme is not used to encourage speculation. In all programmes host governments charge conversion fees which may be as high as 25 per cent for low priority industries and as low as 5 per cent for export-revenue-earning projects. Some schemes carry provisions relating to the payments of dividends, repatriation and the exchange rate to be used for the foreign currency conversion. In the case of Mexico, debt converted to equity may not be repatriated for 12 years, nor can the resultant dividends exceed 9 per cent for the first three years. From the fourth year, dividends are freely payable and transferable.

Exit bonds

These are to be found mainly in restructuring agreements between commercial banks and debtor countries. They are issued by a debtor government or central bank in place of a bank credit generally exempting the bank from future requests for new money and restructuring. Interest rates on these bonds are below market, so a bank that decides to take up exit bonds instead of participating in a concerted lending package contributes to the debtor country's financing needs by accepting lower interest payments.

The debt reduction measures described here have had only a small impact on the outstanding debt of developing countries. Recognizing the implications of a continuing debt problem for growth, there has been numerous proposals by groups and individuals for its alleviation. In June 1988, the Toronto Summit adopted the following menu of options to be chosen by creditor countries in rescheduling the official bilateral debt of low income countries within the framework of the Paris Club:[14]

1. Partial write-offs: one third of the debt service due during the consolidation period is cancelled and the remaining two thirds rescheduled at market rates, with a maturity of 14 years, including eight years of grace;
2. Longer repayment periods: debt service due during the consolidation period is rescheduled at market interest rates, with a maturity of 25 years, including 14 per cent of grace;
3. Concessional interest rates: the consolidated debt service is rescheduled at market interest rates reduced by 3.5 percentage points or 50 per cent, which ever is less, and with a maturity of 14 years, including eight years of grace.

A number of rescheduling agreements have benefitted from the Toronto terms.[15] In addition, some donor governments have cancelled loans to some low income countries, particularly those in Sub-Sahara Africa. Some IDA-eligible debt-distressed countries have been denied the benefits of the Toronto terms, and this has raised questions about the eligibility criteria. A major criticism of the Toronto terms is that they apply only to a small part of the debt service obligations of developing countries. With respect to the introduction of concessionality into the terms of rescheduling official and official guaranteed export credits, questions have been raised about the adequacy of this concessionality in terms of the overall debt servicing capacity of beneficiary countries. Only debt service payments falling due during the consolidation period benefit from the Toronto terms which critics feel should apply to the entire stock of debt outstanding.[16] Under the Toronto terms creditors are expected to provide additional funds for debt relief, but some are transferring funds from their aid budget for this purpose.

Recognizing the inadequacies of existing schemes to assist debtor countries, including the Toronto terms, a further proposal was put forward by John Major, the then British Chancellor of the Exchequer, in Trinidad in 1990 to the effect that debt service reduction should apply to the full stock of the debt. This proposal, now referred to as the 'Trinidad terms', suggested that up to two thirds of the debt of low income countries could be written off, and the repayment period for the remainder would be 25 years, with 5 years grace. For countries with severe cash flow problems, moratorium interest (interest on restructured debt service obligations) could be capitalized (that is, added to the principal) for five years and later payments could be graduated and linked to the country's export capacity. This proposal no doubt had some influence on the 'enhanced Toronto terms' discussed earlier.

Following the Toronto Summit a number of other proposals were advanced by experts and political leaders but these did not get off the ground.[17]

Recognizing the shortcomings of the 'Toronto terms', Paris Club creditors in December 1991 decided to increase the concessionality of the terms for the poorest highly indebted countries (essentially IDA-only countries). Under the 'enhanced Toronto terms' as this new arrangement has come to be known, a distinction is made between official commercial credits or government guaranteed debt on the one hand and ODA-related debt on the other.[18]

Official Commercial Credits or Credits Guaranteed by Public Agencies

There are three options that are offered for restructuring the payments of principal and interest falling due during the consolidation period (which varies from 12 to 35 months depending on the agreement):

1. Debt reduction: reduction of 50 per cent of debt service obligation, with the remaining half to be rescheduled at market interest rates over a period of 23 years, including a grace period of 6 years.
2. Debt service reduction of 50 per cent of the present value of debt service obligations through rescheduling at reduced concessional rates over a repayment period of 23 years, with no grace period;
3. Commercial option: for budgetary or legal reasons, creditors would choose simply to reschedule debt service obligations over a period of 25 years, including 14 years of grace, at market rates. This option does not provide for any reduction.

ODA-related debt

ODA-related debt cannot be cancelled but concessional rates are applied and the pay back period is extended to 30 years including a 12-year grace period.

Following the G-7 Summit Meeting in Naples, the Paris Club creditors agreed in December 1994 to offer new terms for the poorest and most indebted countries. The so-called 'Naples terms' represent improvement over the earlier enhanced Toronto terms, in that they include an option to reduce debt or debt service by 67 per cent.

Countries eligible for Naples terms are those that have received Toronto and enhanced Toronto terms.[19] To qualify for a 67 per cent reduction the countries must have either a per capita GDP of less than US$500 or a ratio of present value of debt to exports exceeding 350 per cent.

The Naples terms offer creditor countries additional options to those offered under the enhanced Toronto terms. The following new options are available:

- Debt reduction: reduction of 67 per cent of debt service obligations, with the remaining third rescheduled at market interest rates over a period of 23 years, including a grace period of six years;
- Debt service reduction: reduction of 67 per cent of the present value of debt service obligations through rescheduling at reduced concessional interest rates, with a repayment period of 33 years, and no grace period;
- Commercial option: for budgetary or legal reasons, creditors would choose to reschedule debt service obligations over a period of 40 years, including 20 years of grace, at market interest rates. This option does not provide for any reduction.

In exceptional circumstances 'stock treatment' can be applied. If there is sufficient agreement among creditors to reduce the stock of debt, reduction will be achieved through:

- Debt reduction of 50 per cent or 67 per cent, the rest being rescheduled over a period of 23 years, including six years of grace, at market interest rates; or
- Reduction of the present value of debt by 50 per cent or 63 per cent. Debt will be paid at reduced concessional interest rates, over 23 years (including three years of grace) under the 50 per cent option, and over 33 years (including three years of grace) under the 67 per cent option.

With respect to ODA loans, these will be rescheduled over 40 years (including 16 years of grace) under the 67 per cent reduction option, at interest rates at least as favourable as original rates.

The debt to be rescheduled covers medium- and long-term public and publicly guaranteed debt contracted before the cutoff date, that is, the date before which loans must have been contracted in order to be considered by the rescheduling agreement. This date is usually determined at the first rescheduling and remains unchanged in subsequent reschedulings. The scope of the debt covered will be determined on a case by case basis.

Following the adoption of the Naples term in December 1994, the number of countries that went to the Paris club increased substantially in the early part of 1995, but the momentum in concessional rescheduling fell off after this, partly because of the difficulties some countries were encountering in reaching a new agreement with the IMF.[20] When this is seen in the context of countries with proportionately large multilateral and non-OECD official bilateral debt, it is clear that the international debt problem is far from resolved.

The Brady Plan

The Baker proposals, discussed earlier, failed to have the intended impact, mainly because it could not encourage the additional resource transfers which was perhaps the most crucial part of the Plan. Neither was the debt service burden reduced, nor was their significant growth. The austerity programmes being implemented in many cases under IMF/World Bank auspices were also creating social unrest in certain countries.

As indicated earlier, as the 1980s progressed, the attitude of both debtors and creditors towards the debt situation changed, as action to reduce the outstanding debt became more readily accepted. Several banks began writing off large amounts of outstanding debt and increasing the loss reserves provisions. The secondary market emerged, and debtor countries began buying back their debt at a discount with the cooperation of the banks who by then had concluded that many debt papers were not worth their face value.

On 10 March 1989, US Treasury Secretary Nicholas F. Brady advanced some new ideas which explicitly recognized the need for debt and debt service reduction and advocated the use of IMF and World Bank funds (as well as contributions by governments) in support of debt reduction operations. The key proposals included:[21]

1. adoption of sound economic policies, with stronger emphasis on measures to increase foreign and domestic investment and the repatriation of flight capital;
2. timely support from the IMF and World Bank for countries' reform programmes, in part through financing for debt and debt service reduction transaction;

3. active participation by commercial banks in providing financial support through the negotiation of debt and debt-service reduction and new lending, where needed.

Perhaps the most innovative aspect of the Brady proposal was the opportunity it afforded to recover part of non-performing loans. Under the plan commercial bank creditors could exchange outstanding loans for bonds at a discount. This could be done in two ways. The bonds could carry a face value lower than that of the outstanding loans but with commercial interest rates ('discount bonds'); or they could carry the same face value as the original loans but with interest rates below market levels ('par bonds'). There could, of course, be combination of the two.

It needs to be pointed out, however, that a secondary market for developing countries' debt had already began to take shape since the early 1980s. The driving force was the uncertainty hanging over the servicing of loans and the desire by many banks to 'cut their losses' and 'clean up' their books. The discount bid offered would reflect the investors' and banks' confidence in the debtor government.

Like its predecessor the Baker Plan, Brady's adopted the case by case approach to resolution of the debt problem. Rather than it being aimed at only 15 heavily indebted countries, however, it was aimed at all developing countries with debt problems. It is similar to the Baker Plan also in the fact that it links assistance to reform programmes approved by the IMF and the World Bank. It differs from its predecessor in that it calls explicitly for debt and debt service reduction, and this represented a radical change in US thinking which eventually came to recognize a link between debt and the deteriorating social and economic situations in Latin America; between debt and the ability to buy American exports. The effect of debt on the democratization process in Latin America and the implications for a greater flow of immigrants to the US was not lost on the US Government. The Plan was essentially aimed at the Latin American countries with their large commercial debt.

The Brady Plan was not a comprehensive debt strategy. It seemed to focus heavily on middle income countries with large commercial debts. The Plan itself as originally presented was short on many details. The criteria for eligibility for debt reduction were not spelt out. Banks were expected to participate voluntarily in debt reduction and new money arrangements, but the incentives for doing this were not readily apparent. The idea seemed to be that banks which took action to mitigate the burden of debtors will be rewarded through increased security of remaining loans.[22] Despite the uncertainties surrounding the Brady Plan the banks saw in it an opportunity to keep loans as current as possible, to gain time to rebuild capital and revenue and to transform impaired loans into better assets.[23]

Since 1969 a number of middle income highly indebted countries have entered into Brady type arrangements, which involve a range of options, including buy-backs, the exchange of debt for bonds ('exit' or Brady bonds), debt exchanges, and so on. Through these transactions debtor countries have their debt reduced (with corresponding benefits in interest payments), while the creditor banks get improved assets which in some cases carry certain guarantees. In some instances new money has also been forthcoming.

THE POSITION OF THE IMF AND WORLD BANK ON DEBT REDUCTION

One of the practical outcomes of all the discussions and proposals relating to debt was the adoption by the IMF and the World Bank of new policy guidelines which will enable them to finance a variety of methods of debt or debt service reduction. The World Bank agreed to allow some part of its structural adjustment loans to be used for debt reduction of principal. In August 1989, the International Development Association (IDA) of the World Bank established a Special Debt Reduction Facility for low income member countries. Only a few countries (among them Mozambique, Niger, Guyana, Uganda and Bolivia) have utilized this facility to reduce their commercial bank debt through buy-backs or discounted exchanges.

In May 1989 the Fund adopted broad guidelines[24] that could facilitate a reduction in the volume of outstanding debt and debt-service payments. The strategy was based on a case-by-case approach with three basic elements:

1. the pursuit of growth-oriented adjustment and structural reform in debtor countries;
2. the provision of adequate financial support by official, multilateral and private sources; and
3. the maintenance of a favourable global economic environment.

It agreed on a set of guidelines for eligibility, the kinds of debt operations the Fund would support, the degree of access to Fund resources, and the Fund's policy on financing assurances. Fund support for debt reduction operations would be open to all members, subject to the following criteria:

- the sustained pursuit of strong economic policies in the context of a medium-term program supported by the Fund, which includes strong elements of structural reform;
- the likelihood that such voluntary market-based operations will help the country regain access to credit markets and achieve external payment viability with economic growth;
- a determination that support for the reduction of debt and debt service represents an efficient use of scarce resources.

The Board agreed that a certain proportion of Fund resources committed under an extended or stand-by arrangement could be set aside to reduce the stock of debt through buy-backs or exchanges. While this percentage will be determined on a case-by-case basis, it would normally be around 25 per cent. Drawing on the amounts set aside will be phased in line with the member's performance under the adjustment program, although some front-loading may be permitted in certain cases.

Additional access to Fund resources would be allowed in certain cases, provided that such support is decisive in promoting further cost-effective operations and in catalyzing (that is, mobilizing) other financial resources. Such additional access – up to 40 per cent of a member's quota will be used for interest support, in connection with debt or debt-service reduction. Actual access, however, will be determined case by case, in light of the magnitude of the member's balance of payments problems, the strength of its adjustment program, and its efforts to contribute its own resources to support debt and debt-service reduction. Fund resources in support of debt reduction will be disbursed only when the Fund-supported adjustment program is on track.

It should be noted at this point that in January 1994, the Board agreed to modify these guidelines.[25] To facilitate commercial bank debt restructuring for some countries with difficult debt situations, the Board decided to eliminate the segmentation requirements under which the proportions of Fund resources committed under a stand-by or an extended arrangement that were set aside could be used only to support operations involving principal reduction, such as cash buy-backs and discount exchange, while additional resources provided through augmentation could be used only for interest support for debt or debt service reduction and for collateralization of principal in reduced-interest bound exchanges. The elimination of segmentation makes it possible to use both set asides and additional resources from augmentation to support operations involving debt reduction, interest support for debt and debt-service reduction, and principal collateral for reduced interest par bonds provided that such operations satisfy the Fund's criteria.

Through the use of various mechanisms and measures a number of lower and middle-income debtor countries have received some relief. Between 1991 and 1994 US$15 billion of debt was forgiven on a bilateral basis. By 1994 over US$20 billion were rescheduled under the Naples terms and US$185 billion were reorganized or reduced under the Brady framework.[26] The position of the so-called heavily indebted poor countries (HIPCs), however, has been a cause for concern in the international community. 'The low level of development in most of these countries, characterised by structural rigidities, weak institutions and administration, poorly functioning markets, and deficiencies in skills and infra-structure, prevented a rapid and strong response to reform efforts.'[27] In some cases economic performance was also affected by adverse terms of trade, weather conditions, civil strife and poor implementation of adjustment programmes. Most of these countries have little or no access to international capital markets.

In the context of the efforts being made to diffuse the debt problem, it is worth recalling that the multilateral financial institutions generally do not reschedule debt, and this has particular implications for countries with a large share of their debt owed to such lenders. For countries like Benin, Bolivia, Burundi, Burkina Faso, Rwanda, Niger and the Central African Republic over half (in some cases over three quarters) of their outstanding public debt is multilateral. The inability to fully service their debt has resulted in an accumulation of arrears in some cases, and in this situation new loans are not easily forthcoming.

To deal with the particular problem faced by HIPCs, the World Bank and the IMF launched a joint initiative in late 1996 to establish a fund which could help reduce the debt burden of these countries. Bilateral donors and creditors are also being asked to contribute to the Fund.

Issues relating to the external debt of developing countries surface at almost every international meeting, and attempts to find relief are reflected in a whole series of proposals assuming names such as the Toronto terms, the enhanced Toronto terms, the Trinidad terms, the Houston terms, the Naples terms, the Venice terms, and so on. Generally the greatest attention is paid to the most severely indebted poor countries. The middle income debtors tend to be subjected to standard treatment in which rescheduling is a major technique. Rescheduling largely takes place from the perspective of the creditors.

There are two 'institutions' which have become almost synonymous with debt rescheduling and debt relief, namely, the Paris Club and the London Club. The former reschedules credits extended by governments or by private lenders with a credit-government guarantee, while the latter reschedules credits extended by commercial banks without any creditor-government guarantee.[28] The word 'Club' is somewhat misleading in that there are no 'members' but 'participating creditor countries'. The Paris Club was 'born' in 1956 when a group of creditor governments met in Paris to negotiate a debt-relief arrangement with Argentina. It is not an international organization. It is less of an institution and more a set of *ad hoc* procedures for negotiation of debts owed to official creditors who are largely the governments of the major industrial countries.[29] These procedures have evolved since 1956, as an increasingly larger number of countries have sought relief from the Paris Club. In 1982 only five agreements were negotiated involving a rescheduling of US$428 million. Between 1983 and 1995 the annual number of agreements per year averaged 17.

The Paris Club which meets traditionally in the French Treasury operates differently from the bank steering committees. Instead of tailoring a 'term sheet' for each case, the Paris Club agrees to a set of generic term sheets for different classes of debtors, based primarily on their level of income per capita.[30] Among the major changes that have been introduced by the Paris Club in recent years to help low income countries include the following:[31]

- Under exceptional circumstances, the Paris Club will consider cancelling or providing equivalent restructuring of the entire stock of a country's official debt contracted before a cut-off date;
- The interest rate on consolidated non-concessional debt can now be substantially below market rates;
- Longer repayment periods for rescheduled non-concessional debt;
- A menu approach for creditors, under which they can choose the modality of debt relief;
- A move toward equalizing burden sharing among creditors so that each creditor's debt relief agreement would achieve an agreed net present value target.

Participation in the Paris Club does not prevent individual creditor governments from formulating their own individual approach to debt relief on a unilateral basis. In 1992, for example, the French Government assisted four middle income African countries by creating a debt conversion fund of 4 billion francs, which would be partly financed by debt-servicing payments of these countries. The francs would then be recycled to development projects. Under the Enterprise for the Americas initiative the United States government agreed in 1992 to reduce the debt owed by certain Latin American states.[32]

In practice there are three major principles which guide debt relief: imminent default, conditionality and burden sharing.[33]

Imminent default

Creditor governments normally will not entertain a request for debt relief unless there is strong evidence that the debtor country will default on its external payments in the absence of such relief. The test widely used for 'imminent default' is the existence of *ex ante* financing gap:

	Sources		Uses
	{exports of goods and services + workers }		Imports of
Ex	{remittances + private and official }		goods and
Ex- ante =	{transfers+loan disbursements + direct }	<	services
Gap	{investment +borrowing from the IMF + }		+
	{foreign exchange reserves }		debt service
			payments

When a debtor country's uses of foreign exchange, which are usually projected for one year in advance, exceed its sources, there is *prima facie* evidence that a situation of imminent default exists. High reliance is placed on IMF projections.

While the principle of imminent default is used to discourage debtor countries from seeking relief before there is need to do so, it has been the subject of a great deal of criticism, because by the time a debtor meets this criterion, the situation would have deteriorated and arrears started to build up.

Conditionality

Creditors are not simply interested in providing temporary debt relief. They are concerned also with having debtor countries regain a position from where they can service their external debts fully and on schedule. Debt relief by itself does not solve debt problems. If debt relief is not accompanied by a program of sound economic policies, it is argued, debt relief would have been wasted. Creditors could negotiate with a debtor country to obtain the required policy reforms, but in practice they insist on a stand-by or extended arrangement with the IMF whom Paris Club creditors believe is in the best position to help formulate and oversee a package of sound economic policies.

Burden sharing

This principle states that all creditors must provide relief that is commensurate with their exposure in the debtor country. There are four broad group of creditors to consider: (a) multilateral lending institutions; (b) official creditors participating in the Paris Club negotiations; (c) official creditors not participating in these negotiations; and (d) private creditors such as commercial banks.

Multilateral financial institutions (for example, the IMF, the World Bank, the Regional Development Banks) are exempted from undertaking any open or direct debt restructuring. There are two arguments for exempting multilateral institutions from rescheduling. The first is that both debtor and creditor countries are members and therefore they both benefit from any advantages accruing to these institutions. The second is that the institutions bear their share of the burden of relief by continuing to lend to the debtor country. It is argued that exemption is important in helping multilateral financial institutions to maintain strong credit rating which not only make them less dependent on their shareholders for funds, but also allow them to borrow money at favourable rates which are passed on to borrowing members.

The fact that the MFIs do not reschedule does not mean that borrowers do not default, and by so doing lose their borrowing privileges. The IMF, for instance, currently has six countries which are in arrears.[34] In March 1990, the Fund adopted a mechanism under which, *inter alia,*

> it negotiates adjustment programs with countries in arrears that wish to pursue a policy of 'intensified collaboration' aimed at resolving the overdue obligations. The Fund monitors each programme, as it would regular adjustment arrangements, and as long as the programme remains in effect, the country is deemed to accumulate rights to make a drawing once it again becomes eligible, that is, when its arrears are repaid. Meanwhile, bilateral creditors generally provide balance-of-payments support, some of which might be used to at least prevent IMF arrears from growing.[35]

Some creditor countries occasionally provide loans or grants to help countries to clear their arrears.

It has been pointed out that the essential *raison d'etre* of the Paris Club is to ensure burden sharing among participating creditors.[36] But there is no formula for this. Very often debt relief is accompanied by new loans, and how creditors share in this is not always easy to resolve. Sometimes creditors, both within the Paris Club and outside are approached on a bilateral basis, but very rarely, and especially Paris Club members, do creditors adopt this procedure.

With respect to burden sharing by non-participating creditors, Paris Club creditors use a non-discrimination clause in the standard Paris Club agreement. The clause commits the debtor country to obtain relief on the same terms from non-participating creditors.[37]

Burden sharing with private creditors has become necessary mainly because commercial banks have become major sources of funds for developing countries in recent years. Banks being profit oriented institutions lend on terms quite different from governments who may be influenced by a variety of motives. In seeking burden sharing with commercial banks, the concept of 'comparable treatment', is now frequently used. Under this arrangement the debtor government agrees 'to seek a measure of relief from the banks that is as generous in the context of normal commercial lending as the relief offered by creditor governments in the context of their lending.'[38] The concept of 'comparable treatment' is both difficult to measure and enforce.

CONCLUDING OBSERVATIONS

There has been some diffusing of the international debt problem, but it has not gone away. The measures taken by the banks with large exposures, and by the international community has reduced the threat of imminent collapse of the international financial system. Some countries are starting to grow out of their debt, but in a large number of cases, debt remains a critical issue, not only because of the outstanding levels, but because of continued poor economic performance and slow structural change. The inability to access new funds itself has contributed to this situation. In a number of cases debt service payments continue to exceed flows associated with new borrowings. In Africa, for example, the outstanding external debt for this group of countries increased by US$17 billion between 1994 and 1995, but debt service payments in 1995 was US$33 billion.[39] In Latin America net disbursements by the World Bank in the 1990–95 period amounted to US$2.3 billion, but when interest and charges of US$16.4 billion was taken into account, the net transfer was minus US$14.1 billion.[40]

The challenge of financing reform programs, servicing debt and dealing with poverty issues has put both the technical and financial capacity of many developing countries under heavy stress. A large number of them are still unable to attract private investment, and capital programs still rests heavily on state borrowing. With increasing competition for dwindling concessional funds middle-income countries are forced to use resources that not only carry 'harder' terms but may also be associated with policy conditionalities. The solvency problem faced by many poor debtor countries, particularly in Africa, and concern with dwindling funds available for international assistance have led to calls for new approaches in overcoming poverty. One proposal that has been reviewed in recent years was made by James Tobin (who won the Nobel Prize for Economics in 1981) in 1978.[41] Tobin suggested the imposition of a uniform *ad valorem* transaction tax on all spot sales and purchases of foreign exchange in all major foreign exchange markets. He suggested that a tax of 0.5 per cent could have a revenue potential of US$1.5 trillion a year. The tax would have to be worldwide, at the same rate in all markets, or it could be evaded by executing transactions in jurisdictions with no tax or lower tax.

According to Tobin, the proposal had two basic motivations: (1) to increase the weight market participants give to long-term fundamentals relative to immediate speculative opportunities, and the second is to allow greater autonomy to national monetary policy, by making possible larger wedges between short interest rates in different currencies. In this way the tax would reduce volatility of the foreign exchange market.[42]

At the time the proposal was made it did not win broad support in the economics profession 'because its effectiveness in stemming exchange-rate volatility was not assured even in theory, while its distorting effect on resource allocation was clear.'[43] It is considered even less feasible today because of the development of the market in financial derivatives and the complexity of the foreign exchange market, particularly for the major currencies.

Notes

1. See IMF, *World Economic Outlook*, May 1996 (Washington, DC: IMF, 1996), p. 173.
2. UNCTAD, *Trade and Development Report*, 1996 (New York: UN, 1996), p. 66.
3. See IMF, World Economic Outlook, May 1996, *op. cit.*, p. 173.
4. United Nations, *World Economic and Social Survey, 1996* (New York: UN, 1996), p. 344.
5. *Ibid.*, p. 349.
6. H. Hughes, 'The External Debt of Developing Countries,' *Finance and Development*, Vol. 14 (December 1977), pp. 22–5.
7. *Ibid.*
8. G. R. Kincaid, 'Inflation and the External Debt of Developing Countries', *Finance and Development*, Vol. 18 (December 1981), pp. 21–4.

9. *Ibid.*
10. R. Devlin, 'The Menu Approach,' *IDS Bulletin*, Vol. 21, (No. 2, April 1990), pp. 11–16.
11. United nations, *World Economic and Social Survey, 1996, op. cit.*, pp. 350–1.
12. Some of these are discussed at length in the IMF, *Annual Report*, 1990.
13. See, M. Schubert, 'Trading Debt for Equity', *The Banker*, February 1987, pp. 18–20.
14. See UNCTAD, *Trade and Development Report 1989* (New York, UN., 1989), p. 53.
15. *Ibid.*
16. See UNCTAD, *Trade and Development Report 1989* (New York, UN, 1989), p. 53–9.
17. For a discussion of some of these see IMF, *Annual Report 1989*, p. 24.
18. For a description of these proposals see UNCTAD Report, 1989, *op. cit.*, pp. 48–9. See also UNCTAD, *Trade and Development Report 1995* (New York: UN, 1995), pp. 38–9.
19. These countries are Benin, Bolivia, Burkina Faso, Cameroon, Central African Republic, Chad, Côte d'Ivoire, Equatorial Guinea, Ethiopia, Guinea, Guinea-Bissau, Guyana, Honduras, Madagascar, Mali, Mauritania, Mozambique, Nicaragua, Niger, Senegal, Sierra Leone, Togo, Uganda, United Republic of Tanzania, Vietnam, Zaire, Zambia.
20. UNCTAD, *Trade and Development Report, 1996* (New York: UN, 1996), p. 57. By the end of April 1996, 16 reschedulings were agreed under Naples terms – 14 flow reschedulings and two stock-of-debt operations (for Guyana and Uganda).
21. See IMF, *Annual Report 1990*, p. 24.
22. See G. Maier, 'The Brady Plan – A Vicious Circle or a Way Out of the Debit Crisis', *Intereconomics*, Vol. 24 (May/June 1969), pp. 116–19. See IMF, *Annual Report 1989, pp. 24–25.*
23. See D. Carreau and M. N. Shaw, *The External Debt* (London: Martinus Nijhoff Publishers, 1995), p. 140.
24. See IMF, *Annual Report 1989, pp. 24–25.*
25. See IMF, *Annual Report 1994, p. 11.*
26. OECD, *Development Cooperation, 1995 Report* (Paris: OECD, 1996), p. 66.
27. UNCTAD, *Trade and Development Report 1996, op. cit.*, p. 50.
28. See A. Riefel, 'The Paris Club, 1978–1983,' *The Columbia Journal of Transnational Law*, Vol. 23, (No. 1, 1984), pp. 83–110.
29. Ibid.
30. Ibid.
31. Klein. 'Innovations in Debt Relief', *Finance and Development*, Vol. 29, (March 1992), pp. 42–43.
32. See UN, *World Economic and Social Survey, 1994, op. cit.*, p. 109.
33. For a detailed discussion of these principles, see A. Riefel, *The Role of the Paris Club in Managing Debt Problems* Princeton Essays in International Finance No. 161 (Princeton: Princeton University Press, 1985), pp. 4–14.
34. At the end of April 1996, obligations overdue by six months or more amounted to US$2911 million SDRs.
35. IMF, *Annual Report 1994*, p. 143.

36.   See A. Riefel, *The Role of the Paris Club in Managing Debt Problem,* *op. cit.*, p. 12.
37.   *Ibid.*, p. 13.
38.   *Ibid.*, p. 12.
39.   IMF, *World Economic Outlook*, May 1996, *op. cit.*, p. 173.
40.   World Bank, *Annual Report 1995*, p. 92.
41.   See the UNDP *Human Development Report 1994* (New York: Oxford University Press, 1994), p. 70. See also J. Tobin, 'Proposal for International Monetary Reform,' *Eastern Economic Journal*, Vol. 4, Nos. 3–46, (July/October 1978).
42.   Ibid.
43.   UN, *World Economic and Social Survey 1995*, *op. cit.*, p. 137.

Further Reading

Bird, G., 'Debt, Deficits and Dollars: The World Economy in 3-D.' *World Development*, Vol. 19 (February/March, 1995) pp. 245–54.

Carreau, D. and M. N. Shaw. *The External Debt*, Martinus Wijhoff Publishers, London, 1995.

Clarke, J., 'Debt Reduction and Market Reentry under the Brady Plan', Federal Reserve Bank of New York, *Quarterly Review* (Winter, 1993–94), pp. 38–62.

Claudon, M. P., (ed.) *World Debt Crisis: International Lending on Trial*, Ballinger Publishing Co., Cambridge, MA, 1986.

Eichengreen, B., 'Historical Research on International Lending and Debt'. *Journal of Economic Perspectives*, Vol. 5 (No. 12, Spring, 1995), pp. 77–95.

Ezenwe, U., 'The African Debt Crisis and the Challenge of Development', *Intereconomics*, Vol. 28 (No. 1 January/February 1993), pp. 35–43.

Garg, R. C., 'The Case for Debt-forgiveness for Latin America and the Caribbean Countries', *Intereconomics*, Vol. 28 (No. 3, January/February 1995), pp. 30–34.

Girvan, N., M. A. Servilla, M. C. Hatton and E. Rodriquez, 'The Debt Problem of Small Perispherial Economies: Case Studies from the Caribbean and Central America'. *Caribbean Studies*, Vol. 24 (No. 1–2, January–June 1991), pp. 45–115.

Griffith-Jones, S., *Managing World Debt*, St Martins Press, New York, 1988.

Helleiner, G.K., 'The IMF, the World Bank and Africa's Adjustment and External Debt Problems: An Unofficial View', *World Development*, Vol. 20 (No. 6, June 1992), pp. 779–92.

Hussain, I. and R. Faruquee (eds), *Adjustment in Africa*, The World Bank, Washington DC, 1994.

Hussain, I. and I. Diwan (eds), *Dealing with the Debt Crisis*, The World Bank, Washington DC, 1989.

Jones, C. T., 'The Impact of the Debt Crisis on Women and Families in Selected Latin American countries', *Journal of Caribbean Studies*, Vol. 8 (Nos. 1–2, Winter 1990–Summer 1991), pp. 31–45.

Kaminarides, J. and E. Nissan, 'The Effects of International Debt on Economic Development of Small Countries', *World Development*, Vol. 21 (No. 2, February 1993), pp. 227–32.

Korner, P., G. Maas, J. Siebold, R. Tetzlaff, *The IMF and the Debt Crisis*, Zed Books, London, 1987.

Lagos, R., 'Debt Relief Through Debt Conversion: A Critical Analysis of the Chilean Debt Conversion Programme', *Journal of Development Studies*, Vol. 28 (No. 3, April 1992), pp. 473–99.

Latin America Bureau, *The Poverty Brokers: The IMF and Latin America*, Latin America Bureau, London, 1983.

Lombardi, R. W., *The Debt Trap: Rethinking the Logic of Development*, Praeger, New York, 1985.

Nunnenkamp, P., *The International Debt Crisis of the Third World*, Wheatsheaf Books Ltd, Brighton, Sussex, 1986.

O'Cleireacaia, S. (ed.), *Third World Debt and International Public Policy*, Praeger, New York, 1990.

Rogoff, K. 'Dealing with Developing Country Debt in the 1990s'. *The World Economy*, Vol. 15 (No. 4, July 1992), pp. 475–86.

Schultz, J. 'How LDCs Hedge their Bets and Debts', *Institutional Investor*, Vol. XVII (February 1992), pp. 105–10.

Serven, L. and A. Solimano, 'Debt Crisis Adjustment Policies and Capital Formation in Developing Countries: Where Do We Stand?' *World Development*, Vol. 21 (No. 1, January 1993), pp. 127–40.

Serven, L. and A. Solimano (eds), *Striving for Growth after Adjustment*, The World Bank, Washington, DC, 1993.

Shilling, J. 'Reflections on Debt and the Government'. *Finance and Development*, Vol. 29 (No. 2, June 1992), pp. 28–30.

Stiles, K. W., *Negotiating Debt: The IMF Lending Process*, Westview Press, Boulder, 1991.

United Nations, *Debt-Equity Swaps and Development*, UN, New York, 1993.

Williamson, J. and D. R. Cossard, *Capital Flight: The Problem and Policy Responses*, The Institute of International Economics, Washington DC, 1987.

7 International Development Assistance

Aid is much more than just a carefully administered flow of resources. It is a basis for contemporary international relationships, both political and commercial. It is a conduit of goodwill, as well as of influence; a source of dynamism, and dependence; a promoter of new orders, and preserver of old ways. It represents 'business' for development and commercial banks, for exporters in the donor countries and importers in the recipient countries.[1]

INTRODUCTION

Notwithstanding the increasing trends towards an integrated, competitive interdependent global economy there continues to be wide differences in economic performance, levels of development and standard of living among the countries of the world. While some states have made progress, others have lost ground. The case for aid has not disappeared, but the context has changed markedly since the early post-war years, and changed attitudes and approaches now inform the international aid effort. The rise of new economic powers, the decolonization process, the spectacular economic success of a few developing countries, the debt crisis, the end of the cold war, the reintegration of the former 'socialist' states in the world economy and persistent civil strife in some developing countries have in various ways influenced the quantum and delivery of aid, which is influenced as much by political as economic factors.

While assistance by the rich countries to poor ones may originally have been conceived as a simple process or transaction devoid of any sinister motives, the quotation at the beginning of the chapter reflects some of the many dimensions which are now associated with what is now commonly referred to as foreign (overseas) aid or development assistance. In the post-war period the provision of aid was supposed to be a major mechanism for raising the standard of living in poor countries. As such, it has featured prominently in relations between developed and developing countries and has become a major preoccupation of international organizations. Aid is not a post-war phenomenon, but following the end of the

Second World War, it became more organized with the coming into being of the United Nations, and as an increasing number of countries entered the world stage as independent nations. There is now an extensive experience relating to the delivery and impact of aid, and not surprisingly this has generated a range of perspectives on the costs and benefits of aid. Because of this, what aid can and cannot do has become a very controversial subject. Despite this, however, there are no serious suggestions that aid should stop, or the aid effort diminished. On the contrary, the developed countries are continually being urged to increase the level of their assistance to poor nations. Sometimes such proposals have a humanitarian basis. Occasionally the argument is based on moral grounds, that is, the rich countries are morally obliged to help the poor ones, many of whom are former colonies. More frequently, however, the case for aid is argued on the conviction that in the long term developed countries themselves will benefit since improvements in the standard of living of poor societies means an expanded market with greater purchasing power and this can provide even greater incentives to production, exports and employment generation in the donor or giving countries. The latter's concern, however extends far beyond the economic implications of their aid effort. There is a variety of other considerations that influence aid giving, and some of these will be discussed later.

The aid effort itself has blossomed into a major industry with aid now being provided by more than 25 major bilateral and multi-country donors, ten multilateral banks and funds, 20 United Nations organizations and several hundred non-governmental organizations for the benefit of over 150 developing countries recipients.[2] Aid has evolved in a somewhat haphazard fashion and does not come under the control of any central authority, though there has been some effort to coordinate the international aid effort. For instance, in the 1960s, the Development Assistance Committee (DAC) of the Organization for Economic Cooperation and Development (OECD) was set up to coordinate the aid effort of the western donor countries.[3] Between 1950 and 1990, it is estimated that the richer countries staked over US$700 billion on the development process in the poorer ones.[4] Given the cost of sustaining the aid bureaucracy and the conditions under which aid is normally disbursed, it is difficult to pronounce on the net benefits accruing to recipient countries. Some of the intended effect of the aid giver is often lost in what is called 'tying', in the choice of poor projects or incompetent consultants, in corruption and in the insufficiency of skilled human and financial resources in recipient countries. 'Tying' may not only require recipient countries to purchase goods or services from donors at prices way above international market prices, but often stipulates the goods or projects on which the aid can be spent. The goods bought may also have to be transported in vessels of donor countries or insured by their companies as well. 'Tying may force the recipient country to carry out importations and to undertake projects which normally would have had lower priority. The various administrative restrictions connected with tying in their turn obstruct rational planning, involve additional administrative and other expenses and in the long run, divert trade from its economically desirable directions.'[5]

The recent poor growth performance of a large number of developing countries, and the emergence of serious debt problems in many of them, have led to the adoption of structural adjustment programs, which if they are to be sustained, require a certain amount of financial resources. The major international organizations, including governments of some developed countries, have called for increased flows of external resources to supplement domestic savings, particularly resources associated with a high degree of concessionality. While acknowledging that the shortage of development finance is a major obstacle to economic progress in poor countries, there is a widespread view that increasing attention has to be paid to the policy framework. The persistence of large scale poverty in many aid receiving countries has also raised questions about whether aid, as traditionally disbursed, is really benefitting the people who are supposed to benefit. The large net outflow of resources from developing countries has also raised questions about who is helping who, and whether aid donors are really interested in helping to reduce or eliminate poverty which is avowedly the major object of aid.

ECONOMIC CONDITIONS AND PERFORMANCE IN DEVELOPING COUNTRIES

Recognizing the shortcomings of using per capita income as an index of poverty, the UNDP has been producing a 'Human Development Index' which is based on a composite of three basic components of human development: longevity, knowledge and standard of living. The first is measured by life expectancy; the second by a combination of adult literacy (two thirds weight) and mean years of schooling (one-third weight); and the third is measured by purchasing power, based on real GDP per capita adjusted for the local cost of living (purchasing power parity). Countries with an HDI below 0.5 are considered to have a low level of human development, those between 0.5 and 0.8 a medium level and those above 0.8 a high level. As can be seen in Table 7.1, there were 42 countries in 1992 with low human development and 32 with medium human development.

Table 7.1 Distribution of countries by human development group, 1960 and 1992

	1960	*1992*
High human development	16	40
Medium human development	22	32
Low human development	76	42
Total	*114*	*114*

Source: UNDP, *Human Development Report*, 1994.

This was an improved picture over 1960 when 76 countries were described as having low human development.

In an examination of the 50 years since the United Nations was created, a recent UN publication concluded that what emerges 'is an arresting picture of unprecedented human progress and unspeakable human misery, of humanity's advance on several fronts mixed with humanity's retreat on several others, of a breathtaking globalization of prosperity side by side with a depressing globalization of poverty.'[6] The report noted that while the world's population more than doubled in the 50-year period since 1945 (increasing from 2.5 billion to 5.5 billion), global GDP increased sevenfold from US$3 trillion to US$22 trillion. Per capita income more than tripled. The share of the world's population enjoying fairly satisfactory human development levels increased from 25 per cent in 1960 to 60 per cent in 1992. Knowledge has been increasing in many fields with dramatic breakthroughs in technology which have revolutionized the way things are done.[7]

Despite all this, however, the Report noted a fifth of the world's population goes hungry every night, a quarter lacks access to even a basic necessity like safe drinking water and a third (1.3 billion) lives in a state of abject poverty. More than a third of the world's children are malnourished and underweight. The richest billion command 60 times the income of the poorest billion. Despite a decline in recent years global military spending (an estimated US$767 billion in 1994) equals the combined income of one-half of humanity each year.[8]

There is no doubting the improvement in material welfare, but both poor nations and rich are being increasingly afflicted by growing human distress – weakening social fabric, rising crime rates, increasing threats to personal security, spreading narcotic drugs, and so on. The damage to the environment and its ability to sustain the growth of world population is an international concern which is now receiving increasingly greater attention. The concept of sustainability is now a critical consideration in development policy.

Notwithstanding the progress being made on some fronts, an on-going concern is the disparity between rich and poor countries. Measured in constant dollars the per capita GDP of the developed market economies was 12.7 times that of developing countries in 1990 as compared to 9.9 times in 1960 (see Table 7.2). If the fast-growing developing countries are excluded the gap will be even wider. Of course, there are wide disparities among developing countries themselves. While in real terms per capita GDP in the developed economies increased by over 30 per cent, between 1980 and 1995, in most developing countries it actually fell.[9] Available data for the period between 1960 and 1990 indicate that the income for the richest 20 per cent of the global population rose from 70 per cent to 84 per cent. Over the same period, all but the richest quintile saw their share of world income fall – and the meagre share for the poorest 20 per cent declined from 2.3 per cent to 1.4 per cent.[10]

In the same way that global per capita income may not give a true picture of global poverty since it ignores the distribution of this income, the same could be said about per capita income at the national level. There are other indices which help to define the state of poverty in any country. One of them is the unemployment level. At the end of 1995 the unemployment rate stood at 3.1 per cent in Japan, 5.6 per cent in the United States, 9.4 per cent in Germany, 8.2 per cent in the United Kingdom, 9.5 per cent in Canada and 4.2 per cent in Switzerland. Figures of 20 per cent or more are to be found in most developing countries. The rates in the transition economies are generally not as low as those of developed market economies, but at the same time they are not as high as the rates prevailing in developing countries. Nutrition and sanitation levels, safe drinking water and health are still below acceptable levels in a large number of developing nations.

> In most parts of the world, nutrition has improved over the past 25 years, as reflected in declining infant and child mortality rates and in declining percentages of the total population suffering from undernutrition. But the improvements in child nutritional status in the 1970s ceased, on average in the 1980s. Some 100 million children under the age of five show protein energy malnutrition; more than 10 million suffer from the severe form that is normally fatal, if not treated. The estimated number of people suffering from severe undernutrition, with

Table 7.2 Growth of GDP per capita, by economic region and income groups of developing countries, 1960–90

Country group	Average annual rate of growth of GDP per capita at 1980 prices			Per capita GDP in 1980 US dollars			
	1960–70	1970–80	1980–90	1960	1970	1980	1990
World	3.2	1.9	1.3	1 601	2 191	2 647	3 000
Developed market economies	3.9	2.4	2.1	5 501	8 042	10 185	12 490
Major industrial economies	3.8	2.5	2.3	5 843	8 492	10 870	13 574
North America	2.5	2.2	1.9	7 223	9 325	11 636	14 071
Europe	4.6	2.7	2.2	5 899	8 554	10 831	13 334
Japan	9.2	3.6	3.4	2 683	6 415	9 109	12 697
Other developed economies	4.2	1.9	1.3	4 284	6 454	7 845	8 911
Eastern Europe and the USSR[a]	6.2	4.2	2.3	1 154	2 101	3,192	4 010
Eastern Europe	5.2	4.5	2.4	1 054	1 743	2 776	3 513
USSR	6.5	4.0	2.1	1 199	2 253	3 363	4 171
China	2.0	4.1	7.5	169	198	290	600
Developing countries	3.3	2.4	0.1	556	763	971	980
Per capita GDP greater than $700 in 1980	3.6	2.3	-0.6	1 175	1 662	2 105	1 980
Per capita GDP between $300 and $700 in 1980	2.0	3.0	1.6	289	345	463	540
Per capita income less than $300 in 1980	0.8	1.6	2.5	189	203	237	300
Least developed countries	1.1	-0.2	-0.3	227	254	249	240

[a] Based on net material product.
Source: UN, *Global Outlook 2000*, New York, 1990.

calorie intakes providing an energy level less than 1.2 times the basal metabolic rate (BMR), increased from 320 million in 1980 to 348 million by 1984 in 89 developing countries (excluding China).[11]

Access to safe drinking water varies widely from country to country. In Asia, for example, less than 60 per cent of the population in 1990 had access to safe drinking water as compared to less than 40 per cent in Sub-Saharan Africa. In the East Asian newly industrializing economies, however, the proportion was 85.5 per cent and in Latin America 73.0 per cent.[12]

While life expectancy has increased in both developed and developing countries, overcoming poverty for a large proportion of the world's population remains a major challenge. The path towards a higher standard of living has not been a steady one. The 1980s witnessed reversals in several countries, with income declining by over 25 per cent in some cases. Over 60 countries experienced negative growth rates in real per capita GNP in the period 1985–94.[13] Many of the countries included in this group have suffered from supply problems, depressed commodity prices or have been burdened with heavy debt service payments, all of which can reduce import capacity with implications for the functioning of the economy and domestic social conditions. Perennial droughts and famines, particularly in Africa, have reduced some economies in this region to shambles. Structural adjustment programs undertaken with the assistance of the international aid agencies have not always had the desired impact. In certain cases they have increased unemployment and worsened social conditions without necessarily strengthening the fabric of the economy. Inappropriate economic policies, mismanagement, corruption and civil wars have contributed in no small measure to the economic and social problems of a number of societies.

Admittedly, poverty does not have a single source. Historical and natural factors, domestic political systems and economic policies and the international trading framework have all contributed in varying degrees. Most of the poor countries in the world today are former colonies that were 'cultured' as suppliers of food and raw materials for the imperial powers who in turn supplied them with manufactured goods. For many of them this role may have become more sophisticated, but has not changed essentially, notwithstanding the attainment of political independence which has not altered the terms of exchange. Many of them continue to produce the same commodities developed in colonial times, and may enjoy some degree of preferential treatment in metropolitan markets, but prices received do not keep up with the cost of production. Mineral producers often do not have the power to bargain in a world tightly controlled by the transnational corporations either for higher prices or for a greater degree of domestic processing or refining. Even when developing countries switch to the production of goods in which they may have a comparative advantage, these products may face tariff and quota restrictions in the markets of developed countries. In the case of textiles, for example, it is estimated that some 67 per cent of the exports of these products from developing countries are affected. The industrial countries, by violating the principles of free trade are costing the developing countries an estimated US$50 billion a year – nearly equal to the total flow of foreign assistance.[14] It is often not enough to produce a good of high quality and at a competitive cost.

Because of their location, some developing countries are the victims of frequent droughts or devastating weather conditions that produce a great deal of human misery. This is often compounded when there are violent political conflicts, civil wars and undemocratic systems that produce refugees and encourage emigration.[15] In such situations the skilled people are the first to leave, and this does not help the functioning of the economy or the development process. To keep themselves in power, undemocratic regimes often incur significant military expenditures at the expense of social and economic programs, which could help to mitigate suffering and uplift the society.[16] The presence of corruption and mismanagement which are to be found both in democratic and undemocratic systems can also retard development and perpetuate poverty.

The need for political and social environments which would discourage people from fleeing their homelands is being increasingly recognized. In 1993 alone, elections were held in 45 countries – in some for the first time. Several countries in Latin America have abandoned dictatorial regimes in favour of democratic ones.

In the race to develop some countries have fallen further behind than others. There is a group of countries recognized as least developed of the developing countries which are given special treatment for certain purposes. From a bilateral point of view donors provide aid for various reasons, and therefore those who need aid most do not necessarily get what they need. Before we go on to discuss these issues, let us define the term 'aid' or 'development assistance'.

DEFINITION OF AID

The terms 'foreign aid' and 'international economic or development assistance' are often used interchangeably to cover a variety of transactions.

Aid can take a number of forms including the provisions of surplus agricultural commodities (food aid), the provision of professional and technical personnel, training, access to markets, and, of course, finance in the form of grants and loans on which most attention tends to be focused. Military assistance is not normally treated as development aid. While aid is generally defined to include identifiable financial transfers it can also take the form of providing commodities (for example, oil) at subsidized prices or the purchase of commodities (for example, sugar) at prices higher than prevailing world market prices. Private investment and loans on credits extended by private financial institutions are generally not classified as aid. Even with respect to official flows, not all would qualify. It depends on the terms. Official flows, which can be made on a bilateral basis (government to government) or through multilateral channels (for example, the World Bank, the IMF, the IDB), can vary from loans made on strict commercial terms to an outright grant. The term 'aid' tends to apply to assistance made available on less than strict market terms and therefore covers a wide spectrum of flows with differing degrees of concession and conditionality. The higher the grant element, the greater the degree of concession. The term Official Development Aid (ODA) tends to cover official flows made available on concessional terms, either bilaterally or through multilateral channels for the avowed aim of promoting economic development and welfare. In practice a grant element of at least 25 per cent is associated with such flows whether they are made directly or through state agencies. It is worth noting that the methods for computing the grant element in a loan can be quite controversial. Published figures relating to aid transfers generally do not mention that these figures include administrative costs and therefore do not reflect actual transfers. A major rationale for the provision of aid through multilateral arrangements is not only to reduce the element of 'political conditionality' but to reduce administrative costs.

A loan is often spoken of as being 'hard' or soft'. There are basically four main factors that determine the degree of 'hardness' or 'softness'. These are: (a) the currency in which the loan is to be repaid; (b) the grace period; (c) the repayment period; (d) the rate of interest. The grace period refers to the interval between disbursement of the loan and the date repayment is scheduled to begin. The repayment period, of course, is the length of time permitted for repayment of the loan. A loan may not have to be repaid either in part or in whole in which case it is a grant. A loan made in foreign exchange but repayable in local currency is a concession sometimes made to countries suffering from foreign exchange problems. The grace period provides a breathing space before repayment begins. The longer the grace and repayment periods, the softer the loan is said to be.

As indicated earlier, aid is rarely unconditional. In the case of a loan or grant the donor country or agency may not only 'tie' the assistance to a particular project, but stipulate the sources from which goods and services are to be procured, the nationality of the ships to be used for carriage of the goods, the nationality of the insurance carrier, the countries from which experts can be drawn, and so on. Donor countries go to great lengths to ensure that their own nationals and companies are not excluded from the opportunities offered by their aid effort. A loan may be for a particular project, or could take the form of a general purpose loan which could be used to support a development programme or a particular sector. A loan may be given to cover only the foreign exchange costs of a project or to pay for imports of capital goods relating to a number of projects outlined in general terms. The individual project approach has certain appealing features. One is that it is easier for donor countries or lending agencies to monitor the project. It also 'provides the lending or granting authority an opportunity to review in detail proposed projects in relation to alternative uses of capital and for its officials to involve themselves more deeply in the development plans for particular sectors of the economy.'[17] Despite this advantage of the project approach, it has been found that a project by itself may not have the expected impact, if complementary actions in related areas are not undertaken at the same time. The building of a school without the training of teachers is a case that comes readily to mind. The construction of agricultural access roads without other forms of assistance to farmers is another.

A HISTORICAL OVERVIEW

Traditionally, the imperial powers provided aid to their overseas territories and even with the granting of independence assistance continued in various forms including financial transfers, trade preferences, technical assistance, and so on. Following the end of the Second World War, the United States emerged as the strongest country in the world, and the Americans took the view that the rehabilitation of Europe was critical to the reconstruction of the world economy. In these early years the atmosphere existed for putting aid within a rational framework capable of addressing both construction and development. The emergence of the Soviet Union as a rival power, however, soon made security a critical concern. The link between economic assistance and security became further strengthened with the outbreak of the Korean War and later the Vietnam War. The ideological rivalry instigated an intense competition to prove that a capitalist based economy was superior to one based on central planning and vice versa. The need to create show-pieces was a major influence on aid dispensation in this period. It would be wrong, however, to conclude that the early intention on aid to raise living standards in poor countries was vitiated solely by superpower rivalry. Perhaps even more damaging was the emergence of the stance by donors that aid must generate a financial *quid pro quo* of some kind. In that context 'tying' became a salient feature of the aid effort. One of the central principles of the 'tying' practice revolves around the view that aid given by a donor country should not redound to the benefit of other developed states, even though as we saw earlier, this could reduce the value of the aid given.

The International Bank for Reconstruction and Development (IBRD) was initially intended to help the reconstruction effort in Europe, while the International Monetary Fund (IMF), was to be the instrument for bringing order to the world's monetary system. Both these institutions were cast in a particular mould in which the guiding objective was a more open world economic system. The fact that the Soviet Union very early chose to stay out of both the IMF and the World Bank indicated that it did not share the vision of its western allies. Soon after the war, the relationship changed from allies to major ideological rivals and aid became an effective tool in the competition for security advantage, sources of raw materials, markets, and so on.

By the mid-1950s, the reconstruction exercise in Europe was near completion and increasing attention began to be given to the emerging developing nations. By the late 1950s/early 1960s the number of donors was increasing. For the new aid givers, however, historical ties and commercial interests were more important influences in determining who received aid and who did not.

The Charter on which the United Nation is founded came into force on 24 October 1945. Its primary aim was and remains global peace. It was evident from the very beginning, however, that the UN could not escape concerns relating to relief, rehabilitation and economic assistance. Beginning in the 1940s a range of specialized institutions have come into being with the aim of addressing particular concerns. Among them are UNESCO, FAO, and the ILO. With the decolonization process there came on the world stage a large number of countries with differing levels of development located in various parts of the world. Raising the standard of living in these countries was seen as a major objective of international economic assistance. There was a basic misconception, however, that development was akin to 'reconstruction' and the same formula that lifted Europe and Japan from the ashes could be used to transform poor societies lacking basic infrastructure, industrial capacity and skills. The simplistic view was taken in these early years both by bilateral donors and the World Bank that growth necessarily leads to development.

That aid would be an effective mechanism in reducing poverty if not in narrowing the gap between rich and poor countries, was inspired by the American's effort in Europe in the early post-war years. Under the Marshall Plan (named after George Marshall, the then US Secretary of State), the US made available to Western Europe (including Germany) over US$12 billion between 1948 and 1952. The significant impact on the production sectors within a short space of time encouraged the view that aid could play a similar role in poor countries, even those lacking in skilled human resources. The dominant role that capital occupied in economic theory provided stimulus to the view that once capital was available, economic growth will take place. 'There is an unstated assumption that growth hinges on capital accumulation, and that additional capital would either provoke or facilitate a more rapid rate of economic development even in circumstances which no one would describe as involving a shortage of capital.'[18] Out of this grew the concept of the capital output ratio which was frequently (either explicitly or implicitly) used to estimate the amount of investment required to achieve a particular rate of growth. In the 1950s and 1960s estimating resource gaps formed an integral part of the planning process. It was generally believed that most developing countries suffered from both a 'savings gap' and from a 'foreign exchange gap'. Not only were domestic savings inadequate to meet investment needs, but given their narrow production base and the high import content of investment foreign exchange was required for economic development. Such thinking had a deep influence not only on development policy, but on the approach to international economic assistance.

THE AID EXPERIENCE

A major pastime beginning with the early post-war years has been to put the whole development problem neatly within the framework of a numbers game. How much aid is needed to bring about transformation in poor countries has long been an international guessing game. In order to raise living standards, it was often projected that per capita income or national product had to grow by a certain percentage. And if this growth rate was to be achieved savings and investment had to achieve a certain volume.

Foreign aid was often rationalized in this context. The fact that the scientific basis of these numbers was not always clearly established, resulted in a great deal of generalization and in a very simplistic approach to development issues, which tended to ignore critical factors bearing on the persistence of poverty.

In 1961 when the first United Nations Development decade was launched, it was proposed that the developed countries should aim at transferring one per cent of their national income to developing nations as financial assistance. This target (which incidentally covered both official and private capital flows) was subsequently adopted by the UNCTAD Conferences of 1964 and 1968 and by certain other forums. The Pearson Report,[19] for example, published in 1969 endorsed the one per cent target and suggested 1975 as the date for meeting it. It, however, went further and recommended that development assistance should be increased from 0.39 per cent of GNP in 1965 to 0.70 per cent in 1975 'and in no case not later than 1980'. When the Second UN Development Decade was launched in 1979, it was urged that 'each economically advanced country should endeavour to provide annually by 1972, for the benefit of developing countries resources transfers in the form of net disbursement of a minimum amount of one per cent of its Gross National Product at market prices, consideration being given to the special situation of countries which are net importers of capital.'[20] Within this overall target a proportion of 0.7 per cent of GNP was set for official development (ODA) transfers. Since the target was first initiated, most of the Development Assistance Committee (DAC) countries have accepted it in principle – some with a time frame, some without. A few countries (including the United States) have not committed themselves. At various international fora including the World Summit for Social Development held in Copenhagen in March 1995 and the Earth Summit in Rio in 1992, most countries have continued to call for new and additional resources for development assistance without committing themselves to a target date for implementing the 0.7 per cent benchmark.

Total net resource flows from all sources are estimated to have reached US$239 billion in 1995. Of this figure, DAC countries accounted for US$167 billion, or 70 per cent. (See Table 7.3). In terms of the composition of the US$167 billion, Official Development Assistance (ODA) accounted for US$59 billion, or 35 per cent, as compared to 65 per cent in 1985 and 35 per cent in 1980. Private flows (at market terms) which had dropped significantly in the mid-1980s accounted for 55 per cent in 1995. In real terms total net flow of financial resources from DAC countries to developing states fell by 8.3 per cent in 1995 over the previous year.

Table 7.3   The total net flow of financial resources from DAC countries
to developing countries and multilateral organizations by
type of flow, 1980–95

(Net disbursements at current prices and exchange rates)

		1980 US$ million	1985 US$ million	1995 US$ million
I.	Official Development Assistance	26 195	28 755	58 894
1.	Bilateral grants and grant-like flows	12 968	17 026	36 152
	of which: Technical co-operation	4 804	5 748	14 311
	Food Aid	680	1 291	1 326
	Emergency and distress relief[a]	353	602	3 062
	Debt forgiveness	1 156	280	3 678
	Administrative costs	808	981	2 889
2.	Bilateral loans	4 015	4 164	4 444
3.	Contributions to multilateral institutions	9 212	7 566	18 299
	of which: UN	2 176	2 349	4 260
	CEC	1 587	1 417	5 370
	IDA	3 106	1 948	5 405
	Regional development banks	1 717	1 246	1 301
II.	Other Official Flows	5 037	3 144	9 802
1.	Bilateral	5 144	3 232	9 014
2.	Multilateral–	−106	−88	788
III.	Private Flows at market terms	40 316	9 505	92 004
1.	Direct investment	10 127	6 523	53 602
2.	Bilateral portfolio investment	17 318	−4 466	33 517
3.	Multilateral portfolio investment	1 469	6 609	−387
4.	Export credits	11 402	839	5 272
IV.	Net grants by NGOs	2 386	2 884	5 973
	Total net flows	**73 935**	**44 288**	**166 674**
	Total net flows at 1994 prices and exchange rates[b]	**129 846**	**85 218**	**152 213**

[a] Except emergency food aid.
[b] Deflated by the total DAC deflator.

Source: OECD, *Development Cooperation,* various issues.

As can be seen in Table 7.3, ODA takes different forms, such as technical cooperation, food aid, bilateral loans, contribution to multilateral institutions, debt forgiveness, and so on. Certain points are worth noting in the Table. For example, while ODA in nominal terms increased by 105 per cent between 1985 and 1995, private flows (mainly investment) increased by almost 900 per cent. Again, while contributions to the multilateral institutions increased by 159 per cent between 1985 and 1992, assistance through these institutions has stagnated since, forcing them to curtail their operations. Bilateral loans have declined since 1992, while bilateral grants and grant-like flows have increased only slightly. When these trends are seen against a background of increasing prices and populations, recent aid flows become even less significant.

Table 7.4 shows that for the DAC countries as a group the ODA/GNP ratio has declined from the mid-1970s, averaging 0.28 per cent in 1994/95 as compared to 0.33 per cent in 1974/75. Only four countries (the Netherlands, Denmark, Sweden and Norway) have met the 0.7 per cent target. The performance of some countries (notably the United States, the United Kingdom, Canada and Australia) has been declining. On the other hand, the ratio for countries like Japan, France, and Austria has increased since the early 1970s. The strongest performance, however, has come from the Nordic countries, which as a group increased their ODA/GNP ratio from 0.51 per cent in 1974/75 to almost 0.80 per cent in 1994/95. The EU's figure (as a group) remained around 0.40 per cent over the period. It is worth noting that even for the Nordic countries, the ratio fell in 1995, as it did for a number of other countries.

In terms of volume (using 1994 prices and exchange rates), Japan was the largest dispenser of ODA with US$13.3 billion (23.5 per cent of the total) in 1994/95 followed by the United States with US$8.6 billion (15.2 per cent) and France US$8.0 billion (14.0 per cent). While aid from some countries (for example Japan and France) has been increasing from others (for example the United States) it has been declining. In real terms ODA of DAC countries increased by only 6.4 per cent between 1984/85 and 1994/95.

Through a number of successive DAC recommendations, members have been urged to provide an increasing grant element[21] in their aid to developing countries. The present target of 86 per cent (the terms test) for ODA commitments, which is still in effect, dates back to 1978. There is also a volume test. Any member who is 'significantly' (in practice 25 per cent) below the DAC average of ODA commitments, expressed as a percentage of GNP is regarded as not having complied with the recommendation.[22] In 1993/94 only three DAC countries (Japan, Belgium and Spain) did not meet the terms test. Some countries also failed to meet the volume test (among them the United States and Portugal). The position can change from year to year.

With respect to the least developed of the less developed countries (LLDCs) the 1978 Terms Recommendation had stipulated that the grant element of ODA commitments to those states should either average 90 per cent, or at least 86 per cent on a three-year average to each LLDC. In 1994 all the DAC countries met the requirements.[23]

Table 7.4 Long-term trends in DAC ODA, 1974/75–1994/95

	Volume of net ODA ($ million at 1994 prices and exchange rates)			Share of total DAC (at current prices and exchange rates, per cent)			Two-year averages net disbursements ODA as per cent GNP		
	1974–75	1984–85	1994–95	1974–75	1984–85	1994–95	1974–75	1984–85	1994–95
Australia	954	1 067	1 120	4.0	2.7	1.9	0.60	0.47	0.35
Austria	245	519	659	0.6	0.8	1.2	0.20	0.33	0.33
Belgium	881	1,059	810	2.7	1.6	1.5	0.55	0.56	0.35
Canada	1 559	2 062	2 146	6.5	5.7	3.7	0.51	0.50	0.40
Denmark	528	976	1,427	1.5	1.6	2.6	0.54	0.83	0.99
Finland	111	327	302	0.4	0.7	0.6	0.17	0.38	0.32
France	3 837	6 625	7 952	10.9	10.8	14.3	0.44	0.62	0.59
Germany	4 579	6 636	6 663	12.8	10.1	12.1	0.39	0.46	0.32
Ireland	21	67	125	0.1	0.1	0.2	0.09	0.23	0.27
Italy	642	2 239	2 129	1.6	3.9	3.7	0.11	0.27	0.21
Japan	5 419	10 592	13 317	9.3	14.3	23.5	0.24	0.31	0.28
Luxembourg	..	21	58			0.1	..	0.16	0.38
Netherlands	1 397	2 484	2 653	4.3	4.2	4.9	0.68	0.97	0.79
New Zealand	144	103	109	0.4	0.2	0.2	0.42	0.25	0.23
Norway	361	871	1,112	1.3	2.0	2.0	0.62	1.02	0.95

Table 7.4 (Continued)

	Volume of net ODA ($ million at 1994 prices and exchange rates)			Share of total DAC (at current prices and exchange rates, per cent)			Two-year averages net disbursements ODA as per cent GNP		
	1974–75	1984–85	1994–95	1974–75	1984–85	1994–95	1974–75	1984–85	1994–95
Portugal	..	..	270	..	..	0.5	..	0.05	0.31
Spain	..	344	1 251	..	0.5	2.2	..	0.09	0.26
Sweden	1 125	1 437	1 666	4.0	2.8	3.0	0.74	0.83	0.86
Switzerland	332	705	953	0.7	1.0	1.7	0.16	0.30	0.35
United Kingdom	2 736	2 716	3 094	6.9	5.2	5.4	0.39	0.33	0.29
United States	10 211	12 124	8 557	32.1	31.8	14.6	0.26	0.24	0.12
DAC TOTAL of which:	35 084	53 000	56 373	100.0	100.0	100.0	0.33	0.34	0.28
EU Members[a]	16 103	25 477	29 059	100.0	100.0	100.0	0.40	0.45	0.40

[a] Data are for DAC countries that were members of the EU in 1995, regardless of the date of their accession.
.. Not available

Source: OECD, Development Cooperation, 1996.

Aid from non-OECD donors has been declining in recent years accounting for less than 3 per cent of total ODA in 1994, as compared to over one-third in the mid-1970s. The two main developments explaining this situation are the less buoyant state of the Arab oil producing economies and the dissolution of the Soviet Union. The latter, which up to 1990 was disbursing over US$2000 million per year, is now more of a recipient than a donor. In 1980 ODA from Arab countries which is highly concentrated in Islamic states amounted to over 3 per cent of GNP, but this has fallen to less than one per cent in recent years. Aid from non-Arab countries such as India and China has also been declining. The share of GNP donated by countries such as Korea and Taiwan and Venezuela varies from year to year.

In terms of the geographical distribution of ODA Table 7.5 shows that two regions (Sub-Saharan Africa and Asia) receive over half of ODA from major sources. Sub-Saharan share increased from 30.8 per cent in 1983/84 to 36.6 per cent in 1993/94. In this group the Sahel region is the major recipient. Asia's share has remained at around 30 per cent, even though it accounts for about 70 per cent of the population. Some countries like China and India are not only givers of aid, but also recipients. While the share going to the Middle East has declined significantly in recent years, Latin America has been receiving a slightly higher portion than it did in 1980.

One of the salient aspects of the post-war aid experience is that aid does not necessarily flow to the countries that need it most. Aid is influenced by a variety of factors relating to both economic and non-economic factors such as security and political considerations. The early post-war aid effort was motivated to a large extent by a recognition that foreign assistance

Table 7.5 Total net receipts of ODA by region, 1983/84 and 1993/94
(percentages)

Regions	1983/84	1993/94	Share of population
Sub-Saharan Africa	30.8	36.6	12.0
Asia	29.5	30.2	69.5
Oceania	3.4	2.8	0.1
North Africa and Middle East	23.5	14.0	5.7
Latin America	11.0	11.0	10.6
Southern Europe	1.8	5.4	2.1
Total	100.0	100.0	100.0

Source: OECD, *Development Cooperation,* 1995.

may help a country overcome poverty. However, with the emergence of the Soviet Union as a world power with its own ideology, aid became increasingly an instrument of influence to secure the donors' objectives, while need became less of a consideration in determining resource flows. The threat of Soviet and Chinese expansionism in the 1950s and 1960s was a major influence on the distribution of United States' aid resources in this period. Political alignment could determine whether a country got assistance or not. So too could location in the context of military security. Whether a country was an important source of critical raw materials or commodities could also determine how much aid it got. There is no doubt that some aid was influenced by concerns about poverty, particularly by donors for whom security or political consideration carried little weight. For the two superpowers security considerations tended to rank high. The colonial powers such as France, Britain, the Netherlands, and Spain have tended to concentrate their assistance on colonies and former colonies. France's overseas colonies and dependencies, for instance, have always received a significant part of French aid. The assistance of the Scandinavian countries which are less influenced by special relationships is more widely spread.

THE EFFICACY OF AID

Aid usually involves the transfer of financial resources or goods and services from 'donor' (or the giving) countries to receiving countries. This can take place through direct channels or through intermediary institutions such as multilateral agencies. As such it involves a cost, but this can be overstated to the extent that donor countries get back some of the benefits. For the receiving countries on the other hand, the provision of goods and services or increased purchasing power represent an increase in wealth and an enhanced ability to make more effective use of domestic resources. As indicated earlier, rich countries make aid available to poor states for a variety of reasons (motives) related to political, security, moral, religious and economic considerations. The poor countries, however, tend to be less interested in motives and more on the volume of the aid and terms and forms on which aid is made available. Sometimes aid is addressed to short-term problems (for example, starvation) or difficulties stemming from natural or man-made disasters. At other times it is aimed at assisting long-term development effort.

Whatever may be the actual reasons for aid-giving one observer has argued that the case for aid can be made on the basis of three propositions:[24] (a) redistributive – this arises from a value judgement that the conditions of life in poor countries are not acceptable and the rich countries should assist in mitigating these conditions; (b) allocative – there are multiple imperfections in the market for capital investment and loan finance in developing countries. The result of this is that areas critical for development could be neglected; (c) stabilization – it can be argued that aid flows will augment world aggregate demand and relieve unemployment, particularly in developed countries. It is worth pointing out, however, that a theory of foreign economic assistance has never been successfully integrated into a theory of economic development, and the two-gap model with all its shortcomings remains the closest attempt to do so.[25]

There is widespread concern, both among donors and recipients, that aid has not had the kind of impact that proponents of this policy initially hoped it would have. This is evident in the number of reports and studies that have been done on the subject over the years.[26] Because of this the approach to aid has not been static. As more is learnt about the nature of underdevelopment both donors and multilateral aid institutions have been making adjustment to their policies not only in terms of operating procedures but also with respect to focus. Such changes are expected to be an on-going process as knowledge increases and more is learnt about the specific needs of poor countries. It should be noted that not all donor countries share the same priorities. Among the objectives which donors claim to support are the following:

1. protection of the environment;
2. prospects and programmes which promote sustainable development;
3. human resource development;
4. poverty alleviation and social sector development;
5. self-help effort;
6. regional integration;
7. development of democratic systems;
8. peace;
9. guaranteeing human rights;
10. enhancing the role of non-governmental organizations (NGOs);
11. improving national governance;
12. development of national technical capacity.

The UNDP has noted, however that donors' programmes do not appear to be directly linked with those objectives. In other words what they say they want to do and what happens in practice are two entirely different things. Let us examine a few of these objectives. With respect to poverty reduction, the UNDP sees the failure here as stemming from the fact that most aid allocations are country-focused rather than objective-focused.[27] The facts show that aid is not targeted at the poor. Donors send less than one-third of development assistance to the ten most populous countries, which are home to two-thirds of the world's poor. One consequence of this is that the richest 40 per cent of the developing world receives twice as much aid per capita as the poorest 40 per cent. The facts also show that aid is not on priority areas of human development, as is often claimed. Bilateral donors direct only 7 per cent of their aid to such priority areas as basic education, primary health care, rural water supplies, nutrition programmes and family planning services. The ratio, of course, varies from country to country. The proportion for multilateral institutions is better, around 16 per cent. The objective of providing technical assistance to build up the technical capacity of developing countries is one of the most scandalous. Technical assistance seems to have built little national capacity in the poorest countries. The UNDP has noted that Sub-Saharan Africa which has been receiving more than US$3 billion a year in technical assistance is associated with human development indicators which are among the lowest in the world. 'Perhaps most disturbing is that, after 40 years, 90 per cent of the US$12 billion a year in technical assistance is still spent on foreign expertise – despite the fact that national experts are now available in many fields.'[28]

The post-war experience with aid indicates that factors affecting the efficacy of aid can be found in the attitudes and approaches of both donors and recipients. The former often take the position that they know more about the situation in poor countries than the latter themselves, and this informs policies adopted with respect to which sectors should be assisted and where priority should be placed in the planning process. Very often the projects chosen are for their visibility and not for the advancement of the objective being targeted. Economic assistance which are avowedly aimed at problems of poverty are often designed with the intention of advancing the interests of the donors. Goods and services often have to be procured from the latter at higher costs than could be obtained elsewhere. Even though their training and background limit their efficacy, consultants used are generally from donor countries. With respect to the volume of aid provided to countries, this is influenced not so much by need, as indicated earlier, but by commercial and strategic interests.

Recipients are often not in a strong bargaining position, and accept assistance even if they disagree with the terms of availability or do not share the perceptions of the donors. The projects they themselves might choose are not always those that can have the greatest impact on development. After more than twenty-five years of political independence in some cases there are a number of poor countries which have few people with expertise in critical areas such as the ability to do feasibility studies, manage a project, make project appraisal and to implement or even formulate or design a project. With the absence of certain kinds of skills the potential for absorbing aid (that is, making the best use of the resources provided) has been limited in many cases. Poor planning and corruption in some instances have also played a role in reducing the impact of aid. Domestic bureaucratic inefficiency and red tape also explain why only limited advantage is sometimes taken of foreign assistance. This is particularly so with respect to scholarships and the use of local consultants. In many countries even informing nationals of the availability of scholarships or training courses is subject to such bureaucratic red tape that many opportunities go begging when deadlines for applications are not met. Because governments insist that all assistance from foreign governments or international organizations, whether intended for the public or private sector, should pass through the state bureaucracy, it is impossible for citizens to express an interest when they may not even be aware of the existence of the opportunities. When offers are used for political patronage the best qualified applicants may not be chosen, and this has implications in terms of the ultimate impact of aid. With respect to consultants, not many countries know what expertise is available locally so that when consultants are required, it is habitual to turn to foreign sources even though the particular skills needed may be available at home. Because aid may not be reaching the people for whom it is intended, donors and international organizations are making increased use of non-governmental organizations (NGOs).

CONCLUDING OBSERVATIONS

Even though there is a constant call to increase the volume of aid resources, full advantage has not been taken of offers of financial and other forms of assistance. This often stems not only from the lack of alertness on the part of poor countries, but from cumbersome rules and regulations underlying access to aid funds. In some cases the conditions to be met are highly unrealistic. These conditions are often formulated on the assumption that all poor countries are at the same level of development or all have the same skill and resource capacity and therefore can all respond in the same way to offers of assistance.

With the end of the Cold War, it was widely believed that there would be a reduction in military expenditure and this would result in the increased availability of resources (the peace dividend) for economic development. There is some controversy over the approach that should be taken in calculating the peace dividend.[29] One calculation was that if the developed market economies, the economies in transition and China had spent the same amount on defence in real terms in the years 1988 to 1994 as they had in 1987 they would have spent a total of US$807 billion more on defence in this period than they in fact did. The comparable figure for developing countries was US$126 billion, giving a cumulative saving of US$933 billion.[30] According to the UNDP it is difficult to track where these funds went. 'Most of the savings appear to have been committed to budget deficit reductions and non-development expenditure, rather than to special development or to environmental improvements.'[31] It is interesting to note that while the industrial countries are urging developing countries to spend less money on arms, they themselves are intensely competing among themselves for the arms business of developing nations.

With respect to the effects of resource transfers from the developed nations, there are questions about the significance of these in the light of the reverse flows taking place. For example, with respect to both official transfers and private capital it has been estimated that the net flow out of Africa between 1984 and 1994 was in the region of US$21 billion. In the case of Latin America and the Caribbean it was US$161 billion.[32] This applies not only to bilateral assistance, but to the multilateral agencies as well. For instance net lending by the IMF to developing countries between 1984 and 1994 was minus US$11.5 billion.[33] In other words repayment of past IMF loans in recent years tended to exceed new resource flows at a time when donors are calling for increased funds to be made available to poor countries in the context of their structural adjustment efforts. World Bank lending in some parts of the world is also associated with negative net transfers. For instance, in Latin America and the Caribbean interest and charges paid to the Bank in the 1990–95 period exceeded net disbursements by US$14 billion.[34]

Given this situation with respect to negative resource transfers, attention has once more turned to an old issue – trade versus aid. Certain commodities from particular developing countries which were marketed under special arrangements in the heyday of colonialism continue to be protected even today as a form of special assistance. Such protection may extend to both market share and/or price paid. Even though the prices received, as in the case of sugar in the Lomé Convention, may be lower than the cost of production, the fact that they are higher than the world market price does result in a level of financial transfer greater than would otherwise be the case. Beneficial as these traditional arrangements are to certain developing countries, however, they are now under threat in the context of the moves towards a more open world trading system. A case in point is the special arrangements enjoyed by certain Caribbean banana producers in the European Community under the Lomé Convention. Prodded by its transnational companies operating in Latin America the United States Government has lodged a complaint to the World Trade Organization to the effect that these arrangements violate international trade agreements.

While recognizing the value of preferential arrangements to high-cost producer developing countries generally, both favoured and non-favoured have long been pleading for greater access to the markets of the rich countries for their non-traditional exports. On the surface, arrangements such as the Generalized Preferential Schemes, the Lomé Convention, the US Caribbean Basin Initiative, CARIBCAN do offer additional opportunities to particular countries. In most cases, however, this access is qualified in terms of the life of the arrangements, the quantity of particular products or groups of products that can be exported, when they can be exported, local value content, and so on. Many forms of non-tariff barriers tend to reduce effective access. Some sectors of particular interest to developing countries (for example, agriculture, textiles, and clothing) are highly protected in the rich countries, notwithstanding their crusade for greater competition in world trade. The Development Committee of the World Bank and the IMF estimates that the 'removal of all industrial country barriers to trade would increase developing-country income by about twice the general value of official development assistance from OECD countries,' that is, more than US$100 billion in lost revenues to developing countries each year.[35] A study in the 1980s by the IMF suggest that a complete liberalization would enable developing countries to increase their textiles by 82 per cent and those of clothing by 93 per cent.[36]

This protection persists in the context of a widespread recognition that increased trade is essential not only if poor countries are to be able to service their foreign debt, but if they are to grow and become increasingly self-reliant in the long term. Structural Adjustment Programmes supported by the major international financial institutions and donor countries put great emphasis on developing a diversified and competitive export sector. But without access to the markets of the industrial countries the attainment of these objectives become more difficult. Being able to make a product that can compete in terms of price and quality does not necessarily ensure that it can be traded in a world where barriers can arbitrarily be imposed to protect particular interest groups operating high cost production structures.

The question does not only relate to manufactured goods. A large number of developing countries depend on one, two or three commodities for their export earnings which in the short term help to define their import capacity. The prices of these commodities undergo severe fluctuations from period to period without any concerted effort being made to stabilize prices. In a situation of falling prices developing countries would find themselves having to export a larger volume for a given amount of foreign exchange. With the steady increase in import prices, this situation results in an effective transfer of real resources from poor nations. What this amounts to is that aid transfers can be offset by outflows taking place through trade and other financial mechanism on a scale that makes nonsense of the whole aid effort. It may well be argued that international price support programmes for the products of developing countries amounts to a form of aid financed by consumers in the importing countries.[37] Even if one were to accept this argument, such implicit transfers would not be under the same kind of donor influence associated with direct assistance.

It is clear from the earlier discussion that the post-war aid effort cannot be described as an unqualified success. The question is being asked if the developed countries are really interested in helping poor nations to develop, and given the shortcomings associated with direct transfers, why are they so reluctant in extending the kind of assistance which can have a more significant impact on the development problem. One area for action is the more effective opening up of their markets – a recommendation that is made year after year. Opportunities 'for increased exports can raise real incomes by making possible a fuller utilization of domestic resources and a realization of the gains from specialization and trade.'[38] Freer world trade, it has long been argued, benefits not only the exporting countries but the importing countries as well. Greater trading opportunities for developing countries may well prove the most effective means of redistributing world income and reducing poverty in these countries.

The failure of most developing countries to attract private investment on any significant scale and given prevailing low domestic saving rates, external assistance can still play a critical role in the development process. The end of the cold war affords the opportunity for a more rational dispensation of aid, notwithstanding the greater competition coming from the states of the former Soviet Union and Eastern Europe. The experience of the early 1990s, however, has shown that there is a tendency to tie aid to a wider range of conditionality which does not sufficiently take into account the social conditions emanating from certain types of policies. The imposition of different sets of conditionalities by different donors and agencies all assumedly pursuing the same or similar aims has created a nightmarish setting for many a poor country. A greater local input in reform policies and greater co-ordination among aid givers can enhance the effectiveness of aid.

Notes

1. S. Brown, *Foreign Aid in Practice* (London: Pinter Reference, 1990), p. XV.
2. *Ibid.*, p. 137.
3. The Development Assistance Committee (DAC) is one of a number of specialized committees set up by the Organization for Economic Cooperation and Development (OECD) which came into being in September 1961, renaming and extending the Organization for European Economic Cooperation (OEEC) set up in the early post-war years for the coordination of the economic recovery programme of Western Europe.

   The aim of the OECD is to promote policies designed:
   ● to achieve the highest sustainable economic growth and employment and a rising standard of living in member countries, while maintaining financial stability, and thus to contribute to the development of the world economy;
   ● to contribute to sound economic expansion in member as well as non-member countries in the process of economic development and
   ● to contribute to the expansion of world trade in a multilateral, non-discriminatory basis in accordance with international obligations.

   The members of DAC are Australia, Austria, Belgium, Canada, Denmark, Finland, France, Germany, Ireland, Italy, Japan, the Netherlands, New Zealand, Norway, Portugal, Spain, Sweden, Switzerland, the United Kingdom, the United States and the Commission of the European Communities. DAC members have agreed to secure an expansion of aggregate volume of resources made available to developing countries and to improve their effectiveness. To this end, members periodically review together both the amount and the nature of their contributions to aid programmes, bilateral and multilateral, and consult each other on all other relevant aspects of their development assistance policies.
4. See S. Brown, *op. cit.*, p. XV.
5. T. Mende, *From Aid to Recolonization* (London: George G. Harrap & Co., 1973), p. 47.
6. UNDP, *Human Development Report, 1994* (New York: Oxford University Press, 1994), p. I.
7. *Ibid.*, pp. 1–2.
8. *Ibid.*
9. See UN, *World Economic and Social Survey 1996* (New York: United nations, 1996), p. 307.
10. UNDP Report (1994), *op. cit.*, p. 35.
11. UN, *Global Outlook 2000* (New York: United Nations, 1990), p. 291–2.
12. *Ibid.*, p. 302.
13. See *World Bank Atlas*, 1996, pp. 18–19.
14. UNDP Report (1994) *op. cit.*, p. 66.
15. It is estimated that at least 35 million people from the South have taken up residence in the North in the past three decades – and around one million

join them each year. The number of international illegal immigrants is expected to be around 15–30 million. The number of refugees is estimated to be around 19 million. See UNDP Report (1994), *op. cit.*, p. 47.

16. Between 1987 and 1984, it is estimated developing countries spent US$1034 billion on military expenditures. See UNDP Report (1994), *op. cit.*, p. 48.

17. Joint Economic Committee, Congress of the United States, *Economic Policies Toward Less Developed Countries*, Studies prepared by R. F. Mikesell and R. L. Allen, US Government Printing Office, Washington, DC, 1961, pp. 11–30. Reprinted in G. M. Meier, *Leading Issues in Development Economics, Selected Materials and Commentary* (New York: Oxford University Press, 1964), pp. 138–42.

18. A. K. Cairncross, 'The Place of Capital in Economic Progress,' in L. H. Dupriez (ed.) *Economic Progress*, Papers and Proceedings of a Round Table held by the International Economic Association, Louvain, 1955,pp. 235, 236–7, 245–8. Reprinted in G. M. Meier, *op. cit.*

19. Partners in Development: Report of the Commission on International Development (Washington, DC: Praeger Publishers, 1969), p. 144.

20. 'International Development Strategy for the United Nations Developing Decade,' Resolution adopted by the 25th Session of the United Nations General Assembly, New York, 1970, A. Res/2626 (XXV).

21. The grant element reflects the financial terms of a commitment, namely interest rate, maturity and grace period. It measures the concessionality or 'softness' of a loan, in the form of the present value of an interest rate below the market rate over the life of a loan. Conventionally, the market rate is taken as 10 per cent. Thus the grant element is nil for a loan carrying an interest rate of 10 per cent; it is 100 per cent for a grant; and it lies between these two limits for a soft loan. If the face value of a loan is multiplied by its grant element, the result is referred to as the grant equivalent of that loan. See OECD, *Development Cooperation 1993 Report, op. cit.*, p. 99.

A 'grant-like' flow is a transaction in which the donor country retains formal title to repayment but has expressed its intention in the commitment to hold the proceeds of repayment in the borrowing country.

22. *Ibid.*
23. *Ibid.*
24. P. Mosley, *Overseas Aid: Its Defence and Reform* Brighton: Wheatsheaf Books Ltd, 1987), p. 12.
25. See A. O. Krueger, C. Michalopoulos and V. Ruttan, *Aid and Development* (Baltimore: The Johns Hopkins University Press, 1985), p. 43.
26. See, for example, *North South: A Programme for Survival*, Report of the Independent Commission on International Development Issues under the Chairmanship of Willy Brandt (Cambridge, MA: MIT Press, 1980).
27. See UNDP, *Human Development Report*, 1994, *op. cit.*, pp. 76–93.
28. *Ibid.*
29. See UN *World Economic Survey, 1995*, (New York: UN, 1995), p. 196.
30. *Ibid.*
31. See UNDP, *Human Development Report*, 1994, *op. cit.*, p. 59.
32. UN, *World Economic Survey, 1995, op. cit.*, p. 44.
33. *Ibid.*, p. 33.

34. World Bank, *Annual Report*, 1995, p. 92.
35. OECD, *Development Cooperation, 1991 Report*, (Paris, 1991), p. 18.
36. See UNDP, *Human Development Report*, 1994, *op. cit.*, p. 66.
37. See R. F. Mikesell, *The Economics of Foreign Aid* (Chicago: Aldine Publishing Co., 1968), p. 198.
38. *Ibid.*

Further Reading

Bhagwati, J. and R. S. Eckaus, *Foreign Aid*, Penguin Books, Harmondsworth, 1990.
Brown, S., *Foreign Aid in Practice*. Pinter Reference, London, 1990.
Byrnes, F. C., *Americans in Technical Assistance*, Praeger, New York, 1965.
Carter, J. R., *The Net Cost of Soviet Foreign Aid*, Praeger, New York, 1969.
Clark, P. G., *American Aid for Development*, Praeger, New York, 1972.
Coffin, F. M., *Witness for Aid*, Houghton Mifflin, Boston, 1964.
Ghosh, P. K., *Foreign Aid and Third World Development*, Greenwood Press, Connecticut, 1984. This work contains a comprehensive bibliography on foreign aid.
Gray, C. S., *Resource Flows to Less Developed Countries*, Praeger, New York, 1969.
Griffin, K., *Financing Development in Latin America*, Macmillan and Co. Ltd, London, 1971.
Hancock, J., *Lords of Poverty*, Macmillan, London, 1989.
Hawkins, E. K., *The Principles of Development Aid*, Penguin Books, Harmondsworth, 1970.
Hayter, T., *Aids as Imperialism*, Penguin Books, Harmondsworth, 1971.
Hiemenz, U., 'Aid Has Not Lived Up To Expectations' *Intereconomics*, Vol. 21, No. 4, July/August 1986, pp. 176–180.
Hyden, G. and S. Reutlinger, 'Foreign Aid in a Period of Democratization: The Case of Politically Autonomous Food Fnds', *World Development*, Vol. 20 (No. 7, September 1992), pp. 1253–60.
Independent Commission on International Development Issues under the Chairmanship of Willy Brandt, *North–South: A Program for Survival*, MIT Press, Cambridge, MA, 1980.
Khan, H. and E. Hoshino 'The Impact of Foreign Aid on the Fiscal Behaviour of LDC Governments', *World Development*, Vol. 20 (No. 10, October 1992), pp. 1481–88.
Krueger, A. O., *Aid and Development*, The Johns Hopkins University Press, Baltimore, 1989.
McKinley, R. D. and A. Maughan *Aid and Arms to the Third World*, Frances Pinter (Publishers), London, 1984.
Meier, G. M., *Problems of Cooperation for Development*, Oxford University Press, London, 1974.
Mende, T., *From Aid to Recolonization*, George G. Harrap and Co. Ltd, London, 1973.
Mikesell, R., *The Economics of Foreign Aid*, Aldine Publishing Co., Chicago, 1968.
Mosley, P., *Overseas Aid: Its Defence and Reform*, Wheatsheaf Books Ltd, Brighton, Sussex, 1987.

Mosley, P. *et al.*, *Aid and Power*, Vol. 1, Routledge, New York, 1991.

Payer, C., *The Debt Trap*, Penguin Books, Harmondsworth, 1974.

Randel, J. and T. German, 'The Realities of Aid: Shrinking Volume and Declining Quality', *Third World Economics*. November, Vol. 76 (November 1993), pp. 15–20.

Report of the South Commission *The Challenge to the South*, Oxford University Press, New York, 1990.

Ridell, R. C., *Foreign Aid Reconsidered*, The Johns Hopkins University Press, Baltimore, 1987.

Seligson, M. A. (eds), *The Gap Between Rich and Poor: Contending Perspectives on the Political Economy of Development*, Westview Press, Boulder, 1984.

Stockmann, R., 'The Long Term Impact of Development Aid: A Neglected Field of Research', *Development and Cooperation* (No. 5, 1993), pp. 21–22.

Takagi, S. I., *From Recipient to Donor: Japan's Official Aid Flows, 1945–1990 and Beyond*. Princeton Essays in International Finance (No. 196), Princeton University, Princeton, 1995.

Toye, J., *Dilemmas of Development*, Basil Blackwell Ltd, Oxford, 1989.

Uvin, P., 'Regime, Surplus, and Self-Interest: The International Politics of Food Aid', *International Studies Quarterly*, Vol. 36 (No. 3, September 1992), pp. 293–312.

Waller, P., 'Aid and Conditionality', *Development and Cooperation* (No. 1, 1994), pp. 4–5.

White, H., 'A Macro-Economic Impact of Development Aid: A Critical Survey', *Journal of Development Studies*, Vol. 28 (No. 2, January 1992), pp. 163–240.

Wilmshurst, J., P. Ackroyd and R. Eyben, *Implications for U.K. Aid of Current Thinking on Poverty Reduction*, Institute of Development Studies, Brighton, 1992.

8 External Development Finance and the Multilateral Financial Institutions

INTRODUCTION

The search for ideas which reduce or eliminate poverty has produced a voluminous literature in the post-war period, as an increasing number of former colonial territories became independent states. One recent study has noted that thinking on development has shifted repeatedly during the past forty years.[1] For most of the post-war years a large role for the state was the dominant strategy. The current emphasis is on the market-driven or market-friendly model which points to the private sector as the engine of growth. In this model, government's responsibility is not to manage development in detail, but to provide a stable macroeconomic foundation and 'to do more in those areas where markets alone cannot be relied upon.'[2] Essentially this means improving the social and economic infrastructure and promoting a framework for sustainable development. It also implies that capital spending by the government is a crucial variable. There are areas for which the private sector will not take responsibility.

Many countries save and invest little, apparently because incomes are low. A long held premise underlying international economic assistance is that if countries are to break out of the vicious circle of poverty, they would have to raise the level of investment. Foreign savings could help do this. The fastest growing economies in the world are saving and investing over 30 per cent of their GDP. Most developing countries are associated with saving rates of less than 20 per cent. Because of the pressures on current expenditure, governments' contribution to the domestic saving effort in a large number of developing countries is nil or negligible. Heavy debt servicing commitments in some cases, have not only reduced the governments' ability to provide an acceptable quality of social services, but has also contributed to the neglect of environmental concerns and the deterioration of the physical infrastructure.

To complement the foreign assistance provided on a bilateral basis, a number of multilateral financial institutions have been established in various parts of the world to provide not only financial but technical assistance. Besides the World Bank which has a global clientele, several regional development banks have been established, and modeled on the World Bank. These institutions not only draw resources from capital contributions of their members (some of whom may be non-borrowing members), but also receive contributions in the form of loans (concessionary and non-concessionary) and grants. They also borrow in international capital markets, and because of this they tend to pay particular attention to their own credit rating which could affect their ability to attract new funds. Development banks are a special kind of financial intermediaries specializing in medium- to long-term lending aimed at assisting economic development. They are not only mobilizers of resources, but increasingly provide technical assistance and advice on macroeconomic policy. The latter two functions are designed to help borrowing countries to make effective use of available resources. The concept of a regional development bank has additional advantages, both from the point of view of donors and borrowers. From the donor's perspective such institutions are often seen as a convenient way of providing assistance. The multilateral institutions reduce the degree of political conditionality usually associated with bilateral assistance. Also, a well structured and efficiently run development institution is likely to attract a greater volume of funds than its borrowing members might be able to raise in an individual capacity. The potential financial backing in the form of callable capital from its members enhances a bank's borrowing capacity. Not to be ignored, too, is the fact that over time a regionally based institution will be able to build up a store of information on its clients that will enable it to make informed decisions which take into account the peculiarities of the countries it serves. The bank itself is likely to be endowed with technical personnel whose skills can be put at the disposal of its clients when the occasion so requires.

The pattern of private flows to developing countries in recent times has placed greater importance on official assistance which is the only source of foreign assistance available to some countries. It has been estimated that 75 per cent of private capital flows to the developing world are concentrated in just twelve countries (and East Asia receives 60 per cent of the total).[3] In the following section, we provide some insights into the structure and significance of the major multilateral financial institutions in the global framework of development finance.

THE WORLD BANK

The 'World Bank' is commonly used in reference to two institutions; the International Bank for Reconstruction and Development (IBRD) and its affiliate the International Development Association (IDA). There are two other affiliates: the International Finance Corporation (IFC) and the Multilateral Investment Guarantee Agency (MIGA). These four institutions now make up what is sometimes referred to as the 'World Bank Group.'

The IBRD, like the IMF, was a product of the United Nations Monetary and Financial Conference held in Bretton Woods, New Hampshire, USA in 1944, and its functions, as can be seen in its name, was to assist in the 'reconstruction' of the war-ravaged economies of Europe and Japan and in the 'development' of the 'less developed' countries by providing loans and technical assistance. The World Bank now sees its central purpose as the promotion of 'economic and social progress in developing nations by helping raise productivity so that their people may live a better and fuller life.'[4]

The Bank was set up with an authorized capital of US$10 billion and had an initial membership of 45, of which 32 were European or Latin American. At the end of June 1996, the Bank's membership (ownership) had grown to 180 countries and had a subscribed capital of US$180.6 billion of which US$11.0 billion was paid up.[5] The total assets of the Bank at the above date was US$152 billion, of which outstanding loans accounted for 70 per cent. Borrowings in the world capital markets represent a major source of funds for the Bank. Out of a total liability of US$152.0 billion, loans outstanding amounted to US$96.7 billion or 64 per cent as compared to 7.2 per cent for equity. A substantial contribution to the Bank's resources also comes from retained earnings and the flow of repayments on its loans.

Membership of the IMF is a prerequisite for membership of the Bank. Each member has 250 votes plus one additional vote for each share of stock held. The subscription by member countries of the IBRD is related to each member's quota in the IMF, which is designed to reflect the country's relative strength. Since capital subscriptions determine votes, the Bank is controlled by a few countries. Out of the total 1.5 million votes at the end of June 1996, the United States held the single largest (17.20 per cent) with Japan (6.10 per cent), Germany (4.71 per cent), France (4.52 per cent) and the United Kingdom (4.52 per cent).

Under the Articles of Agreement of the Bank, all the powers of the Bank are vested in a Board of Governors consisting of one governor from each member country. With the exception of certain powers specifically reserved to them by the Articles of Agreement[6] the Governors of the Bank have delegated their authority to a Board of Executive Directors that performs its duties on a full-time basis at the Bank's headquarters in Washington, that is, it functions in continuous session. The Board consists of 24 executive directors, each of whom selects an alternate. Five of the executive directors are appointed by the five members who have the largest number of shares of capital stock, while the rest are elected by the governors representing the other member countries. These countries are grouped in 19 constituencies, each represented by an Executive Director who is elected by a country or group of countries. The number of countries each of these 19 Directors represent varies widely. The members themselves decide how they will be grouped. The country groups are more or less formed along geographic lines, but political and cultural factors play a part in how they are constituted.

According to a long standing custom, the Bank's President is nominated by the Executive Director representing the United States, but selected by the Executive Directors. Traditionally, the President of the World Bank is a United States' citizen. The present President, Mr James D. Wolfensohn was appointed as the Bank's ninth President in March 1995 for a term of five years, beginning in June 1995.

The President, who is chairman of the Board of Executive Directors, is responsible for the Bank's day to day management and, subject to the general control of the Executive Directors, for its organization, and for the appointment and dismissal of staff. He is assisted by three Managing Directors who oversee operations in specific areas. Formal votes by the Executive Directors are rare since most decisions of the board are reached by consensus. The Executive Directors are responsible for the conduct of the general operation of the Bank, which includes deciding on Bank policy within the framework of the Articles of Agreement and approving all loan and credit proposals. The President is the chief of the operating staff of the Bank and conducts, under the direction of the Executive Directors, the ordinary business of the Bank.

THE INTERNATIONAL DEVELOPMENT ASSOCIATION (IDA)

By the late 1950s, it was apparent that the terms governing the IBRD lending was too onerous for the poorer developing countries and in 1960 the IDA was established to provide 'softer' loans to these countries. Its aim is to promote economic development in the less developed areas of the world included in the IDA's membership by providing financing on terms which are more flexible and bear less heavily on the balance of payments than those of conventional loans. In some ways the IDA is indistinguishable from the IBRD. Like the latter, it helps to finance development projects. IDA has the same staff as the IBRD and the President of the World Bank is also the President of IDA. The IDA, however, has its own Articles of Agreement, different provisions for paying in capital subscriptions, different voting structures, and separate financial resources. The fundamental difference between the two organizations is the way they obtain the funds they lend, and the terms in which they lend to developing countries. The IBRD raises most of its resources on the world's financial markets and lends to developing countries at interest rates somewhat below those of commercial banks and with longer maturities. On the other hand, IDA's funds come from subscriptions, general replenishments from the IDA's more industrialized and developed members and transfers from the net earnings of the IBRD. IDA's loans are referred to as credit to distinguish them from IBRD's resources.

All development credits are made to or guaranteed by member governments or to the government of a territory of a member (except for development credits that have been made to regional development banks for the benefit of members or territories of members of the IDA). Development credits are interest free but carry a service charge of 0.75 per cent, generally have 35 to 40-year maturities and a 10-year grace period for principal repayments. Although IDA does not charge interest, it does charge a small administrative fee of 0.75 per cent against the outstanding balance of credits to meet administrative expenses. There is also a commitment fee of 0.5 per cent or 50 basis points, but this has been waived since 1989. IDA's credits have a grant element of about 85 per cent.

The IDA has become known as the largest single multilateral source of concessional lending to low income countries. Its resources are normally replenished every three years from its richer members.[7] Originally each donor's grant was proportional to its capital in the IBRD. Subsequently, donor contributions to IDA replenishment have been determined through negotiations taking account a number of economic criteria, including donors' GNP, GNP per capita and trade-related indicators.

Membership in the IDA is open to all members of the IBRD. IDA's membership reached 159 at the end of June 1996. Membership is divided into Part I and Part II members. Part I members are non-borrowing members. The five members with the largest voting power in 1996 were the United States (14.98 per cent), Japan (10.76 per cent), Germany (6.97 per cent), and the United Kingdom (5.04 per cent). Total development funds from all sources at the end of June, 1996 amounted to US$100.4 billion, of which US$89.4 billion (89.0 per cent) came from subscriptions and paid in contributions.[8] Outstanding development credits amounted to US$72.8 billion (72.5 per cent) of total assets (total applications of development resources).

Countries are eligible for IDA assistance on the basis of (a) relative poverty and (b) lack of creditworthiness. Per capita income is a major consideration. In order to quality for lending on IDA terms, a country's per capita income must be below a certain level, and this limit varies from year to year. The operational cut-off for IDA eligibility for FY 96 is a GNP per capita of US$865 (in 1994 US dollars) using World Bank Atlas methodology (base period 1992–94). To receive IDA resources countries also meet tests of performance. In exceptional circumstances, IDA extends temporarily to countries that are above the operational cut-off and are undertaking major adjustment efforts but are not creditworthy for IBRD lending. An exception has also been made for specific small island economies which otherwise would have little or no access to Bank Group assistance because they lack creditworthiness. For such countries, IDA funding is considered case by case for the financing of projects and adjustment programs designed to strengthen creditworthiness. Basically, World Bank members fall into three categories: (a) countries eligible for IBRD funds only; (b) countries eligible for a blend of IBRD and IDA funds; and (c) countries eligible for IDA funds only. Depending on changes in per capita income and performance, countries may be moved from one category to another. As of June 1995 there were 62 in the first category, 15 in the second and 63 in the third. In the first category are countries like Mexico, Brazil, Chile, Jamaica, Trinidad and Tobago, Mauritius, Antigua and Belize. Among those in the second are Nigeria, India, Pakistan, China, Dominica, Grenada, St Vincent and the Grenadines and St Lucia. Among those in the third category are Bolivia, Solomon Islands, Ghana, Guyana, Haiti and Ethiopia.

Until the end of June 1991 the cumulative lending operations of the IBRD and IDA had reached US$268 billion. Between 1992 and 1996 total commitments of the two institutions amounted to US$110.3 billion while disbursements were of the order of US$87.9 billion. Of the US$14.7 billion committed by the IBRD in FY 1996, almost 75 per cent was raised in the world's financial markets. The IDA's commitment amounted to US$6.9 billion.

The IBRD loans generally have a grace period of five years and are repayable over fifteen to twenty years. The interest rates charged are calculated in accordance with a 'guideline related to its cost of borrowing.' The Bank lends only in the currencies in which it borrows and closely matches the currencies of its retained earnings to those of its loans. This minimizes risk due to fluctuations in exchange rates. All Bank loans include a small commitment fee of 0.75 per cent of undisbursed balances, but the Bank can waive part of this.

The Bank's Charter has laid down certain rules which must govern the IBRD's operations. It must lend only for productive purposes and must stimulate economic growth in the developing countries in which it lends. In other words the Bank provides assistance to those projects that promise high real rates of economic return to the country. It must pay due regard to the prospect for repayment. Each loan is made to government or must be guaranteed by the government concerned. The use of loans cannot be restricted to purchase in any particular member country. And the IBRD's decision to lend must be based on economic considerations alone. The Bank's loans should not be influenced by political or other non-economic influences or considerations. As a matter of policy the IBRD does not reschedule payments.

An important part of the Bank's operations relate to its co-financing activities with donor governments, official development agencies, and export credit agencies. The volume of co-financing anticipated in support of World Bank-assisted operations in FY 1996 amounted to US$8.35 billion.

Though the Bank was not set up to make profit, it has made a profit in every year since 1947. Its net income over the last six years (1991–95) has averaged over one billion US dollars per year. The Bank claims that the generation of income and retained earnings contributes to its high credit standing and hence enables it to raise funds on better-than-average terms in the capital markets. The Bank does not pay dividends to its shareholders – member governments. A portion of its profits is used to support IDA activities.

THE INTERNATIONAL FINANCIAL CORPORATION (IFC)

The International Financial Corporation (IFC) was established in 1956 to assist the economic development of less developed countries by promoting growth in the private sector of their economies and helping to mobilize domestic and foreign capital for this purpose. Membership in the IBRD is a prerequisite for membership in the IFC which is legally and financially independent, though it works very closely with other members of the World Bank Group. It has its own Articles of Agreement, shareholders, financial structure, management and staff. The IFC's 'particular focus is to promote economic development by encouraging the growth of productive private enterprise and efficient capital markets in member countries. The IFC finances private sector ventures and projects in developing countries in partnership with private investors and through its advisory work, helps governments create conditions that stimulate the flow of both domestic and foreign private savings and investment'.[9] The IFC provides loans, equity investments and arranges quasi-equity instruments. It finances the creation of new companies as well as the expansion or modernization of established ones. It not only acts as a catalyst in bringing private investors together in projects, but also functions as a business in partnership with the private sector. Providing advisory services and technical assistance to business and governments on investment-related matters is an important part of its functions.

The IFC does not accept government guarantees, and prices its financing and services in line with the market. Although the IFC invests and lends on market terms, it does not compete with private capital. It finances projects unable to obtain sufficient funding on reasonable terms from other sources. Normally, IFC does not finance more than 25 per cent of total project costs so as to ensure that most of the project financing comes from private investors and lenders. And while IFC may buy up to 35 per cent of the stock of a company, it is never the largest shareholder and does not take part in a firm's management. But since IFC does not accept government guarantees, it shares all project risks with its partners.

The IFC is the largest multilateral source of loan and equity financing for private sector projects in the developing world. Since its founding in 1956 the IFC has provided US$16 billion in financing for 1595 projects in 114 developing countries. Between 1986 and 1995 alone the IFC approved 1434 projects with a total financing of US$27 billion. Of this, 16 billion was for IFC's own account, while the other US$11 billion came from underwriting and syndications. For every US$1 in financing approved by IFC for its own account in fiscal 1995, other investors and lenders will provide US$5.73. Some of this financing will be in the form of co-financing through loan syndications. Syndication is the primary means by which IFC mobilizes third-party funds for projects in developing countries. Through syndicated loans IFC shares the commercial risks of projects with co-financing partners and provide its lender-of-resort umbrella. In this way IFC is able to secure financing for many borrowers that would not otherwise have had access to long-term project funds on reasonable terms from the international financial markets.[10]

IFC's financing covers a broad range of sectors, but its priority is on infrastructure and capital markets. It assists domestic financial institutions through loans and equity investments in commercial and investment banks, leasing companies, discount houses, insurance companies and venture capital funds. The total assets of the IFC at the end of June 1995 was US$18.2 billion, of which loan and equity accounted for 36 per cent, derivative instruments 34 per cent and deposits and securities 26 per cent.

Borrowings accounted for 44 per cent of total liabilities as compared to 10 per cent for paid-up capital. Paid-up capital as of June 1995 amounted to US$1.9 billion, contributed by 165 members. The five largest holders are the United States (21.96 per cent of the votes), Japan (7.38 per cent), Germany (5.57 per cent), France (5.23 per cent) and the United Kingdom (5.23 per cent).

THE MULTILATERAL INVESTMENT GUARANTEE AGENCY (MIGA)

The Multilateral Investment Guarantee Agency (MIGA) which was established in 1988 is intended to encourage equity investment and other direct investment flows to developing countries through the mitigation of non-commercial investment barriers. MIGA's facilities include guarantees of insurance against non-commercial risks. It also advises developing member governments on the design and implementation of policies, programs, and procedures related to foreign investments, and sponsors a dialogue between the international business community and host governments on investment issues. As of 30 June 1995 MIGA had a membership of 128 with the United States having the largest percentage of votes (17.39 per cent).

How does MIGA rationalize its establishment? MIGA thinks it can help to improve the functioning of international investment markets.

Political risk insurance responds to a unique kind of imperfection in the workings of international markets. Private investors are generally competent and confident in their ability to assess and manage commercial risk in their field of business. However, uncertainty about the continuity and future course of the political, legal and regulatory regime governing foreign direct investment (FDI) constitutes an often intractable form of risk from the point of view of prospective foreign investors. Host government authorities are equally concerned about how to demonstrate the credibility and continuity of their policy reforms. Without some kind of 'intervention' to resolve this credibility and continuity problem, international markets will perform sub-optimally and international investment flows will be reduced to a level far below their full potential.[11]

In this field some of the demands from international investors are met by national and private political risk insurance agencies. The advantages of multilateral political risk insurance of the kind offered by MIGA 'lie in

MIGA's ability to act as a trusted neutral party, owned by 128 member countries that represent the entire spectrum of developmental experience, and its capacity to tap the human and technical resources of the entire World Bank Group.'[12] Also, while private insurances tend to provide short-term coverage, MIGA provides longer term (up to 15, sometimes 20 years). MIGA can also provide coverage against potential losses arising from currency transfer delays, war and civil disturbance which private insurers may find difficult to provide. MIGA can also supplement the coverage other insurers provide through various co-insurance and re-insurance arrangements.

THE PERFORMANCE OF THE WORLD BANK

The IBRD started its operations as a highly conservative institution. Until the late 1960s loans made available to developing countries were largely for projects in basic infrastructure, for example, electric power, ports, transport and communications, and so on. A significant proportion of the bank's resources is still concentrated in these areas, but the bank is now lending for a wider range of activity, for example, the environment, the social sector (including population, health and nutrition), financial and private sector reforms and so on. Growing poverty in some areas and the crippling debt problem affecting some poor countries have forced the bank to review its policies in certain areas, including the issue of debt alleviation.[13]

It has been estimated by one source that although inroads have been made in reducing poverty between the late 1980s and the early 1990s the gains have been small. While the incidence of poverty is estimated to have fallen from 30.1 per cent in 1987 to 29.4 per cent in 1993, the number of poor has increased from 1.23 billion to 1.31 billion. Not surprising,[14] questions are being raised by both donors and recipients whether aid has been having the desired impact. In this context, the operation of the World Bank has not been without controversy. The projects for which it lends, the terms of lending, policy conditionalities, the cost of loans in the context of the profit it makes, the size of its bureaucracy and the fact that annual repayments exceed disbursements in certain areas have all raised critical questions.

There are many who feel that the Bank (like the IMF) is simply an arm of the industrial countries, particularly the United States, which because of its economic clout, exerts a major influence on policy. This was particularly so in the cold war period, and it is felt that the Bank has been slow to adjust to the new context and to incorporate lessons of the post-war development process in its lending policies.

There are indications, however, that the Bank is increasingly taking a more open critical view of itself and the effectiveness with which it delivers services.[15] Donors themselves have become concerned about the performance of multilateral institutions generally and the seeming lack of impact in many countries, and are calling for wide ranging changes. The eleventh IDA replenishment (1997–99) endorses a package that will allow concessional lending of US$22 billion to poor countries which is half that of the tenth and reflects some of the disaffection and aid-fatigue that have emerged.

OTHER MULTILATERAL FINANCIAL INSTITUTIONS (MFIS)

Besides the World Bank, which is a global institution, a number of other financial institutions have been established to serve particular regions of the world. The early emphasis of the IBRD was on reconstruction, and despite the setting up of the soft loans window (IDA) in 1960 to accommodate poor countries, the World Bank was always seen as a 'distant' institution unable to properly address the diverse conditions prevailing in its various member states. The *modus operandi* of the Bank itself with emphasis on fairly large loans, militated against small countries with limited resources and technical skills.

In the post-war period the main regional MFIs that have been set up in developing countries[16] are the Inter-American Development Bank (IDB) in 1959, the African Development Bank (ADB) in 1963, the Asian Development Bank (AsDB) in 1966, the Caribbean Development Bank (CDB) in 1970 and the European Bank for Reconstruction and Development (EBRD) in 1990. There are, of course, a number of other development agencies (for example, the United Nations Development Programme) that operate within the UN system.

Though modelled on the World Bank, the regional MFIs have differences among them, but also share certain similarities. They provide both financial resources and technical assistance, and their general aim is to mobilize resources for social and economic development. Recognizing the disadvantage faced by their less developed members in raising finance in the market place, they all operate special facilities (or funds) which provide highly concessional assistance. This aid feature tends to be kept separate from banking operations. A common aim is to encourage private and public investment and to promote regional cooperation. They lend mainly to governments, but differ on the extent to which they borrow to finance their operations. The EBRD has a different mandate from the others – one in which the donors had a major influence. The aim of this institution is to promote fundamental principles of multiparty democracy, the rule of law, respect for human rights and market economies in Central and Eastern European countries. It would promote private and entrepreneurial initiatives and assist in implementing economic reforms, including demonopolization, decentralization and privatization. The Bank's Agreement specifies that not more than 40 per cent of its lending should be to the state sector.

Both the World Bank and the regional MFIs are modelled on joint stock companies, with capital contributions determining voting rights. Economic importance play a major part in the allocations of contributions. The paid-up capital is normally a small part of the subscribed capital, but the difference (the callable capital) serves as back-up in the event that the bank runs into problems. Since the purpose of a development bank is to mobilize funds on a relatively large scale, their charters make provision for regional and non-regional membership. The latter are not expected to exercise borrowing rights. In its early years the African countries confined membership of the ADB to only African countries, but after some agonizing, and realizing that this policy was affecting the level of operations, it was changed in 1982. In order to maintain their regional character, regional MFIs tend to stipulate a majority shareholding for regional members. They also, of course, insist that lending should be confined to regional members, and the President of the Bank should be a regional person. Even in a minority position, however, the non-regional members can still exert some influence on policy since they are represented on the board of governors. With respect to the division of shareholding between regional and non-regional members, the actual proportions can vary a little from the stipulated figures. In the ADB, the regional proportion is two thirds, in the CDB, 60 per cent, and in the AsDB 60 per cent. In the IDB a minimum proportion of 50.005 per cent has been stipulated for regional developing countries, 30 per cent for the United States and 4 per cent for Canada. In the remaining 15.995 per cent for non-regional members, Japan has 5.001 per cent.

Table 8.1 gives some indication of the size of leading international and regional development financial institutions. It is worth pointing out, however, that the World Bank is a global institution and its impact on particular regions may be less than that of the regional institutions. In the Latin American and Caribbean region, for example, gross disbursement in the period 1991–96 amounted to US$21.3 billion, but after repayments, interest and other charges the net transfer was minus US$15.0 billion. In the same period the IDB disbursed US$18 billion, but net disbursements after repayment was US$6.5. The IDB's lending was also spread over a large number of countries. In Africa, too, the World Bank disbursed some

Table 8.1   Selected data on multilateral financial institutions (MFIs),
1995 (in US$ million)

Institutions	Resource commitment 1995	Net disbursements 1995	Cumulative lending from inception	Total assets 1995	Subscribed capital
World Bank					
IBRD	16 853	897	281 980[a]	168 579	176 438
IDA	5 669	5 205	96 942[a]	101 635	86 236[b]
Inter-American	7 303	1 626	78 214[c]	39 361	66 399
Development Bank					
African Development Bank	669	...	27 843[d]	...	20 972[e]
Asian Development Bank	5 759	...	...	...	30 151[f]
Caribbean	108	–16	1 874[c]	353	648
Development Bank					
European Bank for Reconst.					
& Development	3 283	591[i]	6860[h]	...	11 670[g]

...   Not available.
a   To fiscal 1996.
b   Subscriptions and contributions.
c   To fiscal 1995.
d   To fiscal 1993.
e   At end of 1993.
f   At end of 1993.
g   Authorized capital.
h   To fiscal 1994.
i   Gross to fiscal, 1994.

Source: Annual Reports of the various banks; UN *World Economic and Social Survey*, 1996; *Europa Yearbook, 1996*.

US$17 billion between 1991 and 1996, but the net transfer was only US$5.6 billion.

As far as the sources of funds are concerned, these differ from bank to bank. In the case of the IDB and the IBRD, outstanding loan liabilities account for over 60 per cent of total assets. In the case of the CDB, capital and reserves amounted to 80 per cent in 1995 as compared to 18 per cent for borrowings.

ISSUES IN DEVELOPMENT BANKING

The concept of a development bank marries the twin functions of development banking and being a development agency. On the one hand, the bank acts as a catalyst for mobilizing financial resources, and on the other it provides technical and policy advice to its members. Without the latter, the provision of finance would have had only a limited effect. One of the criticisms frequently levelled at regional MFIs is that they act too much like the World Bank, placing too heavy an emphasis on their banking functions and neglecting their development role. The typical response of the banks is that since they derive a significant proportion of their lending resources in private capital markets, they need a good credit rating and their operations have to meet certain banking criteria. Without funds they would be of little use in either capacity.

The criticisms of the MFIs come from several perspectives. The persistence of poverty in member states challenges the position of the banks as an agency of change and development. To be sure, the banks themselves are one of the number of players and factors affecting development. In this situation it is difficult to assess the effectiveness of one of the players in isolation from the contributions of other elements, including the policies implemented by the recipient countries themselves. Another of the criticisms is that the banks have been slow to change in meeting challenges emanating from developments in the social and economic environment. With the emergence of structural adjustment and rising poverty in some cases, it is felt that the banks, despite their initial steps, still do not sufficiently address poverty concerns. Despite the critical role assigned to the private sector in the market driven paradigm most of the banks are not structured to lend directly to the private sector.

With the inability to attract private investment or to raise money on capital markets, a large number of countries depend on bilateral official assistance and on the MFIs. The insufficiency of funds in relation to the needs of borrowing member countries is a constant challenge facing all development banks. Non-regional members have not only played a critical role in providing funds through equity, but in channelling concessional funds through a variety of different funds which often test the administrative capacity of the banks. The competition for development finance has been increasing, and MFIs are always under pressure to find new sources. One of course is to attract new members who are able to contribute. When this is not successful, another is to increase capital contributions from existing members. A major problem here, of course, is that members' ability to contribute through this means would vary widely, and this would also bring into question the voting structure in the bank and who should be in control of its policy and orientation. In other words, those who have the capacity to increase their capital are not necessarily those whose voting power borrowing member countries may want to increase.

An alternative to increasing paid-up capital is to borrow in international capital markets or in the markets of member countries. In this situation the bank has to pay particular attention to its creditworthiness which would hinge not only on its capital base, but on its financial policies, its profitability, its support and recognition by other highly rated financial institutions, risk ratio, and so on. There is always a fear, however, that the bank in trying to create a particular image as an efficient institution might lose sight of its original objectives. The pressure to do everything and satisfy the varied needs of its members is ever present. The challenge in a development context is to conduct its operations in a way that could maintain the confidence of its contributors and creditors while meeting the needs of the members it was set up to serve. This is not always easy. Donor countries may contribute not only through capital but by making funds available for special purposes. These contributions often carry specific conditions relating to the loan or grant, but may also stipulate the borrowers. These conditions, however, do not always conform to the lending policies the bank may wish to pursue.

In view of the growing demands for development finance, a number of questions have been raised with respect to the operations, role and orientation of development banks. One of these concerns relates to the net injection of funds into developing counties, given the volume of repayments being made. In the Middle East and North Africa, for example, gross disbursements by the IBRD between 1991 and 1996 amounted to US$7.5. billion. After repayments and interest charges the net transfer was minus US$2.5 billion.

In the case of the Caribbean Development Bank net transfers were negative (US$44.4 million) between 1991 and 1995. In the case of the Inter-American Development Bank, repayments amounted to 50 per cent of disbursements in the five year period 1991–95. Given the importance attached to their credit rating, development banks tend to be extremely careful in assessing projects and pay a great deal of attention to the ability to repay. Never having had a default on a loan is one of the 'selling points' used by the IBRD when it borrows on the capital markets. The questions remain, however. Are the development banks lending as much as they can; are they lending for projects that can have the greatest social and economic impact on borrowing member countries; is the work of the banks being done in the most efficient (least costly) way; is the technical assistance being provided succeeding in raising the range and level of skills in borrowing countries, or is it merely providing jobs for consultants; are the most appropriate consultants being used? The low level of lending is

sometimes blamed on failure to identify projects and other local constraints, but to what extent has technical assistance succeeded in improving absorptive capacity in poor countries? Have the banks been lending for
the 'correct' mix of projects as they relate to infrastructure and the productive sectors? Given the new role being given to the private sector as the
engine of growth, are the banks geared to providing greater financial and
other assistance to the private sector, given that their structures and pro-
clivities equip them to deal largely with governments and government-
owned institutions.

In areas served by more than one bank, as is the case in the Caribbean
the question of duplication of functions and unnecessary costs has been
raised. More specifically, it has been asked whether lower costs of administration will not result from a rationalization of their activities within a
stronger collaborative framework. The administrative expenses for three
banks in recent years were as follows:

	US$ million
Caribbean Development Bank (1995)	10.6
Inter-American Development Bank (1995)	230.8
World Bank (fiscal year 1995)	1,409.0

In regions where more than one bank is operating, it has been suggested
that the respective banks might concentrate their lending activities in areas
where they have a comparative advantage. For example, in the Caribbean
the suggestion is that the Inter-American Development Bank should concentrate on large infrastructural projects and channel its resources for edu-
cational and other social projects through the Caribbean Development
bank which should be left free to develop new areas of lending in which
other institutions are not particularly interested.[17]

CONCLUDING OBSERVATIONS

The early history of post-war development assistance is noted for the
heavy emphasis placed on infrastructure which was closely linked to economic growth seen in many circles as being synonymous with development. The practice of development banks has been to lend essentially to
governments or government agencies in the perception that the government was the main agent of change. It is now widely recognized that there
are other important actors such as the non-governmental organizations
(NGOs) and the private sector which are now being put at the forefront of

the development effort. It is also now widely recognized that there is more to development than growth. The gains from growth do not always 'trickle down'. Expenditure on areas other than infrastructure (for example, human resource development) can also often be more critical in contributions to growth and development. Growth cannot be sustained if it is pursued at the expense of the environment or people. The philosophy of lending has been shifting towards more broad-based lending, but there is still a long way to go. One of the major challenges facing development banks, particularly those heavily dependent on borrowing is how to maintain their credit rating and their financial integrity while lending to more risky but essential areas that are critical to breaking out of the poverty circle. Given the growing aid bureaucracy and creeping aid-tiredness, the need to deliver aid more effectively and more cost effectively has to be taken seriously. The recipient countries themselves have to adopt policies which not only provide a framework for more efficient use of resources, but which also ensure benefits to the population at large on a sustained basis. Corruption, inefficiency and poorly formulated policies in borrowing countries have also contributed to the failure to achieve significant change in many cases.

Notes

1. World Bank, *World Development Report, 1991* (New York: Oxford University Press, 1991), p. 4.
2. *Ibid.*
3. World Bank, *Annual Report 1996* (Washington, DC: World Bank, 1996), p. 11.
4. *Ibid.*, p. 6.
5. The difference between 'subscribed capital' and 'paid-up capital' gives what is called 'callable capital'. The latter is a resource that can be called upon in the event the bank runs into trouble. It serves as a guarantee to the bank's creditors.
6. For example, power to admit new members, suspend a member, or increase or decrease the capital stock.
7. IDA has had eleven replenishments so far. The current one which covers the period 1997–99 endorsed a package that will allow concessional lending of US$22 billion to poor countries over the period.
8. In addition to the resource of the IDA, a Special Fund (which was kept separate from IDA resource) was set up on 26 October 1982. The Fund was constituted by funds contributed by members of the IDA and administered by the IDA to supplement the regular resources available for lending by the IDA. Member contributors to the Special Fund totalled US$596 million at June 1995.

On 31 May 1996, the Special Fund was terminated and all its assets, liabilities and capital were transferred to the IDA.

9. IFC, *Annual Report*, 1995, p. 5.
10. *Ibid.*, p. 6.
11. MIGA's *Annual Report*, 1995, pp. 9–10.
12. *Ibid.*, p. 10.
13. In 1906 the World Bank agreed to contribute around US$2 billion to a trust fund aimed at assisting highly indebted poor countries. The Bank also makes grants from a debt-education facility for IDA only countries.
14. World Bank, *Annual Report 1996, op. cit.*, p. 48.
15. See World Bank, *Annual Report 1996*, p. 15.
16. In the context of the integration exercise in Western Europe, the European Investment Bank (EIB) was set up in 1958, and has as one of its main objectives the development of the Community's less privileged regions.
17. See H. Brewster, 'Caribbean Development Bank Strategy and the Future role of the Caribbean Development Bank.' Paper presented at the 25th Anniversary Symposium of the Caribbean Development Bank, Kingston, Jamaica, May 1995.

Further Reading

Al-Shaikhly, S. (ed.), *Development Financing: A framework for International Cooperation*, Frances Pinter (Publishers), London, 1982.

Berg, R. J. and D. F. Gordon, *International Development: The United States in the Third World in the 1980s*, Lynne Rienner Publishers, London, 1989.

Bourne, C., *Caribbean Development to the Year 2000: Challenges, Prospects and Policies*, Commonwealth Secretariat, London, 1988.

Culpeper, R., *The Multilateral Development Banks – Titans or Behemoths?* Lynne Rienner Publishers, Boulder, Colorado, 1987.

Cunningham, G., *The Management of Aid Agencies*, Croom Helm, London, 1974.

English, E. P. and H. M. Mule, *The African Development Bank*, Lynne Rienner Publishers Boulder, Colorado, 1996.

Griffin, K., *Alternative Strategies for Economic Development*, Macmillan, London, 1989.

Hardy, C., *The Caribbean Development Bank*, Lynne Rienner Publishers, Boulder, Colorado, 1995.

Hunt, D., *Economic Theories of Economic Development – Analysis of Competing Paradigms*, Harvester Wheatsheaf, London, 1989.

Hutchful, E. (ed.), *The IMF and Ghana – The Confidential Record*, Zed Books, London, 1987.

Kappagoda, N., *The Asian Development Bank*, Lynne Rienner Publishers, Boulder, Colorado, 1995.

Meier, G., *Problems of Cooperation for Development*, Oxford University Press, London, 1974.

Payer, C., *The World Bank: A Critical Analysis*, Monthly Review Press, London, 1982.

Ramirez-Faria, C., *The Origins of Economic Inequality Between Nations*, Unwin Hyman, London, 1991.

Report of the Independent Commission on International Development Issues (The Willy Brandt Commission), *North–South: A Program for Survival*, MIT Press, Cambridge, MA, 1980.

Richards, J. H., *International Economic Institutions*, Hold, Rinehart and Winston, London, 1990.

South Commission Report, *The Challenge to the South*, Oxford University Press, London, 1990.

Toye, J., *Dilemmas of Development*, Basil Blackwell, Oxford, 1980.

Tussie, D., *The Inter-American Development Bank*, Lynne Rienner Publishers, Boulder, Colorado, 1995.

9 Private Foreign Investment (PFI)

INTRODUCTION

In recent years there has been renewed interest in the role of private investment in stimulating growth and providing employment. There is a growing consensus that private sector led economies are more efficient than those dominated by state ownership and encumbered by various kinds of restrictions. Liberalization is being directed not only to the movement of goods, but also to services. It is recognized that certain measures affecting trade also influence investment, and because investment decisions could be influenced by non-market forces these measures are increasingly being brought within the purview of liberalization. Both in developed and developing countries, the government's role is becoming increasingly more circumscribed, as efforts are being made to define a more limited role for the state and as economies are being reorganized to operate along the lines of market principles. In the present phase of the evolution of the world economy the pendulum has swung in favour of the private sector, as governments relinquish decision-making in a number of areas. Even in the developed countries the tendency is to encourage private initiatives in delivering 'public goods'.

The ideological divide which for most of the post-war period pitted western capitalism with a restricted role for the state against the socialism of the Soviet Union and Eastern Europe with their massive state intervention, has now given way to a near universal recognition that private enterprise has to play a more central role in raising living standards. In developed and developing countries alike, policies are being geared to encourage both local and foreign private investment as a strategy to resolve growth and unemployment problems. There is competition not only among Japan and the western industrialized countries including the newly industrializing countries (NICs) for foreign investment, but the former socialist countries of Central and Eastern Europe are now in the market. Most developing states pursuing structural adjustment programmes under the IMF and World Bank auspices have as a major objective a greater role for private investment as the State becomes more of a facilitator and less of an engine of growth. A critical concern is to remove the disincentives to saving and investment in a situation where the capacity of the State to save and invest has been weakened by the rapid growth of current expenditure. The high level of public indebtedness in which many governments have found themselves, and a reduced ability to borrow, have also contributed to the willingness to provide greater accommodation to private investment, both local and foreign. A major motivation is that the balance of payments cost of direct (equity) investment in the form of profit remittances is recognized to be a function of the commercial success of a venture and does not take the form of fixed interest payments as is the case with borrowing. Many developing countries have found also, that borrowing, particularly from the multilateral international and regional financial institutions like the IMF, the World Bank and the IDB can also result in a loss of power over decision-making and policy, which they had come to associate with foreign investment.

There are, however, other factors which have contributed to a more favourable climate for international foreign investment. The dismantling of trade restrictions which has been taking place within the GATT framework has not only resulted in a significant increase in world trade, but was bound to have a positive effect on the movement of capital. In fact, in recent years the growth of foreign direct investment has outstripped that of both trade and output. One recent United Nations study has noted that foreign direct investment which has been increasing far more rapidly during the 1980s than both world trade and output, has emerged as a major integrating force in the world economy.[1] This is not surprising, given the close link between capital movements and trade. Nationalistic measures taken by many governments have forced suppliers to invest and produce abroad rather than to supply foreign markets through exports. Developments in technology now allow producers greater flexibility in the location of facilities. The introduction of measures to deal with political risks and the devising of strategies by investors to cope with economic uncertainties help to explain the rapid growth in foreign investment in recent years. Not only are there insurance arrangements and investment treaties to guard against political acts like expropriation, nationalization, civil wars, and so on, but investors have developed a range of techniques to deal with such things like exchange rate risks, inflation, and so on. New investment formulas have been created which not only permit the reduction of risks while retaining control over markets and resources, but they also help to present foreign investment in a new light more acceptable to local aspirations, and reflect a great deal more sensitivity to concerns of sovereignty and fears of exploitation. Because equity investment is not always involved, it is not easy to place a value on the new investments. Their importance however, should not be underestimated. The fact that foreign investors whose presence at one time could not be tolerated have been brought back as managers, or partners in some cases, indicate the extent to which the pendulum has turned.

SOME DEFINITIONS

The term 'investment', like 'capital' can refer to a variety of phenomena. In a narrow sense investment may refer to the acquisition of producer goods (assets) or to expenditure which increases the stock of capital in the 'real' economy. In another context the definition may encompass the acquisition of financial instruments. At the domestic level, while new financial and real (producer goods) assets may be in a continuous process of creation (or destruction), claims over existing one may also be changing ownership. Changes in ownership between residents and non-residents, of course, involve capital movements across national borders.

Foreign investment can take a variety of forms. An investor simply interested in returns (capital gain) can purchase non-participating stocks or shares in a new or existing company, or subscribe to fixed interest securities issued by governments. Such investment is commonly referred to as non-equity or portfolio (or security) investment and is closely associated with the speculative motives of investors. On the other hand an investor may wish to have a say in the decision-making of a firm in which case he may have to acquire a substantial part of the participating shares of that firm, or set up his own enterprise which can take several forms. The term direct investment is used to describe investment in which both capital (long term) and control are involved. Direct investment is a package which often includes not only finance, but management, technology, skills, entrepreneurship, markets, and so on In recent years the transnational corporation (TNC) has become the major vehicle of private direct investment, and thus a significant player in a world economy driven increasingly by private enterprise. The power of the TNC lies in the synergistic manner in which it combines tangible and intangible assets.[2] Capital and technology help define the basic strength of the TNC, but the strategic location of affiliates provide the raw materials and marketing power. A large part of international trade is now intra-firm with the cross-national production networks of goods and services increasingly forming an international production system controlled by the TNCs. By the mid-1980s, over 50 per cent of all international trade was carried out by TNCs among their units and with independent firms.[3] International economic transactions encompass not only trade between independent entities, but increasingly intra-firm exchanges, technology transfer, capital movements, the provision of management, skills and training.

Foreign investment is not a new phenomenon in the world economy. The industrial revolution in the 19th century was accompanied by a significant outflow of capital from the industrial countries to the developing world, aimed at developing infrastructure and sources of food and raw materials. A large part of this was of the portfolio type involving fixed-interest loans and securities. The United Kingdom was the most important creditor nation before World War I. There was some direct investment but this was confined to a few companies. Between the two world wars private capital exports from the industrial countries continued to be largely of the portfolio or security type. The 1920s, however, witnessed an increasing role of the United States as a source of foreign investment. The 1920s also witnessed a boom in bond underwriting, but this was followed by a virtual disappearance of the market for new issues after 1931.[4] The depression of the 1930s affected the growth of both direct and portfolio investment, particularly the latter. In the early years following the end of the Second World War capital movements were deeply influenced by decisions stemming from the war and revolved around reparation loans, debt redemption, reconstruction, and so on. The World Bank and IMF were intended to be major players in this scenario. With decolonization, bilateral assistance became increasingly important for developing countries, private financing largely taking the form of traditional bank credit, while bond issues were rare.[5] The investment climate improved dramatically after the war and direct investment began to assume significant proportions. By the 1960s economic motives had become the major influence behind capital movements which had started to respond to the opportunities being opened up in the economies recovering from the war.

Up until the late 1960s/early 1970s official financing continued to play an important role in developing countries. By 1970 more than 50 per cent of the long-term external debt of developing countries was owed to official creditors, while bank debt and bonds accounted, respectively for about 32 per cent and 5 per cent. In the 1970s, borrowing from the banks increased significantly, so that by 1982, 50 per cent of the long-term debt of developing countries was owed to banks, as compared to 36 per cent to official creditors.[6] By 1995 the banks' share had fallen to 35 per cent.

THE VOLUME AND PATTERN OF CAPITAL FLOWS IN RECENT YEARS

Capital movements are not only associated with a variety of motives, but also enter host countries for varying lengths of time. Speculative capital interested in more immediate gains tends to be short term, and their unpredictability have macroeconomic implications which can challenge governments' management of the economy on a daily basis. Long-term capital tends to be more development oriented and is influenced by a different set of factors.

Most countries are importers and exporters of capital at the same time, and the effects on the overall balance of payments position are not always easy to discern. Capital imports allow a country to sustain a current account deficit over a long period; that is to say a country can spend abroad more than it earns from the export of goods and services, and finance the additional imports with foreign savings in the form of gifts, loans and investment. Foreign exchange inflows that are not spent or used to service debt end up in the country's foreign reserves. There is, however, a relationship between the current account and the capital account which is recognized, but which is not always easily quantifiable. The inflow of capital into a country can lead to the appreciation of the exchange rate where the rate is floating,[7] and this can worsen the current account balance, by reducing the cost of imports to residents and making exports more expensive for non-residents.[8] The inflow of loans and investment also gives rise to subsequent outflows of interest, profits, and dividends which appear in the current account. A persistent current account deficit may not only lead to a debt build-up which can affect a country's creditworthiness, but may also impair a country's ability to attract new capital. A weakening of the foreign reserves position can also trigger a process of capital flight, since the country's ability to meet foreign exchange commitments will also come into question.

Capital flows are not easily predictable, particularly in an increasingly liberalized environment and given the range of factors which influence their direction. Some of these are internal while others are external and outside the control of host governments. Recession in capital exporting countries, changes in regulations and interest rates are examples of external factors. At the internal level, governments seeking to attract foreign capital can adjust the regulatory framework, change the tax laws, undertake appropriate institutional and financial reforms and adopt macroeconomic policies designed to bring a stabilizing influence on key financial variables like the inflation rate and the exchange rate.

Table 9.1 Aggregate net private capital flows to developing countries, 1990–96 (in US$ billions)

Type of flow	1990	1993	1995	1996[a]
Total private flows	44.4	157.1	184.2	243.8
Portfolio flows	5.5	80.9	60.6	91.8
Bonds	2.3	35.9	28.5	46.1
Equity	3.2	45.0	32.1	45.3
Foreign direct investment	24.5	67.2	95.5	109.5
Commercial banks	3.0	–0.3	26.5	34.2
Others	11.3	9.2	1.7	8.3
Memo items				
Aggregate net resource flows	100.6	212.0	237.2	284.6
Private flows' share (%)	44.1	74.1	77.7	85.7

[a] Preliminary.

Source: World Bank, *Global Development Finance*, Vol. I, 1997.

Depending on the source, one can get different estimates of the amount of capital flows taking place. According to figures provided by the World Bank (see Table 9.1) net portfolio flows to developing countries increased from US$5.5 billion in 1990 to US$80.9 billion in 1993 (almost 15 fold), while net foreign direct investment increased from US$24.5 billion to US$67.2 billion (almost 3 fold) in the same period. In the following two years, however, portfolio investment fell drastically following the uncertainties created by the Mexican peso crisis, but has started to grow again, as has commercial bank loans. Private flows as a percentage of aggregate net resource flows to developing countries increased from 44.1 per cent in 1990 to an estimated 86 per cent in 1996.

In developing countries balance of payments current account deficits between 1985 and 1995 amounted to US$560 billion. The relative importance of various types of flows in external financing varies from country to country and from year to year. In one period, for example, direct investment might be the dominant flow, while in another period portfolio investment or government borrowing or repayment of past loans may be the major activity influencing the capital account balance. For example, net direct investment flows to developing countries averaged US$12.6 billion per year in the period 1983–88 as compared to US$4.3 billion for net portfolio investment, but in the period 1989–95, the latter had increased to US$41.5 billion per year as compared to US$39.8 billion for the former.[9]

In 1996 Asia and the Pacific region are estimated to have received almost half of the private capital flows, as compared to around 30 per cent for Latin America and the Caribbean. Twelve host countries, with China at the top of the list, account for almost 75 per cent of all private flows which included portfolio investment as well as direct investment and bank loans.

RECENT TRENDS IN FOREIGN DIRECT INVESTMENT

Given the need to expand productive capacity and become more competitive, developing countries are placing great emphasis on attracting direct investment which is less volatile than short-term capital flows. The Mexican experience in 1994 has made emerging countries more wary of capital seeking a quick return. More importantly, however, foreign direct investment has the potential to change the comparative advantage of countries, given its association with technology, managerial skills, financial resources, and so on.

Control over production does not necessarily depend on equity, and therefore estimating the amount of direct investment taking place is not a simple task. Published figures are generally estimates. New forms of investment that does not necessarily include equity investment involve joint ventures, licensing agreements, franchising, management contracts, turnkey contracts, product-sharing arrangements, risk service contracts and international sub-contracting.[10] A recent report has noted that 'as the global environment is changing and strategies of transnational corporations (TNCs) evolve, new configurations of TNC activities are emerging.'[11] One manifestation of this is in the recent surge of mergers and acquisitions (MIA) both in developed and developing countries. It is estimated that the value of all cross-border transactions (including those involving portfolio investments, doubled between 1988 and 1995, reaching US$229 billion in 1995.[12]

During the 1970s foreign direct investment, domestic output and domestic investment grew at similar rates. 'During the early 1980s, the rate of growth of FDI began to diverge from that of domestic output and domestic investment and since 1985 the rate of growth of FDI has accelerated, outpacing that of the other two.[13] Between 1986 and 1990, the annual growth rate of FDI inflows was 24.7 per cent per year, as compared to 10.8 per cent for GDP, and 10.6 per cent for gross fixed capital formation. This trend has continued into the 1990s with FDI inflows averaging 12.7 per cent per year in the period 1991–94, as compared to 4.5 per cent for GDP and 4.0 per cent for gross capital formation. FDI has also been

Table 9.2   FDI inflows and outflows, 1983–95
(billions of US dollars and percentage)

Year	Developed countries		Developing countries		Central and Eastern Europe		All countries	
	Inflows	Outflows	Inflows	Outflows	Inflows	Outflows	Inflows	Outflows
			Value (billion dollars)					
1983–87	58.7	72.6	18.3	4.2	0.02	0.01	77.1	76.8
1988–92	139.1	193.3	36.8	15.2	1.36	0.04	177.3	208.5
1990	169.8	222.5	33.7	17.8	0.30	0.04	203.8	204.3
1991	114.0	201.9	41.3	8.9	2.45	0.04	157.8	210.8
1992	114.0	181.4	50.4	21.0	3.77	0.10	168.1	203.1
1993	129.3	192.4	73.1	33.0	5.59	0.20	207.9	225.5
1994	132.8	190.9	87.0	38.6	5.89	0.55	225.7	230.0
1995	203.2	270.5	99.7	47.0	12.08	0.30	314.9	317.8
			Share in total (per cent)					
1983–87	76	95	24	5	0.02	0.01	100	100
1988–92	78	93	21	7	0.77	0.02	100	100
1993	62	85	35	15	2.70	0.09	100	100
1994	59	83	39	17	2.60	0.24	100	100
1995	65	85	32	15	3.80	0.09	100	100
			Growth rate (per cent)					
1983–87	37	35	9	24	–7	68	29	35
1988–92	–4	3	15	16	298	46	1	4
1993	13	6	45	52	46	99	24	11
1994	3	–1	19	17	7	179	9	2
1995	53	42	15	22	106	–45	40	38

Source: UN, *World Investment Report, 1996*, New York, 1996.

growing at almost three times the rate of growth of exports of goods and non-factor services.

In 1995 world FDI inflows reached US$315 billion as compared to an annual average of less than US$100 billion in the early 1980s (see Table 9.2). The outward stock in 1995 was estimated to be US$2.7 trillion (see Table 9.3). The bulk of foreign direct investment originates in developed countries which account, on average, for over 80 per cent of outward movements. Six countries (France, Germany, the Netherlands, Japan, the United Kingdom and the United States) account for over 60 per cent of outward investments. The main developed countries which are often categorized as a triad (the United States, Japan and the European Community)

Table 9.3   Stock of foreign direct investment, by region and country, 1980–95 (billions of US dollars)

Region/country	1980	1990	1994	1995[a]
A. Outward				
Developed countries	507.5	1 614.6	2 243.8	2,514.3
European Union	213.2	777.2	1 076.5	1 208.8
United States	220.2	435.2	610.0	705.6
Japan	18.8	204.6	284.3	305.5
Developing countries	6.2	69.4	167.4	214.4
Central and Eastern Europe	0.0	0.2	1.0	1.4
World	513.7	1 684.1	2 412.2	2 730.1
B. Inward				
Developed countries	373.5	1 373.3	1 728.8	1 932.7
European Union	185.0	712.2	916.1	1 028.1
United States	83.0	394.9	504.4	564.6
Japan	3.3	9.8	17.8[a]	17.8
Developing countries	108.3	341.7	593.6	693.3
World	*481.9*	*1 716.9*	*2 342.2*	*2 657.9*

[a] Estimated
Source: UN, *World Investment Report, 1996,* New York, 1996.

for some purposes are also the major recipients, accounting for over three quarters of the inflows. Japan, however, is more of a source than a recipient. Despite recent attempts to open up the Japanese economy, many sectors remain closed to foreign investment. Traditionally, Japan has relied more on royalty and licensing agreements to access technology, rather than equity investment.

In the first half of the 1980s the United States and the United Kingdom were the dominant sources. But in the second half Japan was the single most important source followed by the United Kingdom and the United States. In the 1990s the United States has emerged as the most important investor, with outflows from Japan showing a significant decline from the late 1980s. Investment from the UK has shown a steady increase since 1991.

The explanation why the developed countries invest so heavily in each other's economy has its basis in a wide range of structural and cyclical factors.

Among the former are sustained technological and cross-borders, intra-industry production; significant economic developments in those countries, such as the regionalisation of markets with the EC and its extension to EFTA countries; the United States–Canada Free Trade Agreement and the inclusion of Mexico in a wider North American Free Trade Agreement; privatization and deregulation in services industries and their opening to FDI; and fears of rising protectionism as regional markets grapple with their relations with the rest of the world. High growth rates relative to most other regions of the world are among the cyclical factors.[14]

As indicated earlier, investment flows are concentrated in a few countries. The ten largest host countries received two thirds of total inflows in 1995 and the smallest 100 recipient countries received only one per cent.[15] The share of developing countries has increased since the late 1980s, reaching US$100 billion or 32 per cent of the total in 1995. While FDI inflows into Asia (excluding China) increased by over 200 per cent between 1990 and 1995, and inflows to Latin America more than doubled. Investment flows to China increased more than tenfold in the period. About a dozen developing countries receive about three quarters of the foreign direct investment inflows. An example of this concentration can be seen in Latin America where three countries (Argentina, Brazil and Mexico) have accounted for over 60 per cent of the foreign direct investment in the region in recent years. Forced to compete in an increasingly liberalized world economy, firms from developing countries are expanding their activities abroad. FDI outflows from developing countries which averaged US$7.6 billion in the 1984–89 period increased to US$47.0 billion in 1995.

FOREIGN INVESTMENT AND THE ECONOMIES OF EASTERN EUROPE

The group of countries now referred to as 'economies in transition' comprise the countries of Eastern Europe and the former Soviet Union, which are in the process of moving from centrally-planned economies in which the state was the dominant economic actor to economies based on market principles and private enterprise. The population of these countries in 1995 was estimated to be around 400 million with an average per capita GDP (in 1988 US dollars) of US$3639 in 1995. Despite the decline in real per capita income in these countries in recent years, this figure is still higher than that of most developing countries in various parts of the world. The comparable figure for all developing countries in 1995 was US$988, for Latin America US$2092, for Africa US$657, for West Asia US$3328, for South and East Asia US$867 and for China US$664.

Because of inadequate domestic savings, the 'economies in transition' are making strong efforts to attract foreign private capital. With this will come, they hope, modern technology, managerial and other skills and even access to foreign markets. The attraction is not only tax laws with greater incentives and large domestic markets for consumer goods, but natural resources, skills and labour costs. It has been estimated that foreign direct investment inflows in all transition countries increased from about US$200 million in 1989 to about US$12.6 billion in 1995. The stock was estimated at US$33.6 billion in 1995.

Not all the transition countries offer the same attraction, and therefore some (for example, Hungary, the Czech Republic, Poland) have been more successful than others in attracting investors either as partners in existing enterprises or as owners of new enterprises. Policy and institutional reforms have not proceeded at the same pace in all states and this is reflected in the uncertainty to be found in some investment environments which still lack adequate commercial and investment legislations. Foreign investment still favours only a few countries. By the end of 1994, the number of foreign affiliates had reached 55 000.

THE GROWTH OF THE TRANSNATIONAL CORPORATION

As indicated earlier, the transnational corporation (TNC) has emerged as the most important vehicle for foreign direct investment. The number of TNCs has been increasing steadily and it is estimated that by the mid-1990s there were some 39 000 TNCs in the world with over 260 000 foreign affiliates.[16] These affiliates generated approximately US$6.0 trillion in worldwide sales in 1993. This compared with world exports of goods and non-factor services of US$4.7 trillion, of which a significant proportion took the form of intra-firm trade.

Of the 39 000 TNCs noted, 34 000 (or more than 80 per cent) are based in developed countries, mainly Germany with 7000, Japan with 4000, Sweden with 3520 and the United States and Switzerland with 3000 each. Not all TNCs are large companies, and it is estimated that the developing home countries with the largest numbers were the Republic of Korea with 1049 followed by Brazil with 800, Hong Kong with 500 and China with 379. It is worth noting that while developing countries are home to only about 10 per cent of TNCs, more than 40 per cent of foreign affiliates are located in these countries. There are about 400 TNCs (one per cent of the total) based in Central and Eastern Europe.

Why the growth of TNCs and what is the significance for the world economy? One of the salient features of the post-war world economy, particularly in recent years, has been the deliberate efforts aimed at reducing trade barriers and removing the various types of impediments to capital movements. The effect of these actions has been an increasing interdependence and a growing integration of national economies. This process has been helped by the formation of regional groupings, and their tendency to expand. Technological developments in transport and communication have made it easier for transnational corporations to rationalize global production within structures best capable of achieving their objectives. Competition for markets and resources lead not only to larger and larger companies but to the formation of strategic alliances which may not necessarily be a formal part of the company's structure. It is estimated that about one third of the world's private sector productive assets are under the governance of TNCs.[17] A significant part of world trade are in fact intra-company transactions using transfer pricing that reflect the corporation's own strategic interests rather than arms length valuation. Such a practice puts transnationals in a particularly strong bargaining position *vis-à-vis* host countries, particularly where taxation is concerned.

Worldwide sales of TNCs' foreign affiliates exceed US$6 trillion. Fortune Magazine's 500 largest corporations in the world in 1995 had a total revenue of US$11 378 billion, total profits of US$323 billion, total assets of US$32 137 billion and employed over 35 million.[18] In terms of revenues, trading companies rank at the very top followed by motor vehicles (and parts), commercial banks, petroleum refining, electronics, (including electrical equipment) and insurance, in that order. In terms of assets, however, commercial banks are way ahead of any other group. In fact they are among the largest corporations in the world (see Table 9.4). There are only a few non-financial companies in the top 50, when ranking is done by assets. Among them are Ford Motor (US), General Motors (US) and General Electric (US). In the top 100 are Mitsubishi (Japan), Royal Dutch/Shell Group (Britain/Netherlands), Toyota Motor (Japan), Hitachi (Japan), Nippon Telegraph & Telephone (Japan) and Matsushita Electric Industrial (Japan). Not all corporations depend to the same extent on international business. A ranking of non-financial transnational corporations on the basis of foreign assets in 1994 identified the following five companies as the largest: Royal Dutch Shell (Petroleum refining), Ford Motor (motor vehicles and parts), Exxon (petroleum refining), General Motors (motor vehicles and parts), and IBM (computers), in that order.[19]

Transnational corporations are to be found in every field of activity. Some of them are engaged in several lines of business at the same time. In terms of revenues the biggest company in the world is a trading company,

Table 9.4 The world's twenty largest corporations ranked by assets and revenues, 1995

	Ranked by revenues				Ranked by assets		
Rank	Corporation	Country	Total revenues US$ billions	Rank	Corporation	Country	Total assets US$ billions
1	Mitsubishi	Japan	184.4	1	Sumitomo Bank	Japan	524.7
2	Mitsui	Japan	181.5	2	Sanwa Bank	Japan	520.1
3	Itochu	Japan	169.2	3	Dai-ichi Kanyo Bank	Japan	515.7
4	General Motors	United States	168.8	4	Fuji Bank	Japan	508.4
5	Sumitomo	Japan	167.5	5	Deutsche Bank	Germany	503.0
6	Marubeni	Japan	161.0	6	Mitsubishi Bank	Japan	497.4
7	Ford Motor	United States	137.1	7	Sakura Bank	Japan	494.7
8	Toyota Motor	Japan	111.0	8	Novinchukin Bank	Japan	431.1
9	Exxon	United States	110.0	9	Credit Agricole	France	386.1
10	Royal Dutch/Shell Group	Britain/Netherlands	109.8	10	Industrial Bank	Japan	380.7
11	Nissho Iwai	Japan	97.9	11	Nippon Life Insurance	Japan	364.8
12	Walmart Stores	United States	93.1	12	Zurich Insurance	Switzerland	357.6
13	Hitachi	Japan	84.2	13	HSBC Holdings	Britain	352.4
14	Nippon Life Insurance	Japan	83.2	14	ABN Amro Holding	Netherlands	340.8
15	Nippon Telegraph	Japan	81.9	15	Credit Lyonnais	France	339.6
16	AT&T Telephone	United States	79.6	16	Dresdner Bank	Germany	337.7
17	Daimler-Benz	Germany	72.2	17	Union Bank of Switzerland	Switzerland	335.2
18	IBM	United States	71.9	18	Banque Nationale de Paris	France	325.4
19	Matsushita Electronic	Japan	70.4	19	Fed. Natl. Mortgage Assn.	United States	316.6
20	General Electric	United States	70.0	20	Tokai Bank	Japan	309.7

Source: Fortune, 5 August 1996.

Mitsubishi Corporation of Tokyo which had revenues of US$184 billion in 1995. In terms of assets, however, Mitsubishi whose activities embrace manufacturing, mining, agriculture, tourism and a host of other services and industries was ranked 103 among the world's 500 largest corporations in 1995. The assets or annual revenues of some transnationals exceed the Gross Domestic Product (GDP) of many countries. The gross product (value added) of TNCs' foreign affiliates in 1995 was estimated to be over US$1400 billion.[20]

The power of TNCs derive not only from the capital resources they are able to mobilize, but from the technology they produce and control, from their managerial skills and from the marketing network they develop. The world economy is being integrated through the TNC which can now rationalize its operations in an increasingly liberalized environment which has weakened the power of governments to dictate the terms of entry. With governments unable to finance expansion in infrastructure and resource industries and to acquire state of the art technology, they have adopted more open policies designed to sharpen the competitive edge. The world in the 1990s is a far different place than it was in the 1960s, the 1970s and even in the greater part of the 1980s.

CHANGING PATTERNS OF FOREIGN INVESTMENT

As indicated earlier, a great deal of global foreign direct investment takes place among the developed countries themselves. With respect to flows to developing countries in recent years, these are concentrated in a few countries. For various reasons some areas are more attractive than others. East, South and South East Asia which include some of the fastest growing economies in the world is a major area of interest. China, Kong Kong, Singapore, Taiwan, Thailand, Malaysia and Indonesia are hosts to the major share of direct investment flows to developing countries. In Latin America the largest countries, Mexico, Argentina, and Brazil have attracted a significant share of investment to the region. Africa's attractiveness has declined in recent years as a result of political turmoil and poor economic performance. The two countries of any major significance are Egypt and Nigeria, both of which are oil exporters.

A great deal of the foreign investment of the 19th and early 20th century was directed to developing sources of foodstuffs and raw materials which also required investments in infra-structure such as railways, public utilities, and so on. Resource industries accounted for most of the direct investment that took place in this period. On the eve of the First World

War Britain accounted for some 40 per cent of the stock of foreign investment, followed by France (20 per cent), Germany (13.2 per cent) and the United States (8 per cent).[21] Belgium, Netherlands and Switzerland accounted for 13 per cent. Since there was more foreign investment in the United States than the United States had abroad, this country was a net debtor country. In fact the United States and Canada were host to almost 25 per cent of total foreign investment as compared to 27 per cent for Europe, 19 per cent for Latin America and 14 per cent for Asia. Net capital exports from traditional capital exporting countries fell significantly in the inter-war years, as the world economy adjusted to the aftermath of the First World War.

Following the end of the Second World War, foreign private investment, particularly from the United States picked up once more. This was helped by the removal of controls on trade and payments. The major part of this investment was intra-developed countries, but some did go (largely in the form of direct investment) to developing countries in search of markets and raw materials. From the early 1960s, however, as many of the former colonies began to win their political independence, there was a marked change in the attitude towards private foreign capital. Concern with sovereignty and the growth of nationalism resulted in policies which called for greater controls over private foreign capital. Nationalization of the 'commanding heights' of the economy (natural resource sectors and key industries) became an integral part of development policy in some cases as it was felt that public control was essential for development. State ownership was often inevitable because of the critical nature of the resource industries and the size of the investment, and also because the traditional local private sector may either have been seen as being too closely aligned with foreign interests, or not truly committed to national development. Foreign direct investment was also seen as inimical to the emergence of a local entrepreneurial class and the existence of small business.

The reaction of foreign investors to the restrictions adopted by developing countries was to develop new techniques (some of which were mentioned earlier) to maintain access to raw materials and markets. Most of these new forms of foreign investment are not predicated on control and may therefore not involve equity participation. They are a reaction not only to policies and opportunities in the host countries, but to uncertainties in the economic environment, and structural changes in the world economy. These new forms represent innovative ways of combining finance, technology, management and marketing skills in the context of the need to minimize political and economic risk in a rapidly changing global environment.

With the nationalistic policies adopted by many developing countries, there was a marked slow down in the flow of private investment, and governments turned increasingly to borrowing from commercial banks to finance not only investment, but consumption as well. By the early 1980s a number of debtor countries were finding it difficult to service their debt, and bank lending dropped significantly in the mid-1980s. Policies towards foreign investment changed radically in this period, as increasing emphasis began to be placed on private sector flows. Inadequate domestic saving rates and the failure of the import substitution model, not to mention the pressures from international financial agencies, have encouraged host countries to abandon a range of protective instruments and policies creating a new international environment more conducive to trade and the movement of capital. The international context is changing rapidly, as increasing interest is being taken by investors in developing countries. The liberalization of both the real and financial sectors and the removal of a whole gamut of trade, currency and financial controls as well as 'anti-foreigners' sentiments would not only have opened up these economies, but also raised the prospective return on real investment. In the case of Asia the region not only contains some of the fastest growing economies in the world but also some of the most dynamic exporters. It has been observed that the relationship between direct investment and the growth of exports in Asia is stronger than in Latin America. Direct investment is more export-intensive. For example, it has been observed that while the US firms in Asia export more than one-half of their output, those in Latin America export only about one quarter of their domestic production.[22]

FOREIGN INVESTMENT AND GOVERNMENT POLICY

At one time in the not too distant past the activities of transnational corporations came under heavy criticisms as they were seen as 'agents of imperialism' exploiting developing countries and transferring the wealth of poor countries to the developed nations. Their presence in many cases were seen as inconsistent with national development, or of a form that needed changing in order to increase the benefits to the local economy. There are many examples of conflicts between TNCs and host governments, which in some cases involved the governments of the TNCs' home country. This was particularly the case in resource-based industries from which host governments felt that they not only needed a greater share of the benefits generated, but that this would require a greater measure of control. In 1974 the United Nations General Assembly adopted a set of resolutions aimed at establishing a 'new international economic order' which was intended to encourage a more equitable relationship between developed and developing countries and to regulate the conduct of TNCs, *inter alia*.

With the stagnation or decline besetting a large number of developing economies in the late 1970s and 1980s, and the corresponding weakening in the bargaining strength of governments, the whole tenor of that debate changed. The term 'new international economic order' which was viewed with hostility by some developed countries, has now largely gone out of currency, as poor countries compete among themselves and with the rich countries for the favours of the TNCs who with their capital, technology and know-how can initiate enterprise and undertake risks on a scale which many governments cannot.

The widespread abandonment of the import substitution strategy, and the adoption of a development paradigm which places greater reliance on the private sector as a generator of growth, has forced governments to privatize a large number of enterprises in various sectors. This situation has created enormous opportunities for foreign investors. Foreign direct investment from privatization in developing countries amounted to over US$17 billion in the period 1989–94. More than 75 per cent of this was in the Latin America and Caribbean region.[23] Privatization has allowed foreign firms to acquire interest in a number of industries from which they were previously excluded, including infrastructure related activities.

Growing populations and rising expectations are putting increasing pressure on governments to create jobs and to improve the standard of living. Some countries have made spectacular progress compared to others. In a number of countries welfare actually fell during the 1980s. In this kind of situation it was not surprising that a number of countries began to rethink their development strategies and policies with the aim of reversing the trends that had emerged in the 1980s which was viewed in Latin America as the 'lost decade of development'.

In the early 1990s competition among nations has become fiercer. There is not only competition among individual countries, but there is also competition among groups of countries based in various regions. In the western hemisphere the formation of the North American Free Trade Area which includes the United States, Canada and Mexico and which is likely to get larger is seen as counter move to the European Community and the countries in Asia. There is also increased competition among the TNCs themselves as the trade and investment barriers are lowered not only in country groupings, but internationally. The freeing-up of the markets in services as envisaged in the results of the Uruguay Round is also likely to lend to greater foreign investment, since generally services have to be produced where they are consumed. One effect of liberalization and deregulation will be the rationalization of TNCs' structure which would have been deeply influenced by restrictive national regulations and the need to fashion a strategy consistent with their global objectives.

In order to attract private foreign capital, developing countries are using a variety of approaches in transforming the internal environment. Failed policies are being dropped or modified. Discrimination against foreign investors are also being removed, and more appropriate macroeconomic policies adopted. In addition to the changes being made in internal policies several countries have signed investment treaties with other governments providing safeguards against unfair nationalization and expropriation, detailing conditions and procedures for compensation and the settlement of disputes and generally providing a climate favourable to foreign capital. The World Bank has also issued a set of guidelines which host countries are urged to follow. While these guidelines recognize the right to regulate, they suggest that regulations should be simple and that foreign investors should not be the subject of discrimination treatment. The guidelines recognize the right of a State to expropriate, 'but only if this is done in accordance with applicable legal procedures, in the pursuance in good faith of a public purpose, without discrimination on the basis of nationality and against the payment of appropriate compensation'.[24] The OECD is also pushing for a multilateral agreement on investment (MAI) which will be open to both the OECD and non-OECD countries. The agreement is needed 'to respond to the dramatic growth and transformation of foreign direct investment (FDI) which has been spurred by widespread liberalisation and increasing competition for investment capital'.[25]

CONCLUDING OBSERVATIONS

The rules and regulations governing foreign investment in many developing countries are still associated with a great deal of uncertainty and lack of transparency. How to balance the need for greater foreign savings with the desire to maximise local benefits from such savings has always been a challenging task. Whether a framework is in place to enhance the bargaining strength of host countries in the emerging environment remains an open question. Certainly, attempts are being made to develop local capital markets (which remain narrow in most cases) and to encourage stock market activity, but the approach is generally piecemeal. Company laws and banking and financial regulations in many cases remain outdated.

The creation of a more favourable international environment for the movement of capital has not benefitted a large number of countries. In Latin America, for example, of the estimated FDI of US$18 billion in 1995, four countries accounted for 75 per cent. There was a similar pattern with respect to portfolio investment. Another point worth noting, particularly with respect to portfolio investment, is that a significant proportion of such capital does not result in additional capital formation. A considerable proportion of foreign investment seems to have been associated with a change in claims. Countries such as Argentina, Brazil and Mexico have shown no significant increase in the investment/GDP ratio.

Following the Mexican debacle at the end of 1994, the volatility of some forms of capital flows became a major concern. Portfolio flows are not only responsive to internal shocks but are extremely sensitive to international financial conditions, and in the context of a liberalized financial sector pose certain dangers for economic management. With the flight of capital from Mexico in late 1994, the foreign reserves (minus gold) of the country dropped from US$16.4 billion at the end of September to US$6.3 billion at the end of December. The new found faith in emerging financial markets received a serious jolt as questions arose about the quality of the reforms that have taken place and the ability of national monetary authorities to manage the liberalized systems. A basic question is that even with sound macroeconomic policies, are the removal of currency controls, the removal of interest rate ceilings on deposits and loans, the relaxation of restrictions on non-bank financial institutions and the removal of other forms of inhibitions enough by themselves to ensure the kind of intermediation necessary to advance growth in the real sector. It is clear that rapid liberalization without adequate safeguards hold certain dangers for the financial sector which can easily over-extend itself in the absence of adequate prudential safeguards.

Notes

1. See the UN, *World Investment Report 1992* (New York: United Nations, 1992), p. 1.
2. *Ibid.*, p. 5.
3. See UN, *Formulation and Implementation of Foreign Investment Policies* (New York: United Nations, 1992), p. 1.
4. See IMF, *International Capital Markets: Developments and Prospects* (Washington, DC: IMF, May 1991), p. 60.
5. *Ibid.*
6. *Ibid.*

7. Where the rate is fixed, it would of course, come under pressure – hence the argument often heard that a fixed exchange rate regime is inconsistent with the free movement of capital.
8. The opposite would take place when the rate depreciates.
9. See IMF, *World Economic Outlook, May 1996* (Washington, DC: IMF, 1996), p. 35.
10. For a discussion of these arrangements, see Charles Oman, *New Forms of International Investment* (Paris: OED, 1984), pp. 14–17.
11. UN, *World Investment Report, 1996* (New York: UN, 1996) p. xiii.
12. *Ibid.*, p. xiv.
13. UN, *World Investment Report 1992, op. cit.*, p. 51.
14. UN, *World Investment Report, 1992, pp. 20–21.*
15. UN, *World Investment Report 1996, op. cit.*, p. xiv.
16. *Ibid.*, p. 8.
17. See UN, *World Investment Report 1993, op. cit.*, p. 101.
18. *Fortune Magazine*, 5 August 1996
19. See UN, *World Investment Report, 1996 op. cit.*, pp. 30–31.
20, *Ibid.*, p. 5.
21. R. F. Mikesell, *U.S. Private and Government Investment Abroad* (Eugene, Oregon: University of Oregon Books, 1962), p. 22.
22. Bank for International Settlements, *65th Annual Report*, 1st April 1994–31st March 1995, p. 68.
23. UN, *World Investment Report 1996, op. cit.*, p. 6.
24. See UN, *World Investment Report, 1993, op. cit.*, p. 29.
25. OECD, *Towards Multilateral Investment Rules*, (Paris: OECD, 1996), p. 5.

Further Reading

Ahiakpor, J. C. W., *Multinationals and Economic Development*, Routledge, London, 1990.
Barnet, R. J. and R. E. Muller, *Global Reach, The Power of the Multinational Corporations*, Simon and Schuster, New York, 1974.
Black, J. and J. H. Danning, *International Capital Movements*, Macmillan Publishers Ltd, London, 1982.
Dunning, J. H., *The Globalization of Business*, Routledge, London, 1993.
International Monetary Fund, *Report on the Measurement of International Capital Flows*, IMF, Washington DC, September, 1992.
International Monetary Fund, *Foreign Private Investment in Developing Countries*, Washington, DC, 1995, Occasional Paper, No. 33.
Khan, M. S. and C. M. Reinhart, *Capital Flows in the APEC Region*, IMF, Washington DC, 1995.
Lall, S. and P. Streeten, *Foreign Investment, Transnationals and Developing Countries*, The Macmillan Press Ltd, London, 1977.
Michie, J. and J. G. Smith (eds), *Managing the Global Economy*, New York, Oxford University Press, 1995.
OECD *Towards Multilateral Investment Rules*, OECD, Paris, 1996.

Oman, C., *New Forms of International Investment in Developing Countries*, OECD, Paris, 1984.

The Institute of International Finance, Inc., *Fostering Foreign Direct Investment in Latin America*. The Institute of International Finance, Washington, DC, July, 1990.

United Nations, *The Impact of Trade-related Investment Measures*, UN, New York, 1991.

United Nations, *Formulation and Implementation of Foreign Investment Policies*, UN, New York, 1992.

United Nations, *The Determinants of Foreign Direct Investment: A Survey of the Evidence*, UN, New York, 1992.

United Nations, *Explaining and Forecasting Regional Flows of Foreign Direct Investment*, UN, New York, 1993.

United Nations, *Transnational Corporations From Developing Countries*, UN, New York, 1993.

United Nations *World Investment Report, 1993*, UN, New York, 1993.

United Nations, *The Transnationalization of Service Industries*, UN, New York, 1993.

United Nations, *World Investment Report 1996*, UN, New York, 1996.

United Nations, *Transnational Corporations and World Development*, International Thompson Business Press, London, 1996.

World Bank, *Global Development Finance*, World Bank, Washington, DC, 1997.

Index

Africa, 162, 244
  Sub-Saharan, 192, 203, 206
African Development Bank, 225–6
Aid, 187
  definition, 193–4
  tying, 187, 196
  efficacy, 204
Anguilla, 91
Antigua and Barbuda, 91
Argentina, 145, 169, 178, 243
Asian Currency Markets, 130
Asia-Pacific Region, 240
Australia-New Zealand Trade
  Agreement, 22
Austria, 200

Bahamas, 14, 91, 150, 151
balance of payments accounts, 27–33
Baker plan, 147, 166, 167, 174
'Bancor', 59, 60
Bank for International Settlements, 6,
  12, 148
Bank of Credit and Commerce
  International, 142
Banco Latina, 142
Banque Commerciale Pour l'Europe du
  Monde, 150
Barbadian dollar, 94
Barings Bank, 142
Basel Committee Concordat, 143
begar-thy-neighbour polices, 57
Belgium, 143, 200
Benin, 11, 177
'Big Mac' Standard, 104–5
black market rates, 94
Bolivia, 17, 175, 177
Brady Bonds, 175
Brady Plan, 147, 167, 173–5, 177
Brazil, 43, 145, 155, 159, 169, 243,
  244
Bretton Woods Agreement, 12, 14, 54,
  57, 59, 61, 68, 83, 87, 118
Buffer Stock Financing Facility, 72, 75

Burundi, 177
Burkina Faso, 91, 177

Canada, 143, 190, 200, 226
capital controls, 5
capital movements, 5, 6
capital flight, 129, 165
capital mobility, 26
Caribbean Development Bank, 35,
  225, 226, 229, 230
Cayman Islands, 91, 150, 151
CARIBCAN, 201
Caribbean Basin Initiative (US), 201
Central African Republic, 177
Central Bank of West African States,
  91
CFA Franc, 91
Chile, 145, 169
China, 2, 55, 192, 203, 204, 240, 243,
  244
Citicorp, 131
Commercial Banks and the Debt
  Crisis, 143
convertibility, 2
Columbus C., 5
compensatory and contingency
  financing facility, 72–3
Cosa Nostra, 151
Cote d'Ivoíre, 91
Council for Mutual Economic
  Assistance, 1
Credit Tranche Policies, 72
currency options, 8
currency swaps, 8

dollarization, 16
Danish Krone, 45
debt, 155
  debt rescheduling, 151, 160, 167
  debt crisis, 155, 163
  debt service ratio, 159–60
  debt and Latin America, 162
  debt forgiveness, 168

debt *continued*
  debt for export swaps, 168
  debt for nature swaps, 168
  debt buybacks, 169
  debt equity swaps, 169
  debt and the IMF, 155, 173
  debt and the World Bank, 173, 175
  debt and official development
    assistance (ODA), 171–2
  debt reduction facility, 175
  debt and highly indebted poor
    countries, 172
  debt and imminent default, 179
Denmark, 200
deposit insurance schemes, 143
derivatives, 8, 9, 18, 142
devaluation controversy, 118–22
Development Assistance Committee
  (DAC), 187, 198
'Dragon' Bond Market, 11
dollar area, 1
Dominica, 91

Eastern Europe, 3, 216, 234, 235, 243,
  244
Eastern Caribbean Central Bank, 91
Equation of Exchange, 56
enhanced structural adjustment facility,
  71, 75, 76
Enterprise for the Americas initiative,
  178
Euro, 17, 51
Europe, 3, 4
European Currency Unit (ECU), 15,
  110, 111
European Economic and Monetary
  Union, 107
European Bank for Reconstruction and
  Development (EBRD), 225, 226
European Monetary System (EMS),
  15, 109–13
European Union, 200, 241, 242
Euro-currency system, 14, 129, 137,
  138, 144
  and the Bahamas, 138
  and the Cayman Islands, 138
exchange rates, 6
  spot rates, 99
  forward rates, 99

nominal effective exchange rates, 100
  real exchange rates, 100
  real effective exchange rates, 100–1
exchange rate systems, 16, 105, 108,
  114–17
  fixed, 6, 16, 37
  flexible, 16
  managed floating, 99
exit bonds, 170
external adjustment, 39
  and fiscal and monetary policies, 39

FAO, 196
Financial Action Task Force (FATF),
  140
financial centres, 94, 137
  London, 137
  New York, 137
  Tokyo, 137
  Hong Kong, 138
  Singapore, 138
  Switzerland, 138
  Tangier, 141
  Malta, 141
First World War, 56
first United Nations Development
  decade, 198
foreign reserves account, 31, 32
foreign Investment, 236, 250
  definition, 236
  trends, 237, 238, 240, 241
  current flows, 239–40
  treaties, 251
  and Eastern Europe, 243
Fortune Magazine, 245
Franc Zone, 1
France, 13, 200, 204, 241, 242

GATT, 21, 38, 235
Generalized System of Preferences,
  201
Germany, 13, 23, 25, 83, 87, 143, 190,
  197, 219, 241, 242, 244
Glass-Steagall Act, 137
globalization, 1, 3, 4, 17
gold, 54, 55
  gold and the US dollar, 13
  Gold Standard, 13, 14, 55, 56, 58
  gold pool, 13

gold production, 43
Gold-Exchange Standard, 62
Group of Seven, 88, 172
Group of Ten, 13, 26
Guyana, 175

Hong Kong, 23, 24, 91, 244
Human Development Index, 188

ILO, 196
India, 143, 203
information technology, 18
International Banking Facilities (IBFs), 130, 137, 138
International Banking and Regulation, 142
International Development Association, 64, 175, 217, 218, 219, 220, 225
International Finance Corporation, 64, 217, 218, 222
international liquidity, 40
Inter-American Development Bank, 35, 157, 225–7, 224
International Monetary System and Financial Conference of the United and Associated Nations, 59
International Monetary Fund (IMF), 15, 18, 28, 35, 36–9, 43, 61, 65, 67, 85, 158, 163, 165, 167, 173–4, 177, 179, 180, 196, 197, 209, 217, 224, 234, 237
 and developing countries, 68, 78
 and surveillance, 68
 and adjustment, 79–82
 and World Bank, 81
 and United Nations, 81
 and reform, 82, 84
 and debt rescheduling, 151
 and structural adjustment, 155
 and conditionality, 179
International Trade Organization (ITO), 86

Jamaica, 162
Japan, 3, 13, 22, 25, 26, 57, 83, 87, 127, 143, 190, 200, 219, 226, 241, 242, 244

Keynesian Plan, 59
Korean War, 196
Korea, Rep. of, 23, 24, 244

Latin America, 14, 192, 203, 240, 243, 244
LIBOR, 18, 164
London, 58, 177
Lomé Convention, 209
Luxembourg, 143

Major, John, 171
Malaysia, 23
Mali, 91
Manufacturer's Hanover, 145
Marshall Plan, 197
Medellin Cartel, 151
Mexico, 18, 23, 145, 155, 158, 159, 163, 243
 Mexican Peso, 86
 Mexican Crisis, 86, 239
Menu Approach, 167
Middle East, 229
money laundering, 141
Montserrat, 91
Moscow Narodny Bank, 150
Multi-lateral Investment Guarantee Agency (MIGA), 217, 223, 224

NAFTA, 22
Naples terms, 172, 177
Netherlands, 143, 200, 214
NGOs, 207, 230
Niger, 91, 101, 175
North America, 34
North Africa, 229
Norway, 142, 200

Official Development Assistance (ODA), 198–9, 200, 203
Optimal Currency Arrangements, 113–14
Organization for Economic Cooperation and Development (OECS), 156, 187, 211, 209, 251

Panama, 14, 91, 151
Paris Club, 18, 170, 172, 177, 179–181
Peru, 165

purchasing power parity, 101–102
Portugal, 200

regional trading arrangements, 22
Russia, 55
Rwanda, 177

savings gap, 197
Saudi Arabian Rial, 45
Second World War, 1, 12
Singapore, 23, 24
Scandinavian countries, 204
South and East Asia, 2, 3, 244
South African Rand, 45
Soviet Union, 3, 13, 195, 203, 204, 243
Spain, 200, 204
Special Drawing Right (SDR), 14, 16, 17, 35, 36, 43, 44, 62, 70
  SDR Basket, 45
St. Kitts-Nevis, 91
St. Lucia, 91
St. Vincent, 191
Standard Chartered Bank, 131
Structural Adjustment Facility, 75
Structural Adjustment Programs, 155
  and IMF, 155
  and World Bank, 155
Sweden, 200, 244
Switzerland, 244
Systemic Transformation Facility, 72, 75

Taiwan, 23, 24
Thailand, 24
Tobin, James, 182
Toronto terms, 170–172
  enhanced Toronto terms, 171
Transnational Corporation, 236, 237, 240–243

transition economies, 244
Trinidad terms, 171
Trinidad and Tobago, 165

Uganda, 175
United Kingdom, 200, 204, 219, 241
UNDP, 205, 206, 208
UNESCO, 196
UNICEF, 175
United and Associated Nations, 63
United Nations, 156–8, 196, 225, 235, 249
  First Development Decade, 198
  Second Development Decade, 198
United Nations Monetary and Financial Conference, 217
United States, 12, 13, 18, 19, 23, 24, 25, 57, 60, 79, 80, 82, 83, 178, 204, 219, 224, 226, 237, 241, 242, 244
  US banks, 127
  US dollar, 14
  US balance of payments, 15
  US dollar and Bretton Woods, 42
  US dollar and gold, 42
underground economy, 151
Uruguay, 17
USSR, 16

Vietnam War, 196
Venezuela, 145, 147, 162, 165

West Asia, 244
White Plan, 60
Wolfensohn, J., 65, 218
World Bank, 16, 35, 63, 64, 151, 155, 173–4, 177, 180, 194, 196, 216, 218, 220, 226, 227, 228, 229, 237, 239
  Development Committee of, 209